THE ITALIAN ROOM, STOURHEAD, WILTSHIRE, ENGLAND, 1800.

Period Furnishings

AN ENCYCLOPEDIA OF HISTORIC FURNITURE, DECORATIONS AND FURNISHINGS

By C. R. CLIFFORD

FULLY ILLUSTRATED

Published by CLIFFORD & LAWTON
NEW YORK

INTRODUCTORY

IN PRESENTING this work upon the period furnishings of the house, covering historic furniture, fabrics, wall treatments, fitments and accessories, I would lay emphasis upon the fact that the subject cannot be grasped by blind groping or desultory reading. We cannot comprehend by simply memorizing dates and incidents. We must know the underlying origin and impetus and the growth of the styles as influenced primarily by the events of history and all that makes history; the development of nations, their social customs and their characteristics. There are no short cuts to be taken in a spirit of impatience. But to the man who is not easily discouraged at the outset this line of study opens a field of world-wide and compelling interest. If he approaches the subject with an orderly mind he will comprehend from the first the broad distinctions and soon begin to differentiate in the more subtle details of decoration.

Since the study must be systematic, I have prepared charts showing the development of races as well as charts showing the development of nations. These give us a retrospect of relationship which will prepare the student to comprehend the later chronological chart which shows the development of the decorative styles. The differentiation between the periods can be made in many cases only by a knowledge of historic relation. Chronological consistency satisfies one's sense of order, and this is quite as important a consideration in the decoration of a room as comfort in the furnishings.

Decoration must be consistent not only in its construction and application, but in its associations. Ancient architects laid down distinct laws of design covering the five orders, the Ionic, the Doric, the Corinthian, the Composite and the Tuscan. To-day the laws of composition upon which these orders were founded are as effective as ever, for they are not arbitrary, but are based upon the nature of the human mind, the eye and the characteristics of the materials of construction. We must work in accordance with these principles if we are to satisfy the critical taste of men of culture and perception. The outward forms changed from period to period, expressing in their lines, ornament and coloring, the temperament and spirit of the people of the times. Through progressive stages art became altered by elimination, by absorption, and by temperamental interpolations, evolving practically new types and new forms; but running through all these changing styles are the immutable laws of composition and proportion.

We trace with little difficulty the progress of the arts and the development of distinct periods from the days of earliest Babylonia, Egypt, and Assyria, through Greece and Lower Italy, through Asia Minor, through Bagdad and Byzantium, into the Mongol courts of Samarkand. We note the influence of the Saracenic zealots along the Mediterranean. We note the desultory expression of a struggling Gothic art through the dark period of the Middle Ages. We note the awakening finally in Italy during the Fourteenth Century, which expanded into that glorious climacteric era the Renaissance. As the Renaissance developed, carrying with it as an underlying basis the classic arts of Greece and Rome, it was affected by local influences. Religion and commerce alike left their imprint, until finally with the opening of the Seventeenth Century distinct forms varying with the temperament of the nations and of the individual craftsmen, and affected at all times materially by the wealth of suggestion which came through the channels of foreign intercourse, made their appearance. If we would grasp the meaning and the feeling of what, for want of a better term, we call the decorative periods, we must comprehend the influence in each period of the four prime factors in the development of art, namely, temperament, religion, commerce, and education.

If within the limits of this book I have been able to elucidate the subject sufficiently to give the student an intelligent grasp of the essential points, I have accomplished all that I set out to do. For the benefit of those who would pursue the investigation further, I append a list of books to which I have had access and from which I have reproduced many illustrations. I wish to express my sense of personal obligation to the authors of these books, whose original investigations have made them the highest authorities, each upon his own special branch of this subject, and whose works I have found invaluable sources of information.

C. R. CLIFFORD.

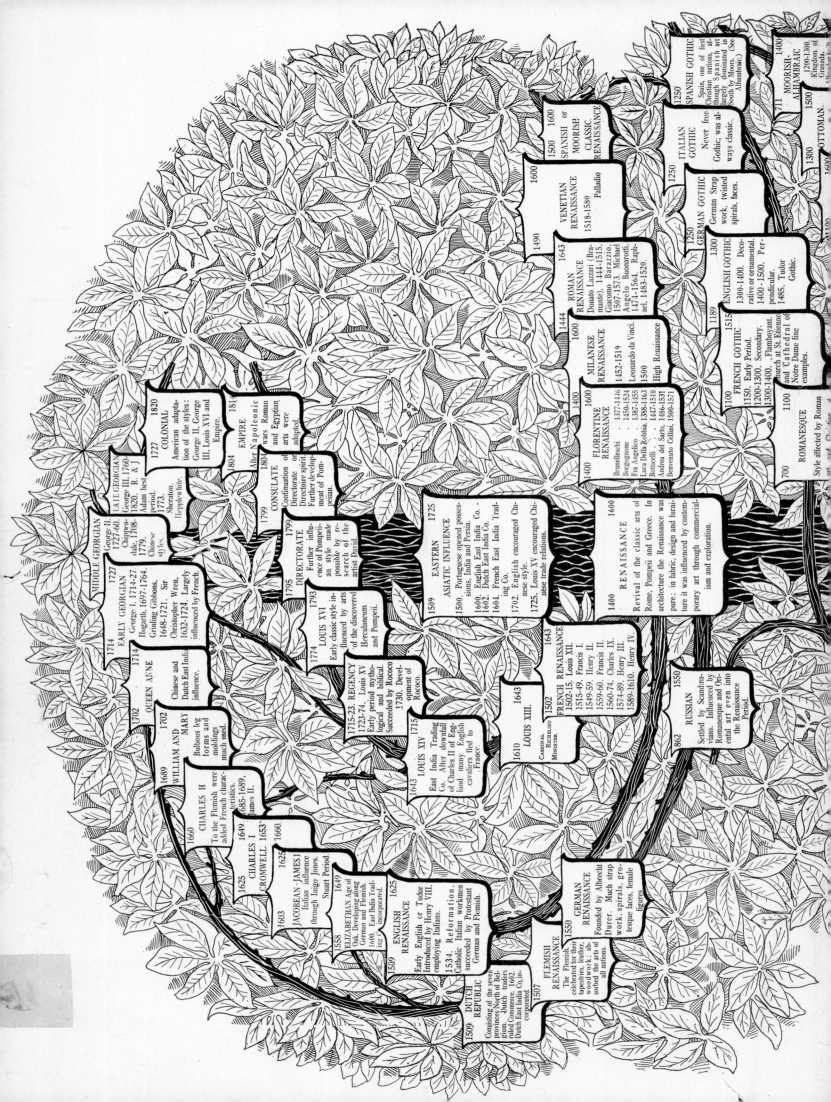

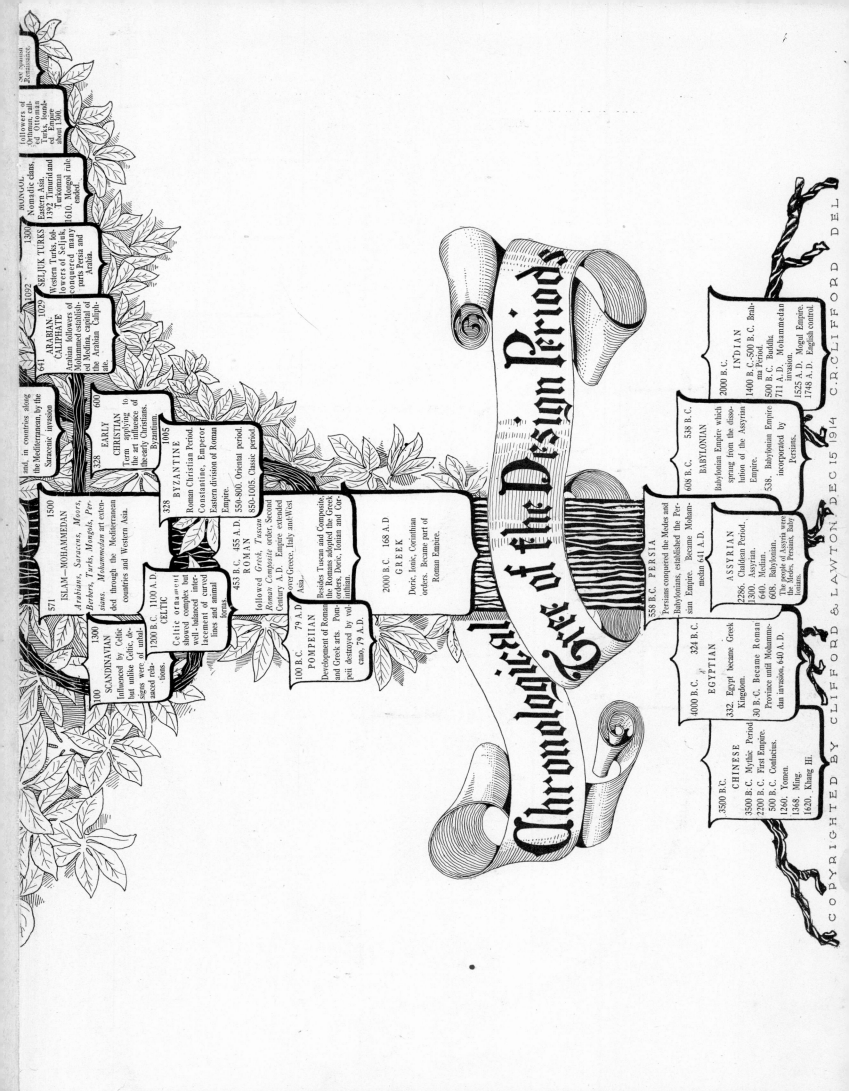

Chronological Tree of the Design Periods.

Spanish Renaissance. (See)

1300 MONGOL Nomadic clans, Eastern Asia. 1392 Timurid and Turkoman 1610. Mongol rule ended.

followers of Orthman, called Ottoman Turks, founded Empire about 1300.

1300 SELJUK TURKS Western Turks, followers of Seljuk, conquered many parts Persia and Arabia.

1029 ARABIAN. CALIPHATE Arabian followers of Mohammed established Medina, capital of the Arabian Caliphate.

and, in countries along the Mediterranean, by the Saracenic invasion

600 EARLY CHRISTIAN Term applying to the art influence of the early Christians. Byzantium.

328 BYZANTINE Roman Christian Period. Constantine, Emperor Eastern division of Roman Empire. 550-800. Oriental period. 850-1005. Classic period.

1500 ISLAM—MOHAMMEDAN Arabians, Saracens, Moors, Berbers, Turks, Mongols, Persians. Mohammedan art extended through the Mediterranean countries and Western Asia.

571

1300 SCANDINAVIAN Influenced by Celtic but unlike Celtic, designs were of unbalanced relations.

100

1200 B.C. 1100 A.D. CELTIC Celtic ornament showed complex but well-balanced interlacement of curved lines and animal forms.

followed Greek, Tuscan Roman Composite order, Second Century A. D. Empire extended over Greece, Italy and West Asia.

453 B.C. 455 A.D. ROMAN

100 B.C. 79 A.D POMPEIIAN Development of Roman and Greek arts. Pompeii destroyed by volcano, 79 A.D.

Besides Tuscan and Composite, the Romans adopted the Greek orders, Doric, Ionian and Corinthian.

2000 B.C. 168 A.D GREEK Doric, Ionic, Corinthian orders. Became part of Roman Empire.

558 B.C. PERSIA Persians conquered the Medes and Babylonians, established the Persian Empire. Became Mohammedan 641 A.D.

608 B.C. 538 B. C. BABYLONIAN Babylonian Empire which sprang from the dissolution of the Assyrian Empire. 538. Babylonian Empire incorporated by Persians.

2000 B. C. INDIAN 1400 B. C.-500 B. C. Brahma Period. 500 B. C. Buddha 711 A. D. Mohammedan invasion. 1525 A. D. Mogul Empire. 1748 A. D. English control.

ASSYRIAN 2286. Chaldean Period. 1300. Assyrian. 640. Median. 608. Babylonian. The people of Assyria were the Medes, Persians, Babylonians.

4000 B.C. 324 B. C. EGYPTIAN 332. Egypt became Greek Kingdom. 30 B. C. Became Roman Province until Mohammedan invasion, 640 A. D.

3500 B.C. CHINESE 3500 B. C. Mythic Period 2200 B. C. First Empire. 500 B. C. Confucius. 1260. Yomen. 1368. Ming. 1620. Khang Hi.

A SERIES OF TABLES TRACING THE ORIGIN AND DEVELOPMENT OF NATIONS, WITH THEIR VARIOUS ARTS, PRODUCTS, ETC.

THE DEVELOPMENT OF NATIONS. 4000 B.C.—100 B.C.

BABYLONIAN.

B.C.
4000. Ancient Babylonian.
1300. Conquered by Assyria.
600. Regained independence after many wars as New Empire of Babylon.
500. Became Persian Province.

EGYPTIAN.

4000. Ancient Kingdom.
3000. Middle Kingdom.
2000. New Empire. Highly civilized.
500. Became Persian Province.
300. Late Art Period. Greek invasion of Alexander of Macedonia. Ptolemy I, general under Alexander, was placed over Egypt and added Lower Syria, Palestine and Cyprus.
100. Conquered by Rome. Egyptian descendants were called Copti.

ASSYRIAN.

3000. Chaldean Period.
2000. Assyrian Period. Colonized from Babylonia.
625. Conquered by Medes.
500. Median Empire covering Lydia and Phrygia in Western Anatolia.
300. Invasion of Alexander.
100. Assyria, Mesopotamia and Babylonia made Roman Provinces.

PERSIAN.

4000. Before the dawn of history in Europe, the Aryan tribes of Asia migrated East as far as India and West to Greece. The Iran Plateau lay between Caspian Sea and Indian Ocean in Central and Western Asia. Those settling in North were called Medes; those South, Persians; those West, Celts.
1200. Bactrians, Medes and Persians occupied the Iran Plateau.
500. Supremacy of Median Period passed to Persians, who formed Empire. Syria, Phoenicia, Cyprus, Judea and part of Arabia paid tribute.
200. Parthian Empire dominated a vast territory from 250 B.C. to 220 A.D. Sassanian Empire held sway 220-640 A.D.

PHOENICIAN.

2000. Highly civilized.
1300. Colonies in Crete, Cyprus and Rhodes.
1100. Tyre, famous city, fell repeatedly under Assyrian rule.
500. Subject to Persia.
300. Invasion of Alexander of Macedonia.

HEBRAIC.

2000. Empire of Shepherd Kings on frontier of Assyria.
1500. Migrated to Egypt.
1100. David King of Jerusalem.
1000. King Solomon.
600. Kingdom divided into Israel and Judea.
500. Jerusalem Jews became subject to Babylonia, Assyria and Rome.
200. Emancipation of Jews.
100. Jerusalem captured by Pompey (63); Jews become Roman subjects.
100. Herod recognized by Romans King of Judea (40).

GREEK.

1900. Pelasgians from Southwestern Asia Minor, original Greeks.
1100. Pelasgians called Hellenes divided into Dorian and Ionian tribes.
600. Spartan Supremacy. Ionic Art Period.
290. Corinthian Art Period.
300. Macedonia having become leading State in Greek Empire 336, Alexander of Macedonia waged war against Persia and the East and conquered all Asia as far as India, spreading Greek culture. Antioch, Syria, Alexandria, Rhodes, Asia Minor became Eastern centers of Greek Art.
200. Macedonia becomes Roman Province.

SPANISH—FRENCH —PORTUGUESE.

2000. Celts settled in and about Spain.
1900. Phoenicians visited Spain.
1300. Portugal was ancient Iberia.
1200. France was peopled by Teuton tribes and called Gaul.
600. Celts dominated Spain.
500. While the Celtic tribes and the men of Gaul (originally Teutons) were all termed Gallic people, they gradually formed distinct divisions.
100. At the opening of Christian era all the Gallic country came under Roman conquest.

ROMAN.

700. Mythical Period.
400. Empire dismembered.
200. Conquest of Spain and Gaul.
100. Destruction of Macedonian Monarchy by Romans. Invasion of England.

ETRUSCAN.

1200. Aryan tribes of Asia living North of Rome and in country now Tuscany.
600. Period of highest development.
Subjugated by Romans, 351 B.C.

TEUTONIC.

600. Tribes of barbarians called Teutons occupied territory now Germany, Prussia, Holland, Belgium, Bavaria, Scandinavia, Northern Italy, Saxony.
500. Scandinavia, covering Denmark and Sweden, occupied by Finnish tribes. In Denmark dwelt Saxons, Angles and Jutes.
200. Dominated by the Romans.

CELTIC.

2000. Aryan tribes from Asia living North of Rome and in country now Tuscany. First of the Aryans to settle in Western Europe. They occupied the country now France, but then called Gaul, and together with Teuton tribes who found their way West and settled there, were included among the Gallic people. Period of highest development.
600. Subjugated Spain.
500. Reached Great Britain.
100. Gallic tribes formed divisions distinct from Celtic tribes and at opening of Christian era were conquered by Caesar, Emperor of Rome.

CHRONOLOGY SHOWING THE

Batavians, 78; British, 86; Burgundians, 28; Byzantine, 10; Danes, Swedes, Norwegians, Finns, 65; Franks, 37; German Kingdom, 33; Saracens, 62; Saxons, Angles, Jutes, 66; Scandinavians, 65; Scotch, 82; Slavs and

A.D.	ROMAN.	BYZANTINE.	ITALIAN.	TEUTONIC.	FRENCH.
100	(1) Destruction Pompeii and Herculaneum, 79 A.D. Roman Empire extended over Greece, Italy, the Grecian Islands, Cyprus, Crete, Rhodes, Cyrene, Carthage, Spain, France, Germanic Countries and Western Asia, including Armenia and Mesopotamia.		(14) Italy originally a term applying to the peninsula divided into Upper, Central, Lower Italy and Islands, Sicily, Sardinia and Corsica. At opening of century Italy was included in Roman Empire.	(25) Teutons occupied territory now Wurtemberg, Bavaria, Bohemia, Saxony, Hesse, Holland, Hanover, Prussia, Swiss and Tyrol Alps and Scandinavia. Religion of nature worship.	(35) Roman province. (36) 170. First Christian church at Lyons.
200	(2) Hadrian successor to Trajan abandoned Armenia and Mesopotamia.			(26) Many small tribes in close relation with Romans.	
300	(3) Constantine, Emperor, became protector of Christians. Accepted Christian religion 328. 330 changed capital of Empire to Byzantium. (See 10.)	(10) Byzantine Empire under Constantine. Byzantium changed to Constantinople. This constituted the Eastern Division of Roman Empire. (See 3.)	(15) 320. Langobards were located on Lower Elbe. (See 30.)	(27) 320. Beginning of migration of Germanic tribes. (28) Alani located on lower Volga; East Goths, Southern Russia; West Goths, Eastern Hungary; Vandals, Southwestern Hungary; Suevi, Bohemia, Moravia and Bavaria; Burgundians on the Rhine; Ripuarian Franks; both sides lower Rhine; Sohe Franks at mouth of Rhine.	(37) 350. Invasion of Franks. (See 28.)
400	(4) Roman Empire dismembered 455. Invasion of Vandals. (See 28.)	(See 16, 17, 18.)	(16) Invasion of West Goths 400. (17) 476. Odoacer became Prefect of Italy. (18) 452. Huns under Attila invade Italy. Venice founded by Italian refugees.	(29) West Goths laid waste Macedonia and Greece, and invaded Italy, 400. (30) Langobards on lower Elbe. (31) 476. Odoacer recognized by Eastern Emperor as Prefect of Italy. (See 17 and 18.)	(38) 400. Invasion of Vandals, Suevi and Alian. (See 28.) 443. Burgundians, Visigoths and Franks settled in upper Rhone. (See 28.) (40) 450. Huns under Attila ravage Gaul. (41) 486. Monarchy established by Clovis.
500	(5) 590. Gregory I Bishop of Rome.	(11) 527. Justinian began twenty-year war which destroyed influence of Goths and Huns. (See 29.)	(19) 568. The Langobards conquered Italy south to Tiber. (See 67.) (20) 590. Gregory I Bishop of Rome. Beginning of Papacy.		(42) 511. Division of Kingdom with four court camps Metz, Paris, Soissons and Orleans. (43) 561. Second Division. Austrasia with capital at Rheims. Population chiefly German. Neustria capital Soissons, Burgundy capital Orleans. Population of last two Celtic.
600					(44) 620. Dagobert. (45) 632. Third Division. Austrasia, principally German Neustria, Northern France, not reckoning Bretagne and Burgundy. (46) 687. Pipin of Austrasia became head of the Kingdom of Franks.
700	(6) 751. Rome independent. First Papal States. (See 21 and 48.)	(12) 700. Lombards (or Langobards) conquered the greater part of the Byzantine Empire in Europe. (See 48.)	(21) 751. First Papal States. (See 48.) (22) 773. Lombardic Kingdom destroyed by Charlemagne, Charles the Great, who became King of Italy. (See 48 and 67.)		(47) 732. Martell, son and successor of Pipin, drove out Arabian invaders. (48) 751. Langobards (Lombards) having conquered almost all Byzantine territory in Europe, excepting Venice, Ravenna, Naples and Rome, Pope Stephen III sought aid of Pipin the Short, who drove back the Lombards and was rewarded by being placed at head of First Papal States. (49) 772. War with Saxons (pagans). Absorption of Saxon land. (See 66.)
800	(7) 800-1200. Saracenic influence prevailed.	(13) Until 1057 Eastern or Byzantine Empire was under Macedonian rule. Byzantine art flourished until the conquest of the Eastern Empire. Muhammed II destroyed Byzantine or Eastern Empire, in 1453.	(23) 800. Charles revived office of Emperor of West.	(32) See 50.	(50) 843. Empire divided into East and West Frankish Empire, which eventually became Germany and France.
900	(8) 966. Dominated by German nations.		(24) 961. First Empire.	(33) 919. Henry I founded German Monarchy. (34) 966. Holy Roman Empire of German nations.	(51) 986. Hugh Capet chosen king of French monarchy. (52) 911. Northmen (or Normans) gained permanent foothold in Normandy with sovereignty over Brittany, and with Rouen as capital. (See 92.)
1000					

Byzantine influence.

Best art period.

Lombardic Romanesque.

Merovingian.

Carolingian, 843-897.

Norman Romanesque.

DEVELOPMENT OF NATIONS

Huns, 18; Irish, 84; Lombards-Langobards, 12; Moors, 62; Normans, 86; Papal States, 21; Poles, Bohemians, Russians, 76; Roman, 1; Finns, 73; Spanish, 55; Teutons, 25; Vandals, 28; West Goths, 21; Norsemen, 52.

SPANISH.	MOORISH.	SCANDINAVIAN.	RUSSIAN.	FLEMISH.	ENGLISH.
		(65) Occupied 500 B.C. by Finns and wandering Teutons. In Denmark dwelt Saxons, Angles and Jutes. At beginning of century, Odin leader of Asas, between Black Sea and Caspian, passed into Scandinavia and subdued Denmark, Sweden and Norway.		(78) Occupied by Batavians.	See also Celtic. (81) England, B.C., occupied by barbarous tribes. Phoenicians visited England at an early period. Celts settled there 500 B.C. Roman invasion, 58 B.C. Roman conquest of Southern England 43 A.D. (82) 81. Roman power extended as far as Scotland.
(53) 205. Spain regarded as Roman province.			(73) Slavs and Finns located between Black Sea and Baltic.		
(54) 406. Invaded by Vandals, Suevi and Alani. (55) 414. West Goths (Visigoths) founded kingdom of Toulouse.	(60) Kingdom of Vandal founded in Northern Africa. Becomes naval power.	(66) Saxons, Angles and Jutes lived in Denmark. In 450 many settled in England. (See 79.)		(79) 449. Angles and Saxons (pirates) settled on Coast of Flanders. Were called in by Britons to help repel their enemies of the North, now Scotland.	(83) 410. Withdrawal of Roman legions. (84) 440. St. Patrick converted Irish to Christianity. (85) 449. Jutes from Denmark and Angles and Saxons from Flanders, pagans came ostensibly to help Britons against their foes. Many Britons migrated to Wales and Gaul, where country of their settlement was called Bretagne (Brittany). (86) 500. Great Britain ruled by petty kingdom of Saxons, Angles and Jutes.
(56) 507. Goth kingdom till 711.	(61) Vandals controlled Coast of Africa. Berbers were the natives of Barbary.	(67) The Lombards entered Italy from Slav territory. Founded powerful nation 568-774 which was destroyed by Charlemagne. (See 22.)	(74) 500. Extended West to Balkan Peninsula, Bohemia and the Tyrol.		
			(75) 623. Slavic monarchy for thirty-seven years. (76) 660. Separate monarchies of Poland, Bohemia and Russia.		600. Christianity preached. Ethelbert, King of Kent, was converted. (87) From Sixth to Twelfth Century Ireland famous in art and literature and sent Christian missionaries over all Europe.
(57) 711. Goth kingdom destroyed by Moors. (58) 755. Caliphate of Cordova brilliant period of supremacy.	(62) 700. Saracens completing conquest of Byzantine Africa, the Berbers who accepted Islam together with other settlers and joined the Arabians under the name of Moors. (63) 711. Moors invade Spain. (64) 755. Establish Caliphate of Cordova.				
		(68) 800. Gorm first King of Denmark, Pagan. Sweden attained greatest power of the Scandinavian kingdom.	(77) 862. Bands of Swedes of Scandinavia subjugated Slavs and laid foundation for future Russia.	(80) 800. Independent Duchies Brabant, Flanders, Guelders, Holland, Zealand, Hainault and the Bishopric of Utrecht.	(88) 827. Egbert First Saxon King. (89) 852. Dublin conquered by Norwegians or Northmen. (90) 828. Ravages of Northmen, Scandinavian vikings.
		(69) 930. Christianity introduced. (70) Denmark. United kingdoms from 850 to 1520. (71) Sweden. Olaf 993. First Christian King of Sweden.			
(59) 1031. Dissolution of Caliphate of Cordova.		(72) Norway. Christianity introduced Norway, 1030, by Irish missionaries.			(91) In 1014, Irish defeated Danes and Norsemen. (92) 1066. Conquest of England by Normans of Normandy (Norsemen). (93) William the Conqueror carrying French art into England.

5

DEVELOPMENT OF NATIONS

ITALIAN.

1000. Western Europe, particularly Italy, threatened by the Northmen, Hungarians and the Saracens as well as by the Feudal system which levied heavy taxes upon cities to support the Lords of the Fief, banded together in protective league and a number of confederations were the result.

Venice, Genoa and Pisa did great Italian trade with the East. A Lombard league was formed of the exiled Milanese and a number of the cities of North Italy.

1032. Kingdom of Germany, Kingdom of Italy and Kingdom of Burgundy constituted the Holy Roman Empire, Germany extending from the Mediterranean Sea north to Denmark.

1100. Venice, which had its beginning in 400 in the huts of refugees who fled from the Huns, became famous.

1261. Period of greatest prosperity for Genoa.

1261. Michael Palaeologus put an end to the Latin Empire.

1300. Venice at height of her power. Supreme on the Mediterranean Sea up to Fifteenth Century, when the conquests of Ottoman Turks destroyed her Eastern relations and the trade went to the countries further West.

1400. Florence famous for its manufacture. Fell into the hands of the Medici.

EARLY RENAISSANCE.

1400-1600. *Florentine Renaissance.*

1400-1600. *Milanese Renaissance.*

1450. Italy came to the close of the Middle Ages with no national government. The greater part of the population was divided between the five States, the Duchy of Milan, the two nominal republics of Venice and Florence, the Papal States and the Kingdom of Naples in the South.

1490-1600. *Venetian Renaissance.*

1444-1643. *Roman Renaissance.*

1453. Flight of Greek scholars to Italy, where they taught Grecian arts, science and literature.

1500-1540. *High Renaissance.*

1540-1643. *Late Renaissance.*

1809. Papal States seized by Napoleon.

1830. United Italian provinces.

1861. First Italian Parliament. Victor Emanuel first King of Italy.

1866. Venetia added to the Kingdom.

1870. France withdrew support of the Pope, Rome became a portion of the Kingdom of Italy and Italy became a united nation.

1871. Papal troops were disbanded. Pope was given the Vatican as a residence and secured in the exercise of his spiritual functions.

FLEMISH-DUTCH.

1000. Netherlands (Lowlands) during large part of Middle Ages were divided into a number of petty principalities.

1300. Flanders came into possession of House of Burgundy and soon all of the other petty provinces were acquired by Charles the Bold, the last Duke of Burgundy. At his death the Netherlands fell to his daughter Mary and finally into the possession of her son, Emperor Charles V of Spain. The great cities of this country were Ghent, Bruges, Mechlin, Liege, Tournai, Courtrai, Brussels and Antwerp of the South provinces and Haarlem, Delft, Leyden, Amsterdam, Utrecht and Rotterdam of the North. Some of them were city republics.

1500. During reign of Charles V, 1515-1555, the Northern Netherlanders were treated with great cruelty in effort to check growth of Protestantism as well as subjugate the people who denied Spanish authority. The struggle lasted forty years.

1576. Holland, Zeeland, Gelderland and Utrecht, the northern provinces of the Netherlands, entered into a union eventually the founding of the Dutch Republic.

1577. All provinces united to drive the Spanish soldiers from the country. Help furnished the Hollanders by the English.

1579. The States of Northern Netherlands became known as the seven united provinces. The Southern States now Belgium continued Catholic and loyal to Spain.

1609. France and England became involved through sympathy with the Netherlands, Philip III granted a truce which became an acknowledgment of the independence of the Northern Netherlanders, who formed the Dutch Republic. The Dutch became famous as great sailors, replacing the Portuguese in the settlement of the trading posts in the East Indies.

1813. Formation of Kingdom of the Netherlands and Austrian Belgium.

1830. The Belgians declared themselves independent of Holland, and the Kingdom of Belgium was established.

SPANISH—PORTUGUESE.

1000. Spain divided by many petty governments, some of them Christian kingdoms, Asturia, Castile, Navarre, Aragon, as well as a number of small Mohammedan States. Portugal part of Spain.

1095. County of Portugal a Spanish peninsular. Under Burgundian control. Son of Count Henry of Burgundy made King of Portugal.

1096. County of Portugal revolted.

1140. Kingdom of Portugal.

1238. The Moors in Spain since 1238 were confined to the Kingdom of Granada.

1383. Greatest power of Portugal. Conquered Tangiers. Formed Christian Kingdom in North Africa. Voyages and discoveries. Following the Turkish conquest of Constantinople, European traders endeavored to discover a direct ocean route to India, which led eventually to the discovery of America.

1400. Through the Fifteenth Century Portugal sailors penetrated into the mysterious tropical seas and discovered new islands off coast of Africa.

1492. Spain conquered Granada. Columbus presented to Portugal plans of exploration, and failing assistance, was about to offer services to France or England when the capture of Granada promised the necessary means from the country of his adoption (Spain) with the result known to history.

SPANISH RENAISSANCE.

1500. Portuguese Renaissance.

1500. Opened possessions in Persia and India. Active in America. Subjugated parts of South America.

1600. Spanish withdrawal from Netherlands.

1610. Moors expelled from Spain.

1640. Following the loss of the Netherlands, Spain lost Portugal.

(Norman Romanesque)

FRENCH.

1060-1108. Philip I. First crusade.

GOTHIC PERIOD.

1108-1137. Louis VI.
1137-1180. Louis VII.
1180-1223. Philip II.

1223-1226. Louis VIII.
1226-1270. Louis IX.
1270-1285. Philip III.
1285-1314. Philip IV.

1314-1316. Louis X.
1316-1322. Philip V.
1322-1328. Charles IV.
1328-1350. Philip VI.
1350-1364. John II.
1364-1380. Charles V.
1380-1422. Charles VI.

1422-1461. Charles VII.
1461-1483. Louis XI.
1483-1498. Charles VIII.
1498-1515. Louis XII.

FRENCH RENAISSANCE.

1515-1547. Francis I.
1529. Reformation. Gobelins manufacture tapestry.
1547-1559. Henri II.
1559-1560. Francis II.
1560-1574. Charles IX.
1574-1589. Henri III.
1589-1610. Henri IV.
1598. *Edict of Nantes.*

1604. French East India Co. established.
1610-1643. Louis XIII.
1611, 1615, 1642. French East India Co. charters renewed.
1643-1715. *Louis XIV.* Gobelins become royal property. Le Brun dictator of styles. Beauvais Tapestry Works established. Chinese characteristics introduced.
1685. *Revocation of the Edict of Nantes and consequent flight of many Protestant work people.*
1715-1774. *Louis XV.* Rococo Period).
1774-1792. *Louis XVI.* (Marie Antoinette).
1793-1795. Revolutionary Period.
1795-1804. *Directoire or Transition Period.* David the prime influence in decoration.
1804-1814. *Empire.* David dictator of style.

ENGLISH.

1066-1087. William the Conqueror.
1087-1100. William II.

1100-1135. Henry I.
1135-1154. Stephen.
1154-1189. Henry II.

EARLY ENGLISH GOTHIC.

1189-1199. Richard I.
1199-1216. John.

1216-1272. Henry III.
1272-1307. Edward I.

1307. *Decorated Gothic.*
1307-1327. Edward II.
1327-1377. Edward III.
1377-1399. Richard I.
1399. *Perpendicular Gothic.*
1399-1413. Henry IV.

1413-1422. Henry V.
1422-1461. Henry VI.
1461-1483. Edward IV.
1483. Edward V.
1483-1485. Richard.
1485-1509. Henry VII (founder of Tudor line).

ENGLISH RENAISSANCE.

1509-1547. Henry VIII (John of Padua, architect).
1534. English Reformation.
1547-1553. Edward VI.
1553-1558. Mary.
Elizabethan.
1558-1603. Elizabeth.

1602. Dutch East India Co. established.
1603-1649. *Jacobean* (many Flemish and German workmen settled in England).
1603-1625. James I (founder Stuart period, beginning of American settlement).
1620. Settlement at Plymouth, Mass.
1625-1649. Charles I.
1653-1659. Cromwellian. Many Royalists fled to France.
1660. Exiled Royalists returned from France.
1660-1685. Charles II.
1660. London East India Co. established.
1685-1689. James II.
1685. Revocation of the Edict of Nantes brought many French and Flemish weavers and woodworkers to England.
1689-1702. William and Mary.
1702-1714. Queen Anne.
1714-1727. George I.
1727-1760. George II.
1776. *American Revolution* and establishment of the United States.
1760-1820. George III.
1830-1837. William IV.
1837-1901. Victoria.

A.D. markers: 1000, 1100, 1200, 1300, 1400, 1500, 1600, 1700, 1800

THE PERIOD STYLES CLASSIFIED BY CENTURIES

Beginnings

OLD BABYLONIAN 4000 B.C.

EGYPTIAN 4000-332
CHINESE 3500

ASSYRIAN 2286-608
  Chaldean Period 2286-1300
  Assyrian 1300-625
  Median 640-558
  Babylonian 608-538
INDIAN 2000
GREEK 1900 B.C.-168 A.D.
  Doric 700, Ionic 600, Corinthian 290

JAPANESE 1200
ETRUSCAN 1044-238 B.C.
  (Tuscan)
ROMAN 753 B.C.-455 A.D.
  Following the Greek orders, Doric,
  Ionic and Corinthian; also the Tus-
  can and Roman Composite

PERSIAN EMPIRE 558 B.C.
BUDDHA PERIOD, India, 500

CELTIC 200 B.C.-1100 A.D.
POMPEIIAN 101 B.C.-79 A.D.
PARTHIAN EMPIRE, Persia, 250
  B.C.-220 A.D.

Developments

FORTIETH CENTURY B.C.
THIRTY-FIFTH CENTURY B.C.
Mythic Period 3500-2200
Egyptian Middle Empire 3000-2100
TWENTY-SECOND CENTURY B.C.
First Emipre Chinese 2200
Assyria included the Medes, Persians,
  and Babylonians
Chaldean Period 2286-1300
TWENTIETH CENTURY B.C.
NINETEENTH CENTURY B.C.
Graeco-Pelasgic 1900-1384
FOURTEENTH CENTURY B.C.
India Brahma Period 1400-500
THIRTEENTH CENTURY B.C.
Assyrian 1300-625
TWELFTH CENURY B.C.
TENTH CENTURY B.C.
SEVENTH CENTURY B C.
Greek Doric 700
SIXTH CENTURY B.C.
Japanese Empire 660
Median Empire (Assyrian) 640-558
Empire of babylon 608-538
Greek Ionic 600
FIFTH CENTURY B.C.
Chinese Confucius 500
THIRD CENTURY B.C.
Graeco-Roman influence
Greek Corinthian 290
Hellenistic 290-168
Etruscan cities subjugated by Rome 350
SECOND CENTURY B.C.
FIRST CENTURY B.C.
Greek Arts absorbed by Romans
Doric, Ionic, Corinthian, Composite and
  Tuscan: the "five orders"
Pure Greek 100 B.C.-79 A.D.
Egypt became Roman Province

Endings

CHINESE Mythic Period, 2200 B.C.

CHALDEAN Assyrian 1300
GRAECO-PELASGIC 1384

End of Assyrian Period 625
Dissolution of Assyrian Empire 608
BRAHMA Period, India, 500
MEDES Conquered by Persians 558
BABYLONIAN EMPIRE incorporated
  by Persians 538

ETRUSCAN 238
EGYPT became Kingdom 332
Etruscan Art Period 238

NORTHERN AND SCANDINA-
  VIAN 100 A.D.
ROMAN GERMANIC 100-700
SASSANIAN EMPIRE, PERSIAN,
  220-641

BYZANTINE 328-1453

ARABIAN 571
MOHAMMEDAN PERSIA 641

MOORISH 711-1610
ROMANESQUE 700-1100
ROME Independent. First Papal States
  751

FLEMISH 850-1758

FIRST GERMAN EMPIRE 961-1806

SPANISH, FIRST CHRISTIAN
  KINGDOMS 1037

NORMAN OR ENGLISH ROMAN-
  ESQUE 1066-1189
GOTHIC 1100-1550
FRENCH GOTHIC 1108-1515
  Early English Gothic 1189-1307

SECOND CENTURY A.D.
Roman Empire extended over Greece,
  Germanic Countries, Italy and West-
  ern Asia. See Chronology of Devel-
  opment of Nations.
THIRD CENTURY A.D.
FOURTH CENTURY A.D.
Constantine changed name of Byzantium
  to Constantinople 330
FIFTH CENTURY A.D.
ORIENTAL ROMAN
Result of absorption of ideas from
  Armenia and Mesopotamia
SIXTH CENTURY A.D.
Beginning of Mohammedanism, 571
Best Byzantine Period 550-1000
SEVENTH CENTURY A.D.
EIGHTH CENTURY A.D.
Saracenic Conquests in Byzantine Em-
  pire, Persia, India and Spain
Saracenic Conquest of Spain 711
Caliphate of Cordova enjoyed bril-
  liant art period until 1031
NINTH CENTURY A.D.
Arabian or Saracenic Conquests affect-
  ing Sicilian Arts
Russia under Byzantine influence 800
Independent Countship 850-1404
TENTH CENTURY A.D.
Russia under Celtic influence
ELEVENTH CENTURY A.D.
William the Conqueror 1066-1087
William II 1087-1100
Active trading with the East
Wars of the Crusaders 1096-1270
TWELFTH CENTURY A.D.
Continuation Romanesque Period
Henry I 1100-1135
Stephen 1135-1154
Henry II 1154-1189
Late Byzantine
Saracenic and Sicilian arts merged

GREEK 168

PARTHIAN 220

ROMAN EMPIRE dismembered 455

SASSANIAN EMPIRE 641

ROMAN GERMANIC 700

BEST BYZANTINE PERIOD ended
  1000

CELTIC 1100
ROMANESQUE 1189

THE PERIOD STYLES CLASSIFIED BY CENTURIES

Beginnings — **Developments** — **Endings**

ALHAMBRAIC PERIOD IN
SPAIN 1200-1300 A. D.
OTTOMAN EMPIRE ESTAB-
LISHED IN ASIA 1258-9
Supremacy 1298
ENGLISH DECORATED GOTHIC
1307-1399
Perpendicular Gothic 1399-1500
FLANDERS 1404
EARLY ITALIAN RENAISSANCE
1400-1500
FLORENTINE RENAISSANCE
1400-1600
MILANESE RENAISSANCE 1400-
1600
ROMAN RENAISSANCE 1444-1643
TURKISH EMPIRE 1453
Byzantium conquered by the Turks
ENGLISH RENAISSANCE 1458-
1603

ELIZABETHAN 1558-1603
HIGH ITALIAN RENAISSANCE
1500-1540
LATE RENAISSANCE 1540-1643
FRENCH RENAISSANCE 1502-1643
SPANISH RENAISSANCE 1500
PORTUGUESE RENAISSANCE
1500
GERMAN RENAISSANCE 1550

JACOBEAN 1603-1649
DUTCH REPUBLIC 1609
(Composed of the seven United
Provinces)
CROMWELLIAN
LOUIS XIII, 1610-1643
LOUIS XIV, 1643-1714
QUEEN ANNE, 1702-1714
GEORGIAN, 1714-1820
COLONIAL, 1727-1820
LOUIS XV
ROCOCO PERIOD, 1715-1774
LOUIS XVI, 1774-1793
DIRECTOIRE, 1795-1804
EMPIRE, 1804-1814
COLONIAL LATE CLASSIC
PERIOD, 1804-1820
VICTORIAN, 1837
ART NOUVEAU, 1898

THIRTEENTH CENTURY A. D.

Height of Moorish Art
Arabians and Saracens dominated by
the Turks and Turkish dominion in
Asia established 1258
Ottoman Empire
Venice became famous as an art center

FOURTEENTH CENTURY A. D.

Covering reigns of:
Edward II, Edward III, Richard II,
Henry IV, Henry V, Henry VI,
Edward IV, Edward V, Richard III

FIFTEENTH CENTURY A. D.

Great Trading Period of Flanders and
Italy.
Florence famous for manufactures
Gobelins established dye works 1440,
which afterward became famous for
manufacture of tapestries

SIXTEENTH CENTURY A. D.

Age of Oak 1500-1660
Portuguese opened East India Trade
1500
Henry VII, Founder ENGLISH TU-
DOR Line, 1458-1509
Henry VIII, 1509-1547
Elizabeth, 1558-1603
Founded by Louis XII, 1502-1515
Francis I, 1515-1549
Henri II, 1549-1559
Francis II, 1559-1560
Charles IX, 1560-1574
Henri III, 1574-1589
Henri IV, 1589-1610
In 1576, Holland, Zealand, Utrecht.
Gelderland, Gromingen, Friesland and
Overyssel became known as the Seven
United Provinces and asserted inde-
pendence. The Southern Provinces,
which form modern Belgium includ-
ing Flanders, which fell to Spain after
the abdication of Charles I, continued
under Spanish domination.
India, Mogul Empire, 1525-1748
Russian Empire, 1547
The Reformation, 1529
Portuguese Settlements in Persia

SEVENTEENTH CENTURY A. D.

Age of Walnut, 1660-1700
Moors Expelled from Spain, 1610
Dutch and East India Trading Com-
panies Organized, 1600
New York Settled by Dutch, 1613
James I (founder STUART
PERIOD), 1603-1625
Charles I, 1625-1649
Inigo Jones, dictator of English
styles, 1625-1652
Commonwealth England, 1653-1659
Inception Queen Anne, 1660. Some-
times called Stuart Period
Charles II, 1660-1685
James II, 1685-1689
William and Mary, 1689-1702
Dutch and East India furnishings largely
imported through Dutch and English
Trading Companies.
Revocation of the Edict of Nantes
brought many French and Flemish
weavers and woodworkers to Eng-
land

EIGHTEENTH CENTURY A. D.

Age of Mahogany, 1730
George I, 1714-1727
George II, 1727-1760
George III, 1760-1820
(Age of Chippendale, Sheraton, Adam
and Hepplewhite)
Flanders subjugated by the French, 1758
Russian Arts under French influence

NINETEENTH CENTURY A. D.

Alhambraic Period 1300
Early English Gothic 1307
English Decorated Gothic 1399

Byzantine 1453
Perpendicular Gothic 1458-1500

FRENCH GOTHIC 1515
High Italian Renaissance 1540

VENETIAN RENAISSANCE ended
1600
English Renaissance 1603
MOORISH 1610
Late Italian Renaissance 1643
French Renaissance 1643
ELIZABETHAN 1603
JACOBEAN 1649
Cromwellian 1659
CHARLES II 1685

William and Mary 1702
Louis XIII 1643
QUEEN ANNE 1714
Louis XIV 1714
Rococo 1774
Louis XVI 1793
FLANDERS subjugated by the French
INDIA MOGUL EMPIRE 1748
Directoire 1804
EMPIRE 1814
GEORGIAN 1820
COLONIAL 1820
VICTORIAN 1901

CLASSIFICATION OF THE PRINCIPAL RACES AND PEOPLES AND DATE OF THEIR ORIGIN

BLACK RACE (Ethiopian or Negro), — Tribes and peoples whose true home is Central and Southern Africa.

YELLOW RACE (Mongolian or Turanian), — (1) Chinese (3500 B.C.), Burmese, Japanese, and kindred peoples of Eastern Asia; (2) Nomad: Tartars, Huns, Parthians, Mongols, etc., of Northern and Central Asia and of Eastern Russia; (3) Turks, Magyars, Hungarians, Finns, ancient *Scythians, Lapps and Basques, of Europe; (4) Malays of Southeastern Asia and inhabitants of many of the Pacific islands; (5) Esquimeaux and American Indians.

WHITE RACE OR CAUCASIAN,

- **Hamites** — Egyptians, 4000 B.C.
  Libyans (Berbers, subsequently Moors), North Coast Africa.

- **Semites** — Assyrians, 2286 B.C.
  Phoenicians, 1100 B.C. (Cyprians, Rhodians.)
  Hebrews, 1900 B.C. Empire of Shepherd Kings in Eastern Egypt (Hyksos).
  Aramaeans (occupying old Syria, Mesopotamia and Babylonia).
  Arabians, 571 A.D. (followers of Mohammed, Saracens).

- **Aryans, or Indo-Europeans**
  - Asiatics....... — Hindus, 2000 B.C.
    Bactrians.
    Medes, 640 B.C.
    Persians, 558 B.C. (followers of Mohammed).
  - Classicals...... — Greeks, 1900 B.C.
    Romans, 753 B.C. } ROMANS } French.
    Etruscans. Spaniards.
    Byzantines. Italians.
    Portuguese.
  - Celts......... originally from Asia, 2000 B.C. — Gauls. } CELTS
    Irish.
    Welsh.
    Scotch. } GERMANIC
    Bretons of Brittany.
  - Teutons....... — Germanic tribes, Franks and Goths, Germans, Flemish, Dutch, Swiss, Scandinavians, Swedes, Norwegians and Danes, Angles, Saxons and Jutes—the English sprung from the four latter tribes.
  - Slavs......... — Russians.
    Poles, etc.

* Authorities differ regarding the Scythians, who 2000 B.C. occupied a vast section of Europe north of the Black and Caspian Seas. Some believe the Scythians were Mongols, others maintain Aryan origin, from which the Slavs descended.

BARBARIC DESIGN

BABYLONIAN ARCHAIC	PHŒNICIAN, OLD ARAMÆAN

WHEN man the barbarian carved some mystic sign upon his club or battle-axe, he had no art in his soul and no conception of Ornament. For centuries that are gone and are still to come, designs or signs or marks, may be regarded as designs to express thought, without any conception of an artistic idea. Hence we must not regard Design and Ornament as analogous terms. Ornament came with civilization. Design was of utilitarian impulse. It was smybolical.

If we contemplate some phases of Oriental art, especially the tribal forms, we find innumerable examples of design that are far from ornamental.

Long before the dawn of history we find two distinct races in Asia, the Turanian or Mongolian, and the Caucasian. The Mongolian or Yellow race includes the Chinese, the Tartars, the Mongols and Turks; the Caucasian race includes the Egyptians,

Assyrians, Arabians, Hindus, Persians, Greeks and Romans. The broad plateau of Iran in Asia was inhabited on the north by the Medians and on the south by the Persians. Many of their people, together with broken tribes of other Aryans, traveled east to the dis-

	MEANING	OUTLINE CHARACTER, B. C. 4500	ARCHAIC CUNEIFORM, B. C. 2500	ASSYRIAN, B. C. 700	LATE BABYLONIAN, B. C. 500
1.	The sun				
2.	God, heaven				
3.	Mountain				
4.	Man				
5.	Ox				
6.	Fish				

trict adjoining India, and in the great sub-division of the Turanian races of China great hordes traveled west, until the Aryan and Turanian characteristics were merged in broken clans, the class that we now term Turkoman.

Where civilization advanced and the arts flourished we have design as a concrete form of decoration and best exemplified in the work of Persia and Arabia, but with the hundreds and thousands of nomadic tribes design had been used to express an abstract thought or symbolism without heed for beauty, and these pictorial forms were at best crude ornament.

As a means of expression the nomads or wandering tribes as well as the savages of all countries early devised a form of picture language, and certain signs understood by them became in time tribal marks or involved possibly religious feeling. Thousands of these people living only by conquest traveled about from place to place in vast ravaging hordes. One can comprehend the conqueror of one band adopting with pride some symbol from the trappings of his fallen foe because this predatory instinct and boastfulness was manifest in the Empire styles, when bits of Italian or Egyptian decoration were strung together to commemorate the conquests of Napoleon.

Then, again, in the crude interchange of tribal courtesies and in the common assimilation of migratory people signs, ideograms and phonograms, having no meaning beyond being the reminder of some experience, were much used. It is natural, moreover, that in the use of simple signs or designs the same thing should be commonly used by many people in many remote parts of the world, and parts of squares and circles have been used universally for thousands of years to indicate various ideas, making it impossible for one to fix a definite meaning for these designs or to determine by their presence a definite point of origin.

The writer some time ago had occasion to illustrate the illusions which arise from the use of angles, and with no thought but to accomplish this purpose

The above is from a Greek tablet and shows apparently the origin of three borders—the water line border, the barber pole and the reciprocal trefoil border.

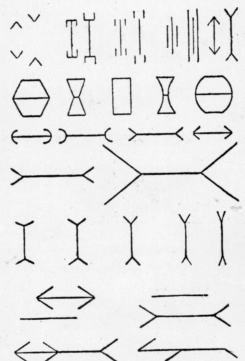

A series of illusions respecting straight lines and angles; similar figures appear in Kurdistan rugs.

Alaskan. "Record of a hunt." See text.

Egyptian.

the accompanying design was prepared to show that notwithstanding appearances the straight lines enclosed between acute or obtuse angles are of the same length.

In the preparation of the story of Oriental design the writer is interested to note that his illusion illustrations, prepared at a time when his mind was far from the Orient, may be regarded as excellent examples of Mongol detail. Every figure in the illusion figures is to be found in Kurdistan designs, emphasizing the fact that simple pictorial expressions are of world usage. They occur to the minds of all people and of all countries, and are not sufficiently intricate to constitute an original thought.

Perhaps the most important influence on the use of design was the common employment of picture-writing. The researches of the Bureau of Ethnology, Washington, incline one to believe that picture language was introduced by prehistoric America to China. Alexander Speltz, in his great work on "Styles of Ornament," encourages this belief by many examples of prehistoric design from North and South America.

The native designs of old Mexico suggest the Anatolian. The native designs of the Aztecs suggest Egyptian, and we commend the reader for further study of this subject to "Unknown Mexico," by Carl Lumholtz, or to the Government Exploration Reports on the Tussayan and Hopi Indians, descendants of those living centuries ago in the deserted villages of Arizona and Mexico, Central and South America.

In the illustration of old Maya designs it is not difficult to trace motifs identical with those of the Mongol districts of the Caucasus. The Maya Indians were the most advanced of the North American aboriginal races. They had books, paper, picture language, were sun worshippers, built well and carved well, had paved roads of stone and communicated by couriers. Their houses were decorated and the temples of Yucatan were built, if we are to believe the archæologists, when Egypt was a wilderness.

The Smithsonian Institute has given to us a great number of illustrations showing the sign language of the Maya, and we find here also the tree of life, the latch-hook, the square and rhomboid, the octagon, the overlapping wave design, the fret, the swastika and the trefoil.

We can turn to Aztec and Peruvian decoration and find designs almost pure Turkestan and Caucasian. Forms of a cross that are often seen in Caucasian rugs are illustrated by Lumholtz as representing conventionalized forms of the Mexican toto blossom. Mexican water motifs are the same as Caucasian, and the use of florals and geometrical figures gives evidence of a common inspiration—an inspiration that nature gives to the primitive mind. There is further interest in the fact that in all countries some flower— the iris, the lotus, the lily, the acanthus, the palm, the poppy, the toto blossom—is utilized for its symbolic significance. With the Mexican Indians flowers, blossoms and birds have a strict religious meaning. Indeed, the Huichol Indians never pluck a flower unless with pious intent. It is safe to assume that no savage ever sat down to the work of ornamentation unless it expressed thought, and such thoughts were naturally simple and confined to simple means. The records of an Alaskan hunt we reproduce as an example from Meyer's "Prehistoric Times." The translation follows:

I go by boat (indicated by a paddle held upright—I sleep one night (hand at side of head denotes sleep)—on island with two huts— I go to another island—two people sleep there— a sea lion I hunt with harpoon—I return by boat with companion (indicated by two oars) to my lodge.

In this system of writing the characters are crude pictures of material objects and no extensive vocabulary is required to cover the needs of a savage people. A picture of an eye would indicate the order of sight, or the personal pronoun, or vigilance, or other meanings, according to circumstances. A lot of zigzag lines falling from a parallelogram would indicate rain.

The great chasm between picture writing and sign writing was partially bridged by the Chinese who, as early as 2000 B. C., employed a system wherein every word of the language was represented by a symbol. Then came the Egyptian system and the Babylonian

Mexican.

Hopi.   American Indian.

Chinese.

system of cuneiform writing, 2000 B.C., a system generally adopted in Western Asia, employing the use of a wedge-shaped stylus. Much of the writing was stamped upon clay. For thousands of years the cuneiform system of writing was lost. In 1618 de Sylva Figueroa, of Spain, investigated the inscriptions and fixed them as Turanian. Hence it is reasonable, in view of the purely angular character of Mongol decoration, to trace much of its inspiration to the early knowledge of cuneiform writing.

In the excavations of ancient Troy, the buried cities of Illios and Hissarlic, certain decorative forms of these cuneiform records, found upon coins and tablets, have been adopted as fetishes of the people, especially in the Kurdistan district, much as the people of America adopt the swastika under the vague impression that it is a good-luck sign.

From the coins and tablets of these old Trojan ruins of Asia Minor we find the swastika so common and in so many forms, or rather alterations, that we believe that the latch-hook of this district and the Caucasus, and even of the Turkoman district, is a lingering swastika influence and not a wave sign. We find in Asia Minor the swastika in its true form as well as distortions of these forms, sprawly shapes, sometimes representing stars or trees or animals. It is impossible to trace the meaning of the signs because we find them among so many people at periods widely separate. The term is thought by some to mean eternity. The swastika enclosed within a circle gives a suggestion of flight, progress. We have seen the swastika with the extending lines leg-shaped, sometimes eight and ten instead of four legged.

Zmigrodski, the anthropologist, classifies these distortions under what he calls related swastikas. Unquestionably the swastika originated as a thought expression, which in time became a fixed symbol of general world use.

The United States Government, in the Smithsonian report of 1894, published the results of its research and showed that the swastika had been found in almost every part of Europe and was identical with the same form used in prehistoric America. It was known in India and ancient Bactria (East Turkestan), in Rhodes, Northern Europe, Southern Europe, Asia

Minor, Greece, Rome, Byzantine, Northern Africa, Great Britain and America. Ancient Troy was full of the swastika, and it appeared on the coins of the classic Orient, Babylonia, Assyria, Chaldea and Persia.

The French Government discovered the swastika throughout Armenia and in the Caucasus district. So any assumption that it has restricted or local meaning is untenable.

In searching for the origin of the star, the octagon and the triangle we are brought frequently to the doors of Constantinople. We may go back to India and the Brahmans and we find the triangle as a sectarian mark. The combination of two triangles gives us the six-pointed star. The combination of two squares gives us the Mohammedan eight-pointed star, and the five-pointed star is supposed to be a Christian symbol. Yet if we go back to the period of Christian enthusiasm in the Byzantine Empire we will find the Brahman and Mohammedan eight-pointed star in universal use. The marble mosaic which covered the floors contained geometrical shapes innumerable. The five-pointed, six-pointed and eight-pointed star is simply a geometrical combination of squares and circles. After the fall of Constantinople the beauty of its decorative system was promptly copied by the Mohammedans, quick to perceive a means of beautifying without the use of animal forms, interdicted by the Koran, and we trace this Byzantine influence through the Anatolian Peninsula and the Caucasus.

Tradition states that the crescent was adopted and used in Constantinople as an omen of protection like the winged asp and ball of Egypt. When the Macedonian hordes approached old Byzantium by stealth the crescent moon arose and revealed their presence and saved the city. The crescent was then adopted generally as a good-luck symbol. In after years when Contantinople fell to Turkish dominion the crescent was seized upon as a valuable symbol.

Geometrical design had a wide influence upon the arts of all Asia, with the exception of Persia. The Arabians developed a remarkable system of strapwork, scroll and circular design strictly geometrical, and even when the Arabian system became floriated it was the juxtaposition of floral details geometrically arranged and interwoven. We find the same system in China, where geometrical forms of the fret similar to the Greek fret, geometrical circles and diamonds and octagons are used universally, but have no relationship with similar designs of the Greek and Roman Empires. We find in China the eight-point decoration that is adopted generally through the Turkoman district and found frequently in Afghanistan rugs. It implies Mongol influence. The same thing is common in Gothic decoration.

Greek.

Design is not always decoration, but decoration is always design. There is much that interests us in aboriginal design in the effort to express some material thought or idea of beauty. But there is greater satisfaction in contemplating a perfected system of decorative unity.

Decoration represents a development of civilization and culture. The Arabians as world conquerors left the imprint of their decorative art for thousands of miles around them, but they absorbed little, and to the end Arabian art was true to its ancient forms.

With Persia, however, the best period of its art progress may be traced direct to the influence of Shah Abbas, who in the Sixteenth Century sent his best artists to Italy, where they studied under the tutelage of the great Renaissance designers. All that is most beautiful in Persian art may be ascribed to the Renaissance and Arabian influences.

We do not forget that for centuries before Christ the Persians were in close intercourse with the Assyrians and Egyptians and their art flourished accordingly, nor that early Persian art was strongly Assyrian and Babylonian.

But this was not the art that became in years afterwards indigenous to the soil, the art which, freed of Mohammedanism, embodies the presentation of nature forms, floral and animal, and presents a unity of design brought into coherent relationship by the principles underlying the best Italian school.

We can continue the work of Arabian and Persian design satisfied with the decorative charm that it possesses. But the mere fact that with most of the Oriental designs we search for the meaning, the symbolic underlying story that is told, shows on its face that the mere picture is not satisfying, and as a decorative composition it does not appeal to us, but only interests because enigmatical.

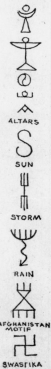

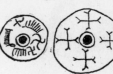

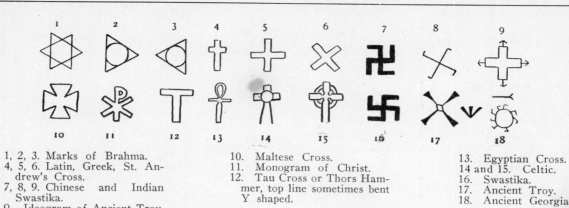

1, 2, 3. Marks of Brahma.
4, 5, 6. Latin, Greek, St. Andrew's Cross.
7, 8, 9. Chinese and Indian Swastika.
9. Ideogram of Ancient Troy.

10. Maltese Cross.
11. Monogram of Christ.
12. Tau Cross or Thors Hammer, top line sometimes bent Y shaped.

13. Egyptian Cross.
14 and 15. Celtic.
16. Swastika.
17. Ancient Troy.
18. Ancient Georgia.

1. Moslem Comb and Star of Bethlehem, Turkish.

2. Knot of Destiny, Chinese origin.

3. Effulgent Star, Caucasian.

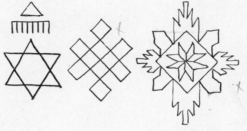

1   2   3

1, 2, 3, 4. Altar designs.
5. Solomon's Signet.
6, 7, 8, 9. Forms of altar, or tree of life.

Kurdistan and North Persian motifs.

Gothic geometric divisions. Note characteristic of Afghanistan.

Old Mexico.

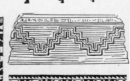

Mexican.   Old Mexico (Huichol). Note similarity to Turkoman, Caucasian and Chinese.

DESIGN CHARACTERISTICS.

EGYPTIAN DESIGN DETAILS.

The top line shows the lotus bud, pad and blossom.

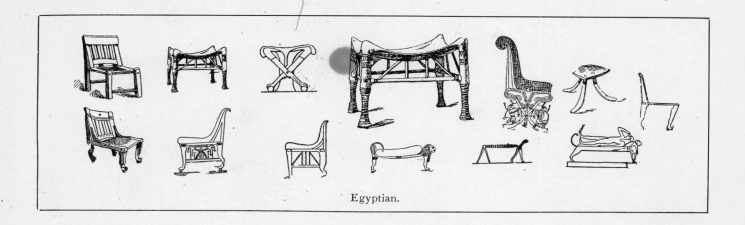

Egyptian.

EGYPTIAN

EGYPTIAN—Old Empire, 4000-3000 B.C. Middle Empire, 3000-2100 B.C. New Empire, 2100-324 B.C. Graeco-Roman Revival, 324 B.C. to 300 A. D.

Egypt, 332 B.C., became a Greek kingdom; 30 B.C. became a Roman province until the Mohammedan invasion, 640 A.D.

EGYPTIAN weaving most ancient known industry. Egyptian linens famous, embroidered with gold, silver and purple.

The moment we leave the age of savagery and man clothed in animal skins, we reach the stage of weaving. Clothing was the first necessity of mankind.

Tombs of Egypt, 2800 B.C., illustrate weavers at work. One shows a man weaving a checkered rug. Monuments of ancient Egypt and Syria show the manufacture of rugs and fabrics, 2400 B.C.

Nine hundred and eight B.C., Egyptian canopy cloths of fine character, embroidered and of a patch character.

The history of lace begins definitely with 900 A. D., but drawn-work and nettings were of prehistoric origin.

Fabrics dating 1000 B.C. are preserved in the Louvre, Paris.

Three thousand five hundred and fifty B.C., building of the pyramids. Following the Stone Age, came the Age of Copper, Age of Bronze, Age of Iron.

As early as 2100 B.C., Egypt was highly civilized. In buildings moldings were seldom used. Chambers were decorated with illustrations representing industries.

Carvings, instead of standing out in relief, were sunken and the ground stood out, a system exactly opposite to the Assyrian system, where the ground was depressed and the subject stood out in relief.

Decoration full of gold and brilliant colors, the triad form being popular (black, yellow and red), (red, blue and white), (dark blue, light blue and white), (cream color, blue and black), (dark red, medium yellow and blue).

Ornaments were frequently in hieroglyphics.

Among motifs and designs were the sun, the beetle, the cobra or serpent, feathers, papyrus buds and reeds, lotus, date-palms, the lily, zigzags for water ways, herbs, animals, fan-shaped ornaments, nude figures, winged human figures, human faces, the ram, sparrow hawk, sacred tree.

Late Egyptian furniture had rope or rush covered seats.

Egyptian wall treatments, confined to frieze decorations against plain walls. Couches were made low; no foot boards; small rests at head to fit under the neck. Stools often had wooden bottoms, but couches were always plaited. Six hundred B.C., seats were of narrow strips of leather plaited; furniture often wood inlaid with metal. Seats were curved to fit the figure.

Egyptian.

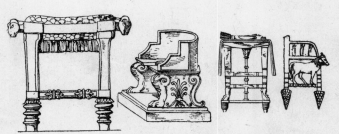

Babylonian-Assyrian.

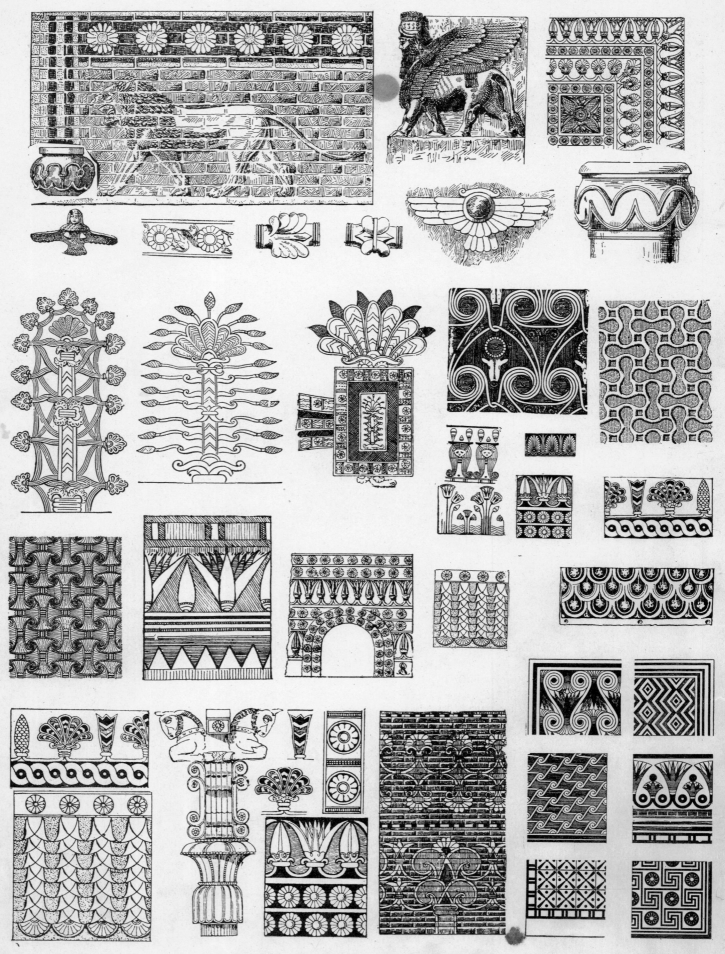

BABYLONIAN—ASSYRIAN.

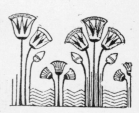

BABYLONIAN—ASSYRIAN—PERSIAN

ASSYRIAN, Persian, Babylonian and even Egyptian arts in the Early Centuries B.C., were so merged as to be indistinguishable to all but the most careful archæological student (see "Chart of origins"). The illustration below is Persian, although it contains distinct Egyptian as well as Assyrian characteristics.

Persian ornament in the popular conception dates from the Islam or Mohammedan period in the Seventh Century A.D.

BABYLONIAN-ASSYRIAN:
Old Babylonian, 4000 B.C. Chaldean Period, 2286-1300 B.C. Assyrian Period, 1300-625 B.C. Median Period, 640-558 B.C. Late Babylonian, 608-538.

EXCAVATIONS in Nineveh, Nimroud and Khorsabad afford proofs of the existence of civilization in Babylonia 4000 B.C. But in this wide country, embracing Assyria, Babylonia, Egypt, Chaldea, Media and Persia, there was such a mixture of peoples, each successively subjugated by first one then another, that the arts of all must be regarded as common to the whole.

Three thousand B.C. in Southern Babylonia a number of independent cities; Erech, Ur, Larsam; Agade, Babylon. Kingdom of Elam, East of Babylonia, supreme 2300 B.C. About 1900 B.C. Kingdom of Semitic Assyrians founded, which later developed the great cities of Asshur and Nineveh.

Six hundred and sixty-eight B.C. Esarhaddon king, Assyria became world power. As in Egypt, so in the adjoining river-valley countries, the lotus flower or the lily played an important role in ornamentation.

In the earliest periods Assyria was famous for its weaving. It is impossible to fix the date of embroideries or fancy needlework, but it is fair to assume that as weaving was, next to the building of the hut and the making of the battle-axe, the first industry, it was likewise the first to partake of decorative character.

In the early period the furniture was of metal and wood or wood inlaid with metal.

Seven hundred B.C. magnificent epoch. At Koyunjik the palace had seventy-one halls and chambers, two miles of wall decorations. Conspicuous features of design were bulls, lions and eagles. At Nimroud the beams of the palaces were of cedar wood carved.

Persian, showing Egyptian and Assyrian influences.

It will be noted that in 993 the walls of King Solomon's Temple were covered with carved cedar and olive wood in styles like the Assyrian stone sculptures, utilizing much winged decoration and lily forms. At this period Hiram of Tyre was famous for his bronze work. Much gold was used in ornamentation. Fabrics were ornamented in minute diaper patterns with bands or borders. The faces in the mural decorations were in profile. The palm, date, vine, fig tree,

Persian.

fern, lily and tall grass were much used. The sacred tree was conspicuous in design, with wave and guilloche ornamentations; fir cones radiated from rosette centers. Carved ivory was plentiful; iron seldom used; emblems usually bronze; ornamentation of vivid color, gold and silver and delicate painting; eagle-headed lions, winged bulls, human figures with wings and eagle heads. Babylonia and Assyria in constant war; their arts were merged. Assyrian ornament copied much that was Egyptian.

Examples of Assyrian furniture are very rare, as the climate did not contribute to the preservation of

Asia Minor. The art that we regard popularly as Persian is the later Islam art of Mohammed.

PHOENICIAN.

THE Phœnicians were commercial people. Two thousand B.C. they were settled on the coast of Syria and had trading stations and colonies in Greece, Italy, Gaul and Africa. They were traders and had no art beyond that of local jewelers.

HEBRAIC.

THE Hebrews of Palestine were dependent on the Phœnicians for their technique, the Mosaic laws forbidding pictures and images prevented the free de-

Ancient Persian, showing Assyrian origin.

woods, which occasionally in Egypt lasted through the centuries. In many places only the bronze and ivory mountings of feet and ends of chairs have been found.

The furniture of the Hebrews was, in the early centuries, of the same character as Assyrian.

PERSIAN—558 B.C. Persian Empire, 558-330 B.C. Parthian Empire, 250 B.C.-220 A.D. Sassanian Empire, 220-641 A. D. Mohammedan Persia, 641 A.D.

DISUNION and unrest, in the Asia of olden times, confused the arts. Ancient Persian Ornament shows few characteristic peculiarities, Egyptian, Assyrian, Babylonian and Grecian influence being all discernible. Indeed, the buildings of the Persian kings were erected by men who were prisoners in the countries of Babylonia, Egypt and the Grecian colonies of

velopment of art among the Jews. King Solomon's palace and the temples were the work of Phœnicians.

INDIAN—2000 B.C. First Period, 2000 B.C.-1525 A.D. Brahma, 1400-500 B.C.; Buddha, 500 B.C. Mogul Empire, 1525-1748 A.D. English Control, 1748-1858 A.D. English Empire, 1858 A.D.

ARCHAEOLOGICAL research reaches no farther back in India than a few centuries B.C. This early art was influenced by Persian and Grecian. The term Indian is geographical and has no ethnological significance. There is no such thing as homogeneous Indian art. It was a country of many races, Aryan and Turanian, of Brahman, Buddhist and Mohammedan development. The Mohammedan phase, which was the most lasting, will be considered later.

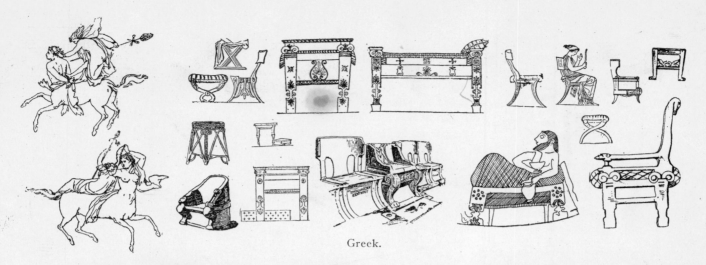

Greek.

GRECIAN—ROMAN—POMPEIIAN

GRECIAN—Graeco-Pelasgic 1900-1384 B.C.; Doric, 700 B.C.; Ionic, 600 B.C.; Corinthian, 290 B.C.; Hellenistic, 290-168 B.C.; Etruscan, 1040-238 B.C.

GREEKS inherited the arts of Persia and Babylonia. Starting with 1900 B.C., the Pelasgic period was based on Assyrian. Early Greek couches nothing more than large stools. In the Sixth Century B.C. Greek and Roman beds were of marble, terra-cotta, bronze, wood, bone and ivory; used for reclining at meals as well as sleeping. Ancient Greeks learned their art from Egyptians, but a purely decorative Greek device is the anthemion, which with the acanthus can be traced back hundreds of years in Egyp-

tian forms. The Greek system was to build within squares. Frets were common. Decorators painted in fresco and in strong colors; blue and Tyrian purple much in use. At an early date conceived a system of applying blue in proportions equal to yellow and red combined, yellow in three parts, red five parts and blue eight parts. First Greek and Roman couches covered with skins or felt materials. Mattresses used Third Century B.C. with coverlets and draperies, in broad stripes of solid colors; pillows various shapes covered with linen, wool, leather and silk. Pillows filled with refuse wool, vegetable fiber, feathers. No record of uses of cotton. Silk much used and draperies described

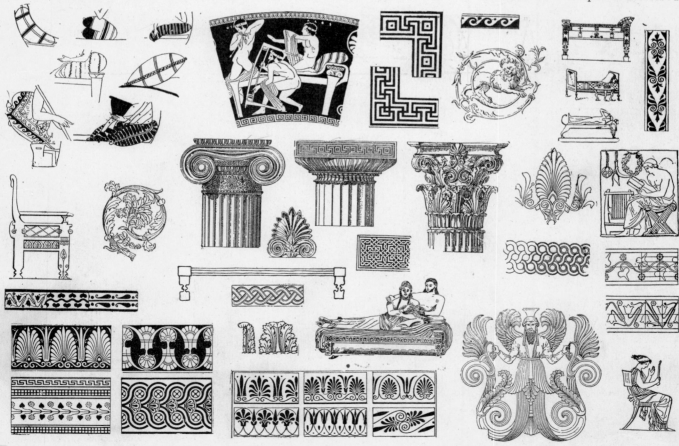

Greek Ornament.

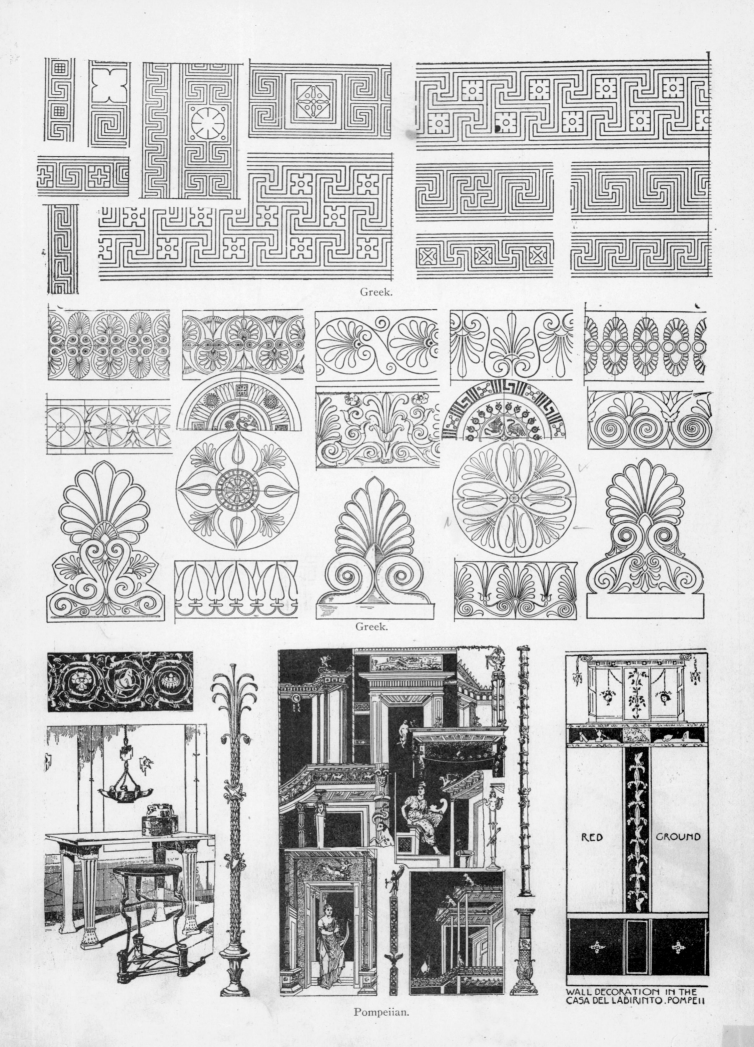

Greek.

Greek.

Pompeiian.

RED GROUND

WALL DECORATION IN THE
CASA DEL LABIRINTO. POMPEII

DETAILS OF ROMAN ORNAMENT.

Roman.

as having nap on one or two sides (velvet) in color-ings of purple, scarlet and gold. Fabrics woven in pattern or embroidered. Thin linens, tapestries. Much material brought from Babylonia.

Greek furniture inlaid with precious metals; bronze and polished silver mirrors. Beds of wood often ornamented in tortoise shell, veneers of fine wood. Wood finished in oil, wax and stains, some-times painted, never varnished; solid carvings.

Tenth Century B.C., Homer the poet referred fre-quently to the bed.

Seventh Century B.C., couches were made with ledges built on a rectangular plan as well as with turned ledges. First they were frame works ledged with a flat surface upon which furs were piled up. Then the upper part was furnished with headboards and footboards.

Sixth Century B.C. gives us beds so draped that the construction of the frame is hidden.

In the Fifth Century B.C. beds and furniture were common, rectangular and turned legs being used. Wood, bronze and other metals. Some authorities maintain that iron was used in beds as early as 427 B.C.

Four hundred B.C., Greek embroiderers produced beautiful results.

Pelasgic Greek was largely based on Assyrian ornamentation. The Greek honeysuckle can be traced to Assyria, also the vitruvian scroll and the guilloche.

Etruscan—A bronze Etruscan bed exists from the Seventh Century B.C.

ROMAN—753 B.C.-455 A.D.

ROMAN. 753 B.C., Roman houses divided into sep-arate rooms for dresses, cupboards, lockers, lounges, articles of luxury. Fabrics of many kinds developed the Greek style. Great love of pomp and splendor. Elaborated the Corinthian principles;

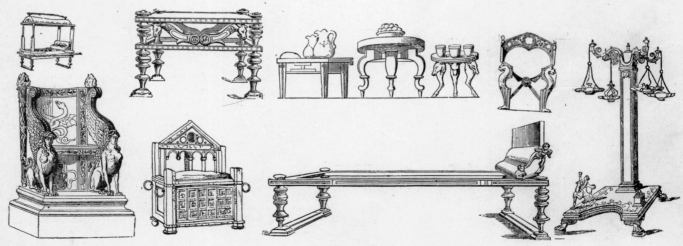

Roman.

22

utilized pineapple, vine, palm, ivy, poppy, winged dolphins, winged horses. Like the Grecians, the Roman wall treatments were confined to frieze decorations against the plain wall. First couches covered with wool material and skins, in time became elaborated beds with head and foot pieces. No upholsterings except movable pillows. Marble couches were common, and wood beds ornamented in precious metals, tortoise shell and ivory. Late Roman furniture had rush and reed plaited seats. Beds used for reclining at meals.

Roman furniture was decorated with paintings and inlay veneer, Tarsia work forming complex decorations. Roman houses were furnished with cupboards, shelves, wardrobes, lockers and general furniture superior in comfort to Fourteenth and Fifteenth Centuries, Europe.

Ancient Phrygian and Lydians occupying western Anatolia made embroideries at a period prehistoric. The Roman word Phrygio means embroiderer.

POMPEIIAN—100 B.C.-79 A.D.

POMPEIIAN. Development of the Roman arts which finally became almost pure Greek; beautiful mosaics, still life, human and divine figures, complete pictures on the walls which were frequently painted in reproduction of oil paintings by Greek masters. Pompeiian wall space divided into dado, middle and upper section, dado generally black with simple ornaments; purple, green, blue or violet middle space enlightened with one or more figures or landscapes, having one or more borders. Upper space usually white. System of dark dadoes and light friezes generally employed. Delicate garlands, fruits, masks, animals, imitating nature. (In England 1762-1792 the brothers Adam almost reproduced Pompeiian style.)

WALL DECORATION.

Grecian and Roman—In Greece much modeling in plaster and stucco, drawn upon a coat of wet plaster spread on the wall and built up. Fresco and tempera or distemper painting widely practiced. Decorative borders frescoed and painted in subjects religious as well as legendary, showing hundreds of Greek and Roman gods; modern or superior deities; the Genii and inferior deities; the demi-gods and heroes, and illustrations of events in Greek and Roman mythology. Statuary and sculpture, as well as paintings, partook of these subjects. Greeks love color. Used it in extravagant proportions in their paintings and frescoes. Massive walls show not only historical and religious subjects, but paintings of still life, city and country scenes, flowers and nature showing perspective. Unlike Egypt and Assyria where walls were all covered, Greek and Roman walls were usually treated with deep friezes or upper thirds. Ceilings were elaborate, divided into geometric sections, octagonal forms and squares. Mosaic brought to its greatest perfection for wall pictures, pavements and floors.

Pompeiian—Pompeii and Herculaneum were centers of late art of highest Roman type. Myth and religion subservient to the beautiful. Perspective scenes elaborately painted; gods, hill and valley, palaces and cottages, water-views, mountains, scenes of travel, commerce and warfare. High dadoes filled with model figures.

In private houses walls were frequently completely covered by paintings executed direct on plaster. Sometimes divided into panels with small pictures in minute panels above larger panels. Mosaic work of most exquisite character.

Pompeiian.

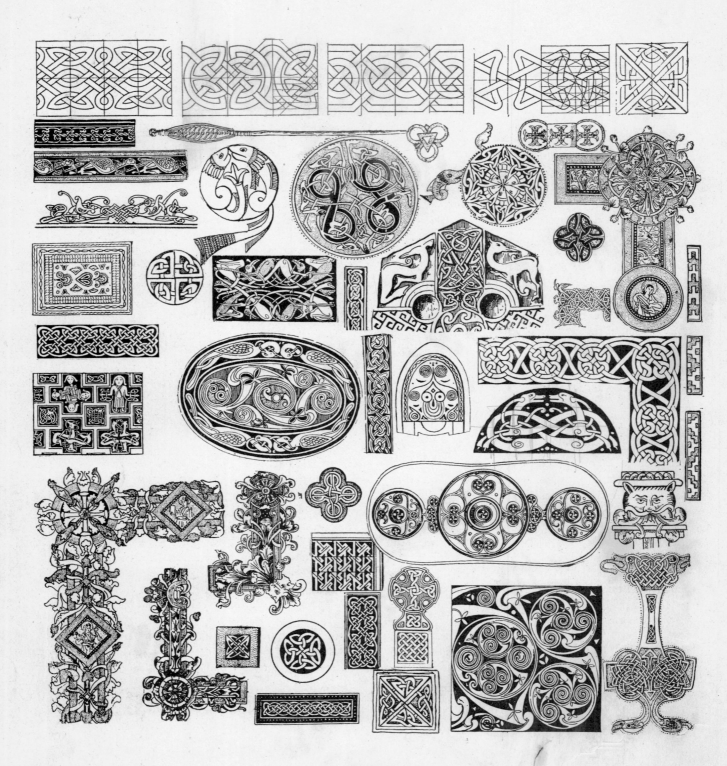

CELTIC ORNAMENT.

The floriated form is the Romanesque influence developing about 700 A.D. The animal form is the Scandinavian influence.

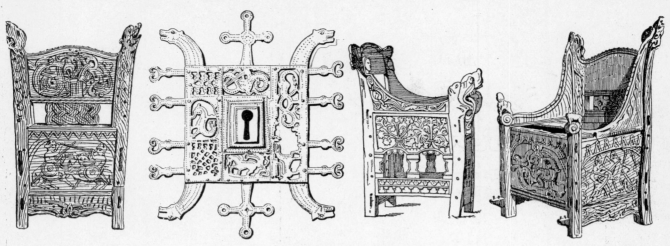

Types of Scandinavian Furniture.

NORTHERN

SCANDINAVIAN OR NORTHERN—100-1299 A.D.

SCANDINAVIAN: A geographical term covering Sweden, Norway and Denmark. Northern or Norseman was an adjective term applying not only to the Scandinavians but to the men of the "North Country."

The term Norman was a contraction of Norseman, the people living just north of the Gallic country.

Scandinavia until nearly 1000 A.D. was pagan. Its art reflected in a realistic manner the traditions of the country.

According to Scandinavian legends there were wrapped in the history of the country's origin intrigue, treasure and murder. It is unnecessary to tell the story (see history), but decorative art utilized a system of interlacements not balanced like the Celtic, but confused lines and chaotic traceries intermingled with figures of the otter, the dragon, the horse, bags of treasures, human figures in conflict.

The Celts and Scandinavians became in time closely related. From 1000 to 1100 A.D. Celtic influence was felt on account of the Celtic missionaries who went north from Ireland and preached the doctrines of Christ in the North country. But after the year 1100 we find plant life introduced, realistic verdure of Roman character, the same that prevailed among the Normans and Anglo-Saxons who at this time were enthusiastic in religion and naturally absorbed the art characteristics of the papal states.

CELTIC—2000 B.C. - 1100 A.D.

THE Celtic nation of Western Europe was annihilated before the Christian era, but the Celts settling in Great Britain, principally in Ancient Hibernia (Ireland) left lasting evidence of their art even

On the left, Scandinavian ornament; on the right, Celtic.

SCANDINAVIAN ORNAMENT.

during the sway of paganism which prevailed up to 400 A.D. Celtic art showed interlaced curved lines sometimes utilizing exaggerated bird forms interwoven, but, unlike Scandinavian, the interlacements showed balanced relation.

From 900 to 1100 A.D. Romanesque influence was strong in Celtic art, due to the enthusiasm and preeminence of the Irish in religion, art and education. Ireland, independent up to 1172, was conquered by the English. Celtic art underwent a radical change by the introduction of Romanesque floral characteristics during the Tenth Century. Intersection was characteristic of the art as in Moresque and Arabian, but intersection in Celtic art, unlike the geometric Moorish, or the flat conventionalized vegetation and leaf forms suggested by Arabian, is always intersection of simple circular or curved bands, sometimes introducing animal or bird forms. When dragons and animal forms are introduced one may detect Scandinavian influence.

Balanced relations prevail in Celtic intersection design.

RUSSIAN—500 A.D.

ORNAMENT of Celtic character is often seen in what is known as Russian art. Russia was settled 862 A.D. by Scandinavians. Russia developed during the Romanesque period up to 1100, a period of high religious fervor, and this period affected the characteristics of Scandinavian art. Subsequent to 1100 Oriental influence was strong in Russia.

NORMAN, ENGLAND—1066-1189 A.D. (See Romanesque.)

THE Normans were the Norsemen and inherited the early Scandinavian arts; but at the time the Normans gained a foothold in Normandy, 911 A.D., and at the time they conquered England, 1066, they were under the French-Romanesque art influence.

BYZANTINE

BYZANTINE—328-500, Roman-Christian, 550-800, Oriental splendor. 850-1005, Macedonian or Roman Classicism.

Chair of Dagobert;
Seventh Century.

BYZANTINE ornamentation covers three periods. The first from 328, when Byzantium, under Constantine, became capital of the Eastern Division of the great Roman Empire, and Christianity was made the established State religion. Most distinctive epoch, under Justinian, was from 527 to about 600. A period of torpor followed until 850, when under Macedonian rule it became classic.

The close historical relations between Byzantine and the Roman-Italian people naturally merged the arts, and we have terms confusing.

Mediæval art is arbitrarily fixed between 450 and 1150.
Romanesque art is the art influenced by the Romans from 700 to 1100, when Gothic began.
Lombardic Romanesque, the Romanesque of the Lombards, began 773.
Early Christian began 330, extending over 200 years.
Norman Romanesque was the Romanesque of the Normans, beginning 911 and finding its best expression in England subsequent to the conquest of the Normans, 1066, hence sometimes called English Romanesque.

Prior to 550 the term Early Christian applied to that period when Christianity was accepted as the State religion by the Byzantine Empire. Christian symbolism soon found its way into Byzantine art, and from the dismemberment of the Roman Empire, 455, these Christian characteristics of design were absorbed and adopted generally outside of Byzantium, but especially by the Goths who ruled Italy until 555, as well as by the Lombards who settled in Northern Italy 568.

Byzantine art was characterized by sharp acanthus foliage united with Christian emblems, circle, cross, crown, vine, dove, peacock; figure sculpture

Byzantine fabric, showing the ogival form of design.

Byzantine embroidery from the tomb of Gunther, Bishop of Bamberg, preserved at Ratisbon.

rarely used, group figures done in mosaics. Interlacing circles, interlacing crosses in fret work, interlacing guilloches finally conspicuous.

FABRICS.

Fabrics precedent of paintings. Ancient Babylon renowned for its needlecraft. All other nations learned their art from Babylon, beginning with decoration of animal skins, embroidering, mat-plaiting and finally weaving.

We can go back to 3000 B.C. for a simple weaving produced by a simple interchange of warp and weft, but the complex manipulation of shuttles producing figures without embroidering or other extraneous aids was not known until 200 A.D., when it was, unquestionably, undertaken by Syrian weavers of the Eastern Roman Empire.

Wool. Egypt, mistress of advanced civilization, employed wool, hemp and flax.

Cotton. Greeks unacquainted with cotton until 333 B.C. The plant was indigenous to India, and not until the invasion of Alexander the Great did it become known to Europe.

Embroidery. In the earliest ages animal skins, before the age of weaving, frequently embroidered or decorated with stitches. Early Assyrians used embroidery. Egyptians and Greeks famous in the art. Ancient Babylon, Egypt and Chaldea understood the art thoroughly.

Beginning with Christian era an active commerce introduced Indian and Chinese stuffs, and the Italian, Teutonic and French craftsmen were quick to adopt Oriental methods. Art of embroidering became generally understood. Appliqué work was also under-

taken as well as tapestry weaving. Byzantine Empire from 350 to 700 A.D. knew no limit to extravagance; decoration conspicuous in griffins, unicorns, lions, tigers, elephants, eagles, peacocks, large and small circular bands, medallion shapes, golden apples, palms, shrubs and flowers. Textile design decorated with wheels or circular bands, lozenge patterns, squares, hexagons, octagons, stripes, beasts and birds.

Biblical and mythological subjects; fabrics largely used for hangings between colonnades as portières.

A favorite arrangement of pattern employed pairs of animals, or pairs of birds confronted and separated by the sacred tree of the Persians.

SILK. Although commonly woven in China, 1200 B.C., not woven in Europe until 500 A.D., when the Emperor Justinian secured through two Persian monks a number of silk cocoons and worms which they smuggled from China.

Six hundred A.D. Sicily, as well as Northern Egypt, was making silks.

Four hundred A.D. Egyptian and Roman tapestries well known. Roman silks, possibly Syrian or Persian manufacture, were sarcenets and taffetas, damasks, brocatelles, lampas and velvets, and the same period produced admirable tapestries and embroideries. Byzantium became the seat for European silk cultivation, and for five centuries, together with Corinth and Athens, was prolific in weave craft.

FURNITURE.

Tables, chairs and beds followed the Roman style, the legs often of turned wood. Ivory, carved and inlaid, and metal, much used; enamels and gold, bronze and inlaid woods employed. Chair of Dagobert (600) a fair example of the elaborateness of the period. It is of gilt-bronze and one of the earliest pieces.

Saracenic. Eleventh Century Silk Damask, showing Persian and Byzantine influence.

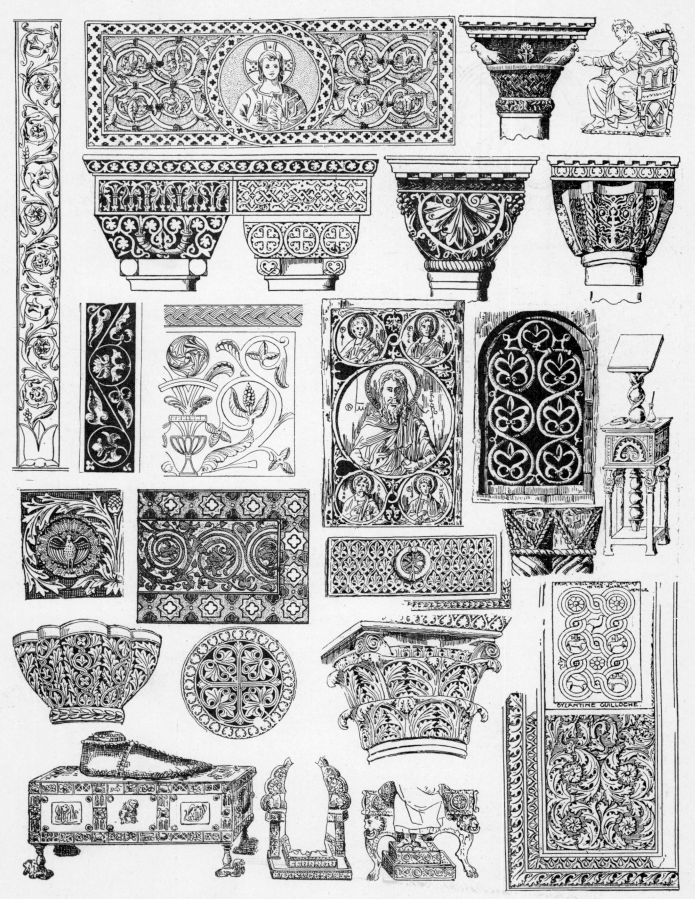

BYZANTINE ORNAMENT.

Showing Oriental as well as Classic influence of Tenth Century.

BYZANTINE ORNAMENT.

No. 1. Perso-Byzantine, 700 A.D. No. 2. Romanesque, 1100 A.D., style of pattern evolved by system of intersecting circles; popular at the beginning of the Gothic period. No. 3. French or German Romanesque, 1100 A.D. No. 4. Section of style showing circles joined together by smaller circles; a system of design in vogue 1000 A.D. No. 5. French, Saracenic influence, 1100 A.D. No. 6. French-Romanesque, 1100 A.D. No. 7. Hispano-Saracenic, 1200 A.D.

EARLY CHRISTIAN—ROMANESQUE

IN THE study of Early Christian, Byzantine and Romanesque art one must never lose sight of the fact that at the beginning and the end of these periods the Orient wielded an influence. In 328, while preparing for battle, Constantine, Emperor of Rome, saw a cross in the sky, and accepting it as an omen he embraced the Christian religion. The capital of his new Empire was Byzantium, which name he changed to Constantinople, and the Byzantine Empire at the outstart covered much of Asia Minor, Arabia, Egypt, North Africa and the country now Bulgaria and Greece. Georgia, that portion of the Caucasus frequently called Iberia, appears first in authentic history in the time of Alexander the Great, but in the Fourth Century it was part of the Byzantine Empire.

From 550 to 800 Byzantine art was gorgeous in Oriental splendor. The Saracens carried Islam art throughout Persia, Palestine, Syria and Egypt in the Seventh Century, over Africa and Spain in the Eighth Century, and Lower Italy in the Ninth Century.

To arrive at a definite understanding of the character of design employed during the early Christian and Romanesque periods we must consider two essentials, Origin and Use.

In the Romanesque period there was no direct relationship between the designs of mosaic, tile, stained glass, furniture, carving, rugs, tapestries, silks and other fabrics.

Tiles had been made for centuries and patterns had been repeated and re-repeated. Colored glass was made by the Egyptians 2000 years B.C., but the earliest stained-glass windows are recorded as 525 A.D. None, however, is known to be still in existence made prior to 1108. Early examples found in Romanesque windows of this date have little medallions with primitive figures and ornaments, the patterns reflecting the spirit of design which had been done in textiles four and five hundred years previously.

In mechanical weaving, a repeated pattern must have fixed dimensions, a restriction not affecting embroidering, tapestry making or mosaic work.

We have already seen that wools and linens, tapestries and embroideries were employed back in the earliest ages. Simple mechanical weaving was known in Egypt 3000 B.C., but the complex manipulation of shuttles whereby figures were produced without embroidering was not practised until 200 A.D.

NORMAN ROMANESQUE. 1000—1100.

GERMAN ROMANESQUE. 1000—1100.

MEDIAEVAL FURNITURE. 450—1150.

Romanesque. 900-1100.

Illustrations 1, 2, 3 are doubtless tile illustrations, following the simple forms used in mechanical textile weaving 200 A.D. The motifs here used are, however, heraldic. The heraldic forms were adopted during the period of the First Crusades, 1096 (the seven Christian Crusades ending 1270).

Illustration 4 follows the textile forms of the early Byzantine, but the details filled in suggest the Saracenic.

Illustrations 5, 6, 7 follow the interlacement system, which beginning with the Roman was revived with the Romanesque and developed with the Gothic.

Illustration 9, like illustration 4, is of Byzantine origin with Romanesque development 1000.

Illustrations 1, 2, 3, 4 and 7 Romanesque, direct Roman origin.

Illustration 5 shows the framing which developed just prior to the Gothic, 1100.

Illustrations 6 and 8 are Romanesque, showing connecting circles, 800.

Illustrations 9, 10, 11 represent the Arabian or Saracenic development of the ogival form of design conspicuous in Lower Italy, 900-1000.

The "ogival" form relates to the form of design developed from 800 to 1100 A.D., where joining circles were brought to acute angles at points of junctures, forming ovals or ogival shapes.

DEVELOPMENT OF MECHANICAL TEXTILE DESIGN UP TO THE GOTHIC PERIOD.

THE development of design was necessarily slow; for many years repeat patterns were of the simplest character.

B.C. Design consisted (1) of repeated lines, spots, bands or stripes; (2) crossed lines or stripes; (3) by changing colors of lines, checks and trellises were produced; (4) by changing proportions, plaids were produced; (5) then came rectangular patterns and diamond shapes.

100 A.D. Development of circular or square frame.

200-600 A.D. Squares or circles filled possibly with floral detail suggested by the Persian and Syrian weavers. The same sort of thing was repeated again five hundred or six hundred years afterwards in simple stained-glass effects.

400-600 A.D. Broken circles or circles joining the upper and lower segments and spread out to form bands.

600-1100 A.D. The use of circles continued, but they were now linked together, large circles being joined together by smaller circles at the points of contact. The designs in and out of these circles became more ornamental, developing by the end of the Romanesque period great elaboration, and

hexagons (Saracenic) arranged with geometrical nicety and elaborated in design.

Up to and including 1100 a common type of design was the persistency of balanced groupings of birds, animals or men, facing or back to back.

From 800 to 1100 saw the development of the ogival form or that form of design where the joining circles were brought to acute angles at points of juncture forming ovals or ogival shapes. The ogival form continued, developing greater and greater elaboration through the Gothic period.

EARLY CHRISTIAN—BYZANTINE—ROMANESQUE

THE accompanying chart shows better than anything else the related periods of design which followed the Byzantine and developed finally into the Gothic. Early Christian naturally expressed the Byzantine or first Christian expression in art where that art symbolized the Christian faith. As time progressed the Romanesque period developed, which was a period of Roman revival.

BYZANTINE.

328—500 Roman Christian Period. Constantine, Emperor, became protector of Christians and the Empire constituting the Eastern divisions of the Roman Empire, 550.

550—800. ORIENTAL PERIOD. This period was largely affected by the Oriental influence surrounding Byzantine.

850—1005. CLASSIC PERIOD. Reflecting the Roman spirit, which had already affected the Italian, German and French arts. Christian symbolism did not again become conspicuous until the beginning of the Gothic, 1100.

EARLY CHRISTIAN.

330—600. Early Christian. A term arbitrarily applied to the art of the countries influenced by the religious enthusiasm of the Byzantine Empire, by the GOTHS of TEUTONIC and SPANISH territory, the early LOMBARDS who settled in ITALY, 568, and the Franks, who under Clovis (the first of the Merovingians to adopt Christianity) became a Christian kingdom about 500 A.D.—750.

The Middle Ages or Mediaeval or Moyen Age is that period usually fixed as between 450 and 1250.

328

600

700

711

774

911

1066

1100

ROMANESQUE.

700—1100. A style affected by the Roman art developing about 700 and lasting until 1100, the beginning of the Gothic.

711. THE GOTH kingdom of Spain was destroyed by the Moors and from this developed a Spanish art which was largely Moorish affected by the ROMANESQUE.

In 774 Charlemagne destroyed the Lombardic Kingdom and became Governor of Italy. The LOMBARDS had entered Italy from Scandinavian territory and founded powerful nation 568 A.D. They conquered almost all of the Byzantine Empire, except Venice, Ravenna, Naples and Rome, and in later years their ROMANESQUE art became more strongly BYZANTINE. The period showed the EARLY CHRISTIAN, the BYZANTINE and ROMANESQUE character.

In the Southern sections of their territory, especially Sicily, there developed by the invasion of the Mohammedans a SARACENIC art.

NORMAN was the ROMANESQUE of the Normans who came down from the North country, gaining a foothold in Normandy and Brittany. In 1066 conquered England where NORMAN ROMANESQUE was often called ENGLISH ROMANESQUE. End of Romanesque Period and beginning of Gothic.

DEVELOPMENT OF TEXTILE WEAVING

300 A.D. Weaving was understood in Egypt. Possibly earlier in Babylonia. Silk weaving introduced from China, where it was practised at a remote period.

200 A.D. Complicated mechanical weaving done by Syrian weavers in the Eastern Roman Empire.

300 A.D. Silks well known to Romans. Persian as well as Syrian manufacture. Egyptian and Roman tapestries in use.

500 A.D. First production of European ornamental silks—sarcenet and taffeta; Roman and Byzantine. Constantinople imported looms for weaving silks in the Persian and Indian styles. Introduced sericulture from Chinese cocoons smuggled into Constantinople by Persian monks, and became a seat for European silk cultivation and manufacture. Produced taffetas, damasks, brocatelles, lampas, velvets, embroideries, tapestries, and for five centuries Constantinople, Corinth, Thebes and Athens were prolific in weave craft.

600 A.D. Northern Egypt made silken fabrics.

700 A.D. Spain in latter part of 700 made progress in silk weaving. Syrian silk merchants opened warerooms in Paris.

800 A.D. Daughters of Charlemagne, France, taught to weave silk.

800 A.D. Abdul-Raman II introduced the use of "tiraz" (silk stuff embroidered).

900 A.D. Sicily and Spain alike showed Saracenic design treatments in fine silks.

1000 A.D. Constantinople, Corinth, Thebes and Athens practically monopolized the making of fine fabrics.

1000 A.D. Roger Guiscard organized a silk factory at Palermo, Sicily, Hotel des Tiraz, with Thebian and Corinthian weavers, and according to some historians it became the greatest silk manufacturing city in the world. Scarcely less renowned were Malaga, Murcia, Granada and Seville. Many Italian towns also took up silk manufacturing,

LATE ROMANESQUE OF LOWER ITALY.

Showing Saracenic Influence.

EARLY CHRISTIAN. 330-600.

Florence, Genoa, Venice, Bologna and Milan. Saracenic and Greek silk weavers located in Germany, the Netherlands, France and Great Britain.

1100 A.D. Towards the end of the Twelfth Century Flemish weavers began the manufacture of wool tapestries. Art developed to Arras, Valenciennes, Tourney, Audenarde, Lille and Brussels. The oldest tapestries in existence are of this era. Two are in the Cathedral, Halberstadt, Germany.

1200 A.D. Persian silks famous throughout Europe and copied generally.

1200 A.D. France began manufacture of tapestries.

1268 A.D. Madrid, Spain, organized tapestry factory.

1300 A.D. Spain began to degenerate as a producing country.

1300 A.D. Arras, city south of France, made valuable wool tapestries up to 1477.

1300 A.D. Lucca, famous for silk weaving, Lucchese weavers emigrated to Germany, the Netherlands, France and Great Britain, in which countries silk manufacture flourished up to 1500.

1300 A.D. Velvet is mentioned in the English inventories and French documents.

1300 A.D. Genoa, the center for Italian trade in the East, introduces Eastern design.

1400 A.D. Spanish and Italian writers referred to "velvets" or velvet stuffs. (See 1500.)

1400 A.D. Asiatic fabrics were taken in great quantities by Europe. During Fifteenth Century Constantinople and Byzantium were the chief markets for supplying Oriental stuffs to Europe.

1400 A.D. While Italian wool tapestries were designed by native artists, the workmen came from Flanders. During 1400, when the Ottomans conquered Constantinople, they infused Orientalism into Southeastern Europe, and the manufacturers in the Ottoman towns—Anatolia—went into the markets of Italy and France, Spain and Flanders. This spirit brought political changes, new commercial relations and the influence over the decorative designs and decorative fabrics of all Europe. This Ottoman type was more Persian than Saracenic. It was strongly floriated.

1432 A.D. Silks of Damascus were famous.

1466 A.D. Lyons, France, established silk looms. Under Francis I silk weaving was encouraged and many Italians employed. Turkey pre-eminent for silks of Broussa, Diarbekir, Beyrout, Aleppo and Damascus, Assyria.

1480 A.D. Beginning of needle-point lace work in Italy.

1500 A.D. Spain weakly reflecting the character of French and Italian styles.

1500 A.D. France, Germany, Holland and England weaving fine silks.

1500 A.D. A continuance of inscriptional styles in gold, "velvet," and satin, superseding brocaded silks of early date. Materials heavier.

1500 A.D. According to the revenue records of Italy, cloths of silk, satin damasks and velvets plain and cut, were made "in a way unknown to the ancients." Prior to this date velvet was a material that had been simply roughed up so as to appear fluffy. England attempted during 1500 to make satin damasks, velvets and cloths of gold, but soon abandoned the enterprise.

1515 A.D. Pope Leo X had tapestries made in Brussels after cartoons by Raphael.

1539 A.D. Francis I established tapestry factory. This was the beginning of Gobelin manufacture.

1600 A.D. Beginning of point Venise laces in Italy. At this time similar laces were made in France and in Flanders and Russia also.

1600 A.D. Showing Italian character of design, strongly influenced by Oriental.
Italian and Sicilian towns famous in silk manufacture. Also Tours, Nimes, Lyons, Avignon, Paris, France. Flemish and Dutch were more traders than producers.

1619 A.D. Mortlake Tapestry Works were established near London by James I. Existed up to Charles I.

1619 A.D. Gobelin Tapestry Works became royal property of France.

1650 A.D. Under Colbert many lace factories established in France for the making of net laces.

1690 A.D. or thereabout, Beauvais Tapestry Works established.

1700 A.D. French characteristics prevailed in French manufactures. Many towns in France undertook manufacturing. The French influence in designs spread to Spain, England, Holland, Germany and Switzerland during the flight of the weavers from France at the time the Edict of Nantes in France was revoked.

1700 A.D. Netherlands, Bruges satins famous.

1700 A.D. Flanders famed for its tapestries.

1750 A.D. Thousands of silk-weaving looms established in England—in Spitalfields, Cheshire, Yorkshire, Essex, Derbyshire, Lancashire and Norfolk. Large quantities of Chinese and Indian silks used in England.

1759 A.D. Manufacture of printed linen authorized and encouraged by French Government. The most famous became known as Toile de Jouy.

1800 A.D. The Germans were great producers at Crefeld, Elberfeld, and Barmen.

1800 A.D. Austria began the manufacture of silk and 1500 looms were soon in operation by imported labor from Genoa and Lyons.

1800 A.D. Some silk was made at Stockholm, but neither Norway nor Sweden had made history in this business.

1800 A.D. Moscow and St. Petersburg established silk looms in Russia.

1818 A.D. Bobbinet first made by machinery.

ASIATIC

ORIENTAL——ISLAM ORNAMENT.

THE term ORIENTAL relates to the Far East or Asia.

The term ISLAM relates to the religion which began with the birth of Mohammed, 571 A.D.

ARABIAN——SARACENIC.

Native of Arabia. Arabian followers of Mohammed, born 571, were called Saracens and located at Medina; established Mohammedan religion 622.

634. Saracens conquered Syria, Palestine, Phoenicia and Egypt.

641. Persia overthrown by Arabians, who also conquered Northern Africa and captured Rhodes.

700. Saracens conquered Byzantium and Northern Africa; the Berbers accepted Mohammedan religion, and with inhabitants of Greek and Roman descent, became amalgamated with the Arabians under the name of Moors; 711, crossed to Spain, establishing the Caliphate of Cordova. Saracenic conquests for many years extended over Southwestern Asia up to the Mediterranean, influencing the arts of Spain, Southern France and Southern Italy. Followed the use of flat conventionalized interlacement of geometric accuracy, thus unlike Celtic or Scandinavian, and unlike the Ottoman form or later Turkish type. The Mohammedan religion interdicted the use of animal forms, and the law of the Koran was strictly followed by the strict Mohammedans, hence Arabian art was confined to conventionalized forms, with occasionally Arabic inscriptions.

MOORISH.

The Moors were the Saracen converts from Northern Africa who in 711 crossed to Spain. The arts are sometimes called early Spanish.

1250. The ALHAMBRAIC period. By 1200 the Moorish form of ornament embodied Arabian ornament superimposed upon geometrical background framework.

1610. Moors expelled from Spain.

TURKISH.

Turks originally Tartan tribe, 226 B.C. Seljuk Turks, a term applied to Western Turks who in 1096 held empire by conquest over many parts of Persia and the West Coast of Arabia.

The Turks had no art excepting the art borrowed from Persia and Arabia. (See Ottoman.)

OTTOMAN.

A band of wandering Turks aided the Seljuk Turks, or Western Turks, in battle and conquered the Arabians 1250. This was the beginning of the Ottoman Empire and the arrest of the Arabian conquests in Asia.

1360. Ottomans conquered Asiatic possessions of the Byzantine Empire and Turkey in Europe.

1453. Surrender of Constantinople to the Ottoman Turks.

1480. Ottoman supremacy on the wane.

The Ottoman arts were the arts of the Ottoman Turks or the Turks of the Ottoman Empire, established 1259. Ottoman art was the development of the Arabian with strong Byzantine influence even to the interdiction of animal life. A characteristic was the use of conventionalized pea forms and leaf and pod.

PERSIAN.

Islam effect upon Persia began 641, when Persia was overthrown by Arabians.

750. Independent principalities sprang up in Persia.

1605. Shah Abbas, ascending throne of Persia, drove out the Ottoman Turks and Mongols and recovered the country.

Islam effect upon Persia 641, when Persia was overthrown by the Arabians. As long as Persia was dominated by the Arabians Persian art was largely Arabian; but in 1605, with the downfall of the Ottomans, Persia, through Shah Abbas, developed to its fullest the native tendencies, even to the adoption of European Renaissance forms and human, animal and bird forms. Persian art had been always liberal, and even when under Arabian control was never flat and conventional, but realistic with florals, notably pinks, hyacinths, tulips, roses, palms, pines, pomegranates, pineapples and dates.

INDIAN.

1400 B.C.   Brahma.
500 B.C.   Buddha.
711 A.D.   Arabian Invasion.
1525 A.D.   Mogul Empire.
748 A.D.   English Control.

Indian art was influenced by Mohammedan up to the Sixteenth Century, and it broke away from the restrictions of the Koran.

ARABIAN ORNAMENT.

ARABIAN—An interlacement of flat and geometric or vegetation forms, distinguished from Ottoman or the late Turkish by being less realistic. Inscriptional work often introduced. Human or animal figures are expressions of outside influence, usually Persian. It is impossible to distinguish between Arabian and early types of Moorish.

MOORISH ORNAMENT.

Moorish (Arabian origin) developed finally the Alhambraic, an elaborate form.

OTTOMAN ORNAMENT.

Ottoman Turkish developed a floriated Arabian form, with the pea vine and leaf as motifs.

PERSIAN ORNAMENT.

PERSIAN—Where Arabian characteristics appear in Persian design they point to the period of Arabian domination. The floriated form expressed a later feeling, when Persia recovered control of much of her territory. Persian art reached its highest type of floriated form in 1500.

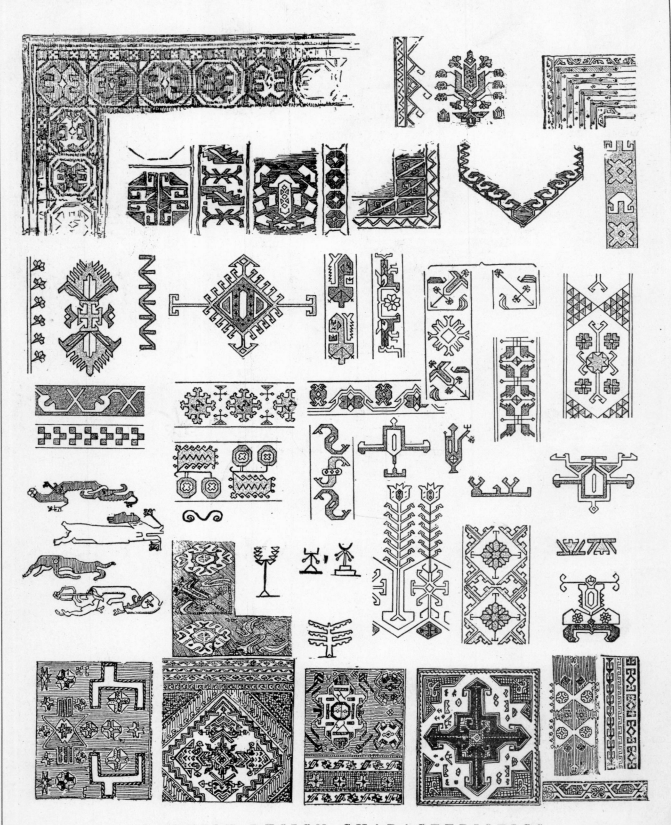

TURKISH DESIGN CHARACTERISTICS.

Chinese Ornament.

CHINESE — INDIAN — JAPANESE — SARACENIC

CHINESE—Mythic Period 3500 B.C. First Emperor 2200 B.C. Confucius 500 B.C.

Sung Dynasty, 960-1127; Han Dynasty, 1127-1279; Yuan Dynasty, 1279-1368; Ming or "Bright" Dynasty, 1368-1628; Wan Lih Period, 1573-1620; Shun Chih Period, 1644-1661; Kang Hsi Period, 1661-1722; Yung Ching Period, 1723-1736; Kien Lung Period, 1736-1796; Chia Ching Period, 1796-1821; Tau Kwang Period, 1821-1851.

CHINESE and Indian art are frequently confused because they have much in common. Possibly this condition may be accounted for by the influences of Buddha. The Chinese employ an endless list of deities, demons, monsters. They have eight immortals and the figure eight is a favorite. They have eight lucky emblems, eight Buddhist symbols, eight ordinary symbols. We note also in Chinese frets and geometrical details, forms identical with Greek.

Mythological art is an art of great study. To comprehend its meaning one would have to be a Confucionist, a Taoist and a Buddhist. Stripped of its symbolism, Chinese art is an art of extravagant nature forms, and in the past four centuries these forms were undoubtedly influenced by Persian nicety and decorative consistency.

INDIAN—Brahma 1400 B.C. Buddha 500 B.C. Arabian Invasion 711 A.D. Mogul Empire 1525 A.D. English Control 1748 A.D.

WOVEN brocades and silks of India were not developed as decorative arts until the Sixteenth Century. While Indian art goes back to the remote past, the art as we understand it is Islam. Having the typical Mohammedan divisions of space, but more flowing, having more freedom and grace, it is less confined than the Arabian style. The Arabian invasion of India began 711 A.D., and from that date Mohammedan domination prevailed; but beginning with 1500 Indian art broke away from the Koran restrictions and we have the elephant, lion, tiger, the peacock and the human figure common accessories in

45

PRINTED COTTON.
INDIAN 18TH CENTY.
S.K.M.

INDIAN ORNAMENT.

CHINESE ORNAMENT.

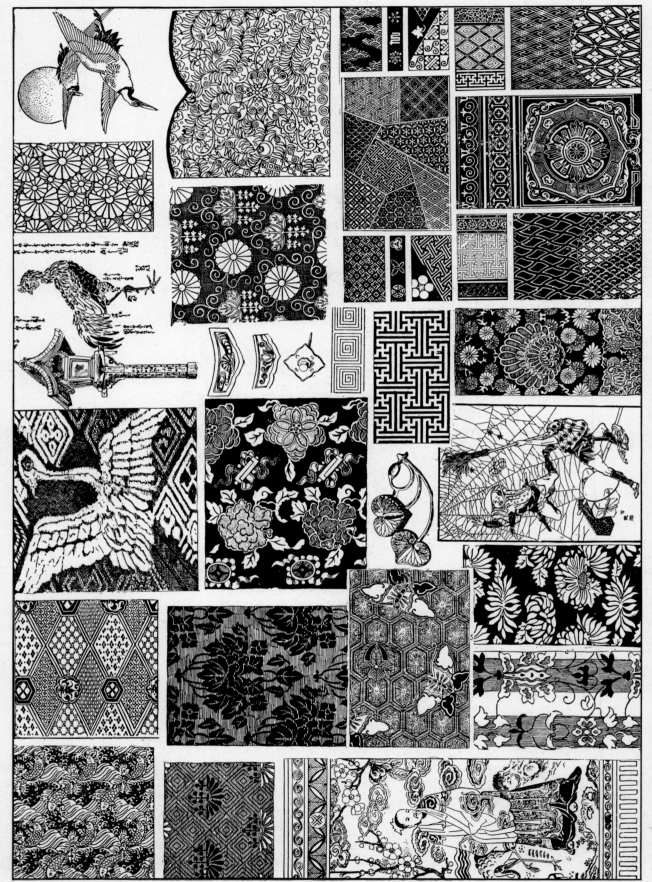

JAPANESE ORNAMENT.

decoration. Indian ornament followed a profuse floral system, and block prints in silk and cotton reached a high degree of perfection during the Seventeenth and Eighteenth Centuries. The details are always worked out finely.

SARACENIC — 641 A.D. Persia was conquered by the Saracens or Arabians, who by 711 had invaded India, Spain, Turkestan and Northern Africa.

827 A.D. Saracens settled in Sicily. Early in Tenth Century extended their incursions into Italy.

IT is impossible to classify Saracenic designs under one grouping, for the reason that the term applies to the Arabian influences covering many years and many countries. (See Romanesque, Gothic and Italian.) To comprehend the term Saracenic one must study the chronological history of the Orient. Wherever the Arabian or the Saracen conquered there he left his influence. The term is adjective. It may apply to much that would be otherwise classified as Romanesque, Norman, Gothic, or Sicilian if the Arabian characteristics permeate the composition. In Southern Italy and in Sicily the style which developed in the Ninth Century was distinctly Saracenic. If we study the Romanesque and the Norman we find in the origin of each the Saracenic superimposed upon Roman or Byzantine and we have as a result a confusion that is often hard to analyze.

A design, therefore, Norman, Romanesque or Byzantine that is conspicuous by its Arabian influence is called Saracenic.

Under the Saracens, textile fabrics reached a high development in color and material. The arts culminated in the period 900-1200. Though Mohammed forbade the wearing of silk, it was largely used, and to evade the injunction cotton was interwoven with it. Sicilian or Siculo-Saracenic fabrics showed bands of birds and animals, foliage, inscriptions, in blue, green and gold on red ground.

Drawn gold thread was not used in early fabrics, but gold leaf on paper and then rolled around a fine thread of silk was manipulated. Sicilian fabrics of the Thirteenth and Fourteenth Centuries are frequently in purple ground of twilled silk with birds and foliage formed by gold thread weft. Saracenic or Hispano-Moresque fabrics of Spain are distinguished by the splendid crimson or dark blue conventional patterns of silk upon yellow ground, and by the frequent use of strips of gilded parchment in place of the rolled gilt thread. Undoubtedly under the influence of the crusades the Sicilian weavers of the Thirteenth and Fourteenth Centuries produced many fabrics enriched with winged lions, crosses, crowns, rayed stars, harts, birds, linked together with floriations or armorial bearings. Late in 1200 this character of design was introduced into Northern Italy. Genoa adopted much that was Persian from the Twelfth to the Seventeenth Century, and in the Fifteenth Century, when Louis XI encouraged the art of weaving in France at Tours and later at Lyons under Francis I, the Persian and Italian fabrics were closely followed, and the vase pattern was adopted.

The Oriental character of design in textiles did not entirely disappear until the gardens of Versailles and the Trianons under Louis XIV gave inspiration to the use of European flora.

Saracenic.

Saracenic.

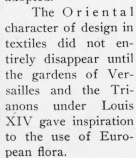

Saracenic.

Japanese Ornament.

JAPANESE—1200 B.C. Empire established 660 B.C.

THERE is a close affinity between the Indian and Japanese arts, for Buddhism, introduced from India, exercised pronounced influence upon the people of Japan. We are inclined also to broadly associate the Chinese and Japanese arts; indeed the differences are not easy to determine.

In 1200 B.C. the Ainos, people occupying islands east of Asia, were conquered by bands from the mainland. The conquerors became known as Japanese, but for centuries their early arts were stimulated by their Chinese progenitors. Little by little, however,

Indian.

they developed a great love of detail, a nice accuracy of expression foreign to the Chinese spirit. They employed less conventionality and more nature. We nevertheless find in both Chinese and Japanese art forms that are almost identical, and where that is the case we can trace it to the influences of India.

We find in indigenous work of the Japanese a great deal of nature study—butterflies, cranes, dragons, peacock-feather patterns, flowers, tortoises, waves—in fact, almost everything in nature, and the methods are in most cases picturesque rather than fixed and formal.

During the last fifty years Japan has studied and complied with the demands of European taste, and native art has consequently weakened.

At its best, it followed the methods of China and India and in most cases was content with reproduction.

Indian Ornament.

GOTHIC INTERIOR, 1300.

From an old painting in Stuttgart, Germany.

FIFTEENTH CENTURY GERMAN GOTHIC FURNITURE.

[CLASSIC.]

[ROMANESQUE]

[SICILIAN.]

[GOTHIC.]

[GOTHIC.]

DEVELOPMENT OF FLORAL GOTHIC MOTIFS.

GOTHIC

Romanesque or round-head Gothic

THE Gothic style was the art expression having root in the spread of the Christian religion, and is full of Christian symbolism. At first crude and heavy, it yielded later to a highly ornate form of treatment.

Regarding the Gothic development there is much confusion. It developed directly from the Romanesque, a style which grew up in Northern Italy; naturally the Romanesque characteristics lingered in its construction. Indeed, the late Romanesque is called the Round - Head Gothic, its arches in architecture being semi-circular, as distinguished from the later Gothic development of pointed arches.

The Gothic period, extending as it did from 1100 to 1550 and influenced as it was by the Byzantine,

   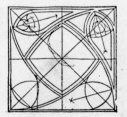

Gothic Fleurs-de-lis.   Three in one.   Quarry.

Saracenic, and finally Romanesque, naturally absorbed many architectural characteristics as the style traversed France, Germany Spain, Italy and England. And yet all phases possessed a common floriation and universal religious symbolism—the trefoil, the quatrefoil, curves and arches, circles, triangles, religious figures—are conspicuous whether of the Gothic of Spain with Moorish arch, or the Gothic of France with pointed spires, or of England with its lancet as well as squat Tudor vaults.

One cannot too strongly emphasize the fact that Gothic art was an architectural art. It was the art of the builder, the sculptor, the wood-carver, as distinguished from the art of the weaver, who up to this period took inspiration mainly from Asia. Thus we find frequently in the furnishings of a church, palace or cottage, Gothic characteristics in all that was of the house or building proper or of the cabinetmaker, and com-

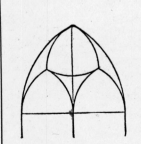 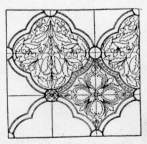 

Gothic Characteristics of Design.

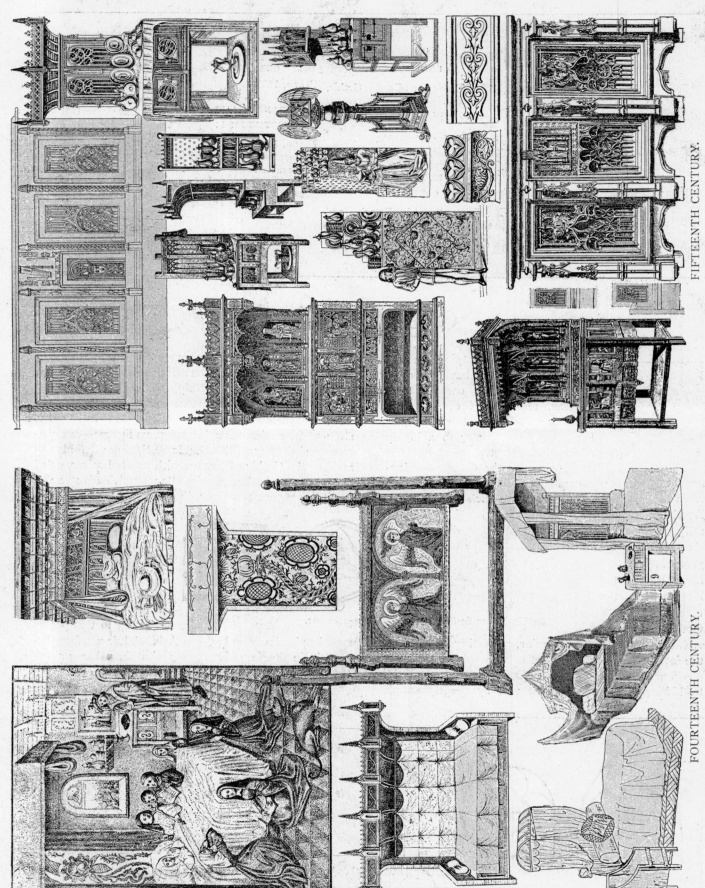

FIFTEENTH CENTURY.

FOURTEENTH CENTURY.

FRENCH GOTHIC.

While the French Gothic period began with the close of the Romanesque (1100), it was not until 1300 that the flamboyant style developed, prior to which the arts were distinctly Romanesque.

A Fifteenth Century room in the Volpi Museum, Florence, the first illustration showing round arch Gothic, the second illustration Transition Gothic. Walls of cosmatic mosaic introduced in the Thirteenth Century by Giovanni Cosmato. Floor, tiles. Furniture, Sixteenth Century.

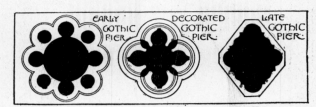

Gothic forms from which the trefoil and quatrefoil details were taken, obtained by the use of circles.

bined therewith textiles and art treasures brought in by the Flemish and Italian traders from far Asia.

It is somewhat difficult to understand the terms used descriptive of the Gothic epochs. In order to assist in a comprehension of these terms we reproduce the classifications of Sharpe, Rickman and De Caumont. We prefer, however, that the student shall follow our own classification. The term "Transitional Gothic" as shown by Sharpe is the same as "Norman," applied by Rickman. The classifications are as follows:

SHARPE.

ROMANESQUE: Saxon, 1066 A.D.; Norman, 1066-1145 A.D.

GOTHIC: Transitional, 1145 - 1190 A. D.; Lancet, 1190 - 1245 A. D.; Curvilinear, 1245-1360 A.D.; Rectilinear, 1360-1550 A.D.

RICKMAN.

ROMANESQUE: Norman, 1066-1189 A.D.; Early English, 1189-1307 A.D.

GOTHIC: Decorated, 1307-1379 A.D.; Perpendicular, 1379-1483 A.D.; Tudor, 1483-1546 A.D.

DE CAUMONT (FRENCH).

ROMANESQUE: Primordiale, 400-900 A.D.; Secondaire, 900-1100 A.D.; Tertiaire, 1100 A.D.

POINTED: Primitive, 1200; Secondaire or Rayonnant, 1300; Tertiaire or Flamboyant, 1400 A.D.

WITH the beginning of Gothic we note the simple crochet form, as it is called, a terminal floriation. At first crude, it soon developed into the Decorative type, characterized by natural foliage of many kinds, with flowing, undulating lines, truer to nature than Early Gothic and treated in richness and profusion. Then came the Perpendicular Gothic, arranged with more fixed geometrical rules of construction, and introduced as motifs we find heraldic forms shields, badges and crests. The space to be carved was divided into rectangular or lozenge shapes and filled with ornament systematically.

At the time of the Norman conquest English houses were usually one room. A hole in the roof served to carry out the smoke from the fire, and indeed many houses lacked chimneys in England as late as 1500.

The tables used were mere planks on trestles.

Chests were common articles of furniture, and may be divided into three classes, which are defined as follows:

First, the chest of the Early Gothic following the Romanesque style banded in iron more for strength than ornament.

Second, the chest heavily banded in iron and painted. These were common during the Thirteenth and Fourteenth Centuries.

The third type began with the Fifteenth Cen-

Group IV (G).   Group IV (G).   Group V.

See table of group classifications, for dates.

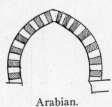

Arabian.   Moorish.   Romanesque or round-head Gothic.   Early English.   Lancet.   Perpendicular.   Tudor.

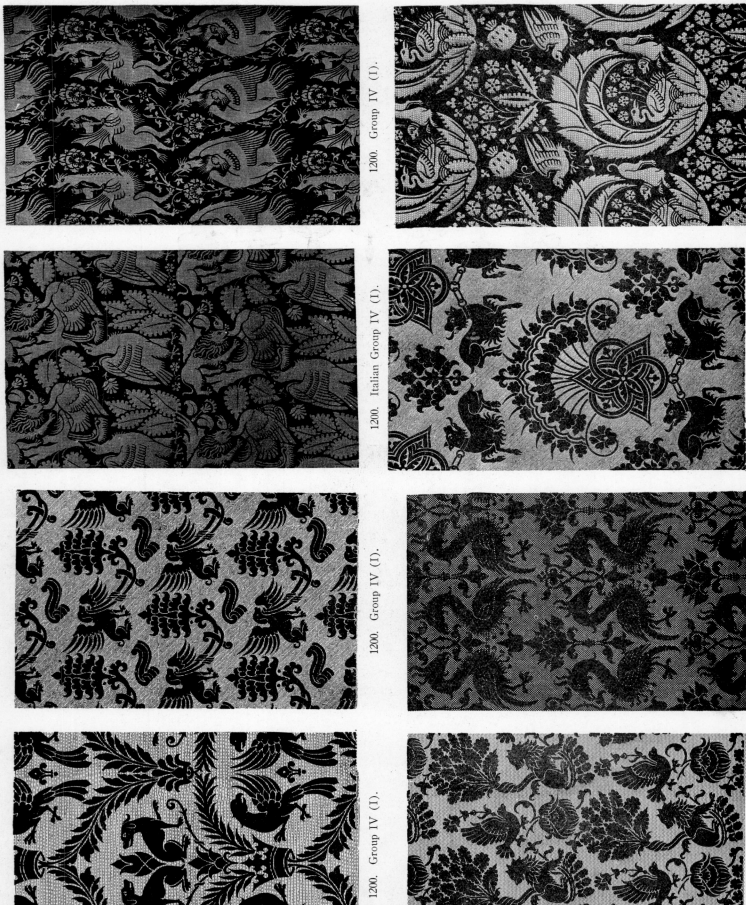

1200. Group IV (I).

1200. Group IV (I).

1200. Italian Group IV (I).

1200. Group IV (I).

1200. Group IV (I).

1200. Italian Group IV (I).

1200. Group IV (I).

1200. Group IV (I).

THIRTEENTH CENTURY ITALIAN AND FLEMISH FABRIC DESIGNS

tury and was carved, following the architectural forms.

Beginning with 1200 the walls of the houses were wainscoted and painted, often decorated with subjects romantic, biblical and traditional.

The very rich used colored glass windows; the wainscotings of the rooms being primitive were frequently hung with tapestries to check drafts..

Domestic furniture was often painted in bright colors or rendered in tempera or wax. Cupboards showed Gothic details of simple character with perforated doors for ventilation, as food was often kept therein.

In 1400 the lower-floor room of a house was a combination dining-room and bedroom. The furniture consisted of a table, a long bench (with canopy called a dossier) seating four persons, a standing cupboard, a bed with heavy curtains at the foot, two buffets, a table for holding toilet articles, a few stools and a *prie-dieu*. The floor was strewn with rushes, or in the halls of the wealthy it was laid with Eastern carpets.

Clothing was kept in an adjoining room, while the bath was taken in a wooden tub drawn up to the open fireplace.

About 1500 the large hall of the house was the general sitting-room, reception-room and dining-room combined, furnished with a long table, and dossier.

Chests, benches and settles with occasionally an individual chair, a buffet, a side table, screen and one or more cupboards, completed the furnishings.

This furniture was primitive, drawers in tables not being introduced until late in 1400, nor was an extension table or a table with added leaves in use prior to 1500. The chest was a favorite piece of furniture. In the Royal presence it would have been a breach of etiquette to sit on a chair, but proper to sit on chest or coffer. Towards the middle of 1400 these chests became decorated with linenfold panels in the form of carving that looked like folds of linen. The linenfold pattern was first used in screens in the churches. Though Flemish in origin, it quickly became identified with English. It was carried well into the Renaissance and lasted from about 1450 to 1550. Towards the close, bunches of grapes and profuse floriation were introduced.

German, Fifteenth Century.

TEXTILE DESIGNS.

THE terms Gothic, Saracenic and Renaissance are laxly applied.

In architecture and woodcarving, Gothic, for example, defines an accurate development, but the fabrics used in Gothic environment, even fabrics woven in Italy, Germany and France, have little Gothic signifi-

The Ball-Flower

Alternate Ball-Flower

Four-Leaved-Flower

EARLY ENGLISH GOTHIC 1189-1307.

To this floral form is added, in ecclesiastical work, religious symbols, the circle, the trefoil, quatrefoil, triangle, crucifix, crown, chalice and cross.

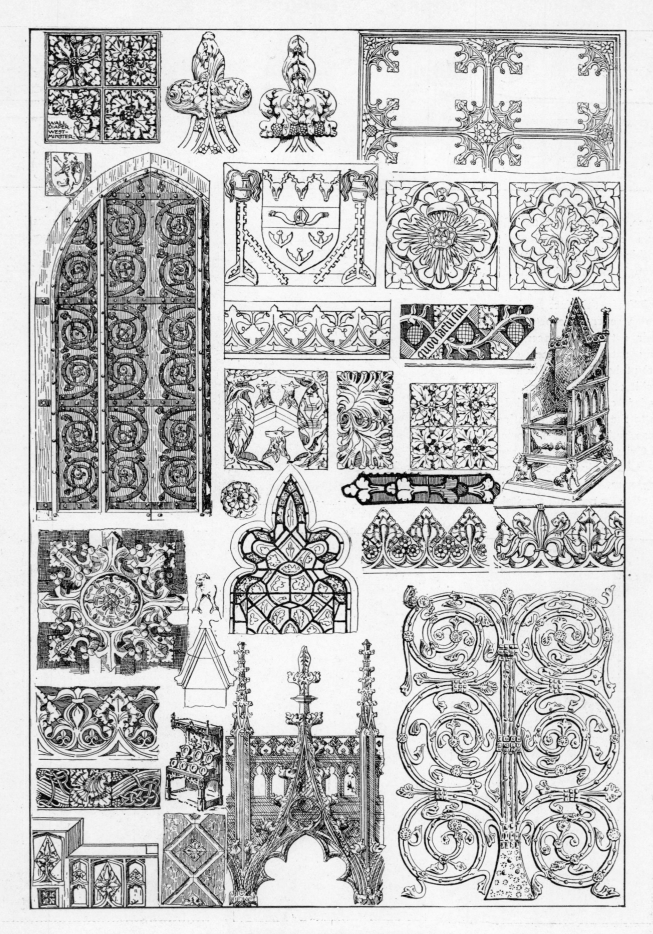

ENGLISH GOTHIC 1189-1509.

cance. Throughout the European countries dominated by Gothic feeling, weaving was strongly influenced by the Saracens. In lower Italy, Sicily and Spain this fact is obvious; the weavers perpetuated in their arts the Saracenic style long after all traces of the Orient had been obliterated by architect and sculptor. The traders of Flanders and Italy, up to the fall of Constantinople were active in the importation of Oriental stuffs, which served as a stimulus for European workmen.

It was not until the Italians

Saracenic, Twelfth Century.

and French had practically lost their Oriental commerce that they turned their attention to home manufactures; and not until this condition arose, were designs produced, consistent with the character of the prevailing arts.

The acanthus forms were taken as motifs.

The Anthemion was generously utilized, as well as fleur-de-lis. Laurel leaves and wreath shapes were adopted, and toward the end of the Sixteenth Century European flora, crowns and urns were a common source of inspiration. (See page 52.)

1300.

North Italian, 1200.

1400.

1450. Group V (L). 1500. Group VI (N). 1500. Group VI (P).

Late Italian Gothic.

Late Italian Gothic.

Late English Gothic developed finally the style known as Tudor (Tudor Gothic), the arches of which were low and squat instead of angular. The panelings showed linenfold effects and the tops of the folds were often elaborated by floral details. Outside the eccelsiastical forms, leaf motifs were the predominating Gothic characteristic. Where the work had religious significance the design harked back to the Byzantine, Romanesque and Celtic. Thus in manuscript decoration of even a later date we frequently note the pea and pea-tendril types, the penman finding special opportunities in the elongated sweeps of the vine.

French — French architecture was bold and elaborate, showing doorways enriched with statues. As a rule the floral leaves were rounded and more full than the English leaves. Clustered pillars were almost unknown in France; observable in Germany and England.

Netherlands—Tyrol—The arts of the Netherlands were influenced by France and Germany. Wrought iron decoration in leaf and plant form was popular. Tyrol Gothic, a type simple and effective, generously utilizing the work of the wood carver.

Germany—Although Germany followed Late-Gothic tendencies, it was not until 1350 in possession of an established style. It followed the vertical more than any other and at an early stage developed a fine system of strap work in metal, in which Gothic lines were closely followed. The use of birds in conjunction with leaf forms was common and twisted spirals and faces and armorial details were often used.

GOTHIC FABRICS.

We have grouped as IV and V, under the heading, "Development of Mechanical Textile Design," page 64, all that may be regarded as contemporaneous with Gothic. Group IV representing fabrics between 1000 and 1350, Group V between 1350 and 1500.

FRENCH GOTHIC.

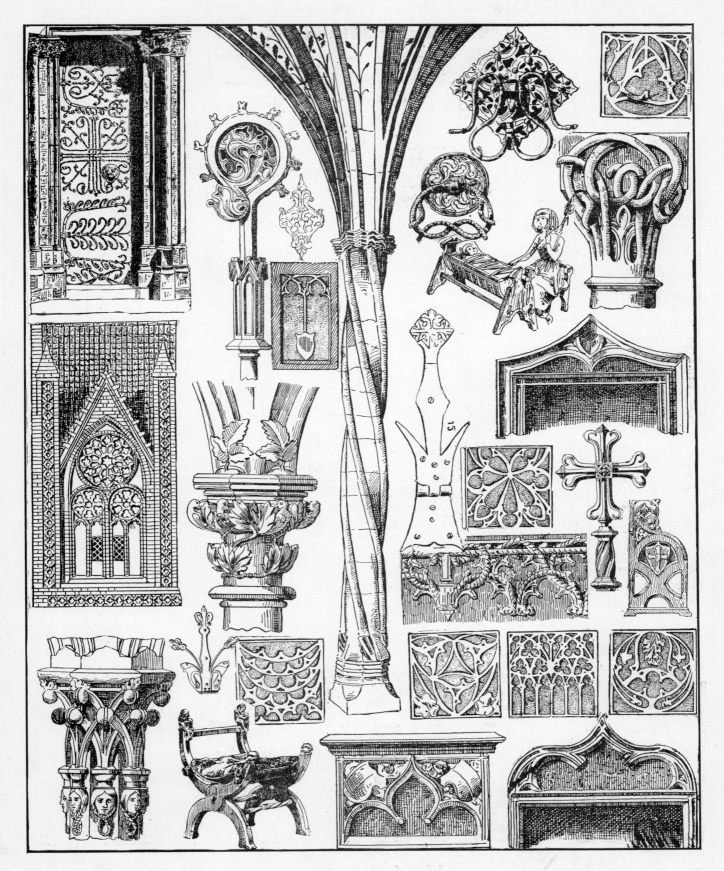

GERMAN GOTHIC.

1450. Group V (J). 1450

GOTHIC FABRIC DESIGNS.

1550. Group VI (P).

1550. Group VI (P).

THE DEVELOPMENT OF MECHANICAL TEXTILE DESIGN--GOTHIC PERIOD

CONSTANTINOPLE, Corinth, Thebes and Athens practically monopolized the making of fine fabrics 1000 A.D. Towards the end of the Twelfth Century Flemish weavers began the manufacture of wool tapestries. France and Spain also undertook the manufacture during the Thirteenth Century. The Orient up to 1400 was famous throughout Europe for its fabric creations, the Crusades being largely responsible for the distribution of fine examples. European weavers copied liberally the Asiatic styles, and when in the Fifteenth Century the Ottomans conquered Constantinople, Orientalism was still further infused throughout Southeastern Europe.

200-400. Group I (A) The development of circle and geometric frames, sometimes filled with simple floral, bird or animal forms.

400-600. Group II (B) The utilization of broken circles spread out to form bands.

600-1000. Group III (C) The use of circles linked by smaller circles, with ornaments inside and out, developing at length (D) the ogival form; often (E) hexagon frame work.

1000-1350. Group IV (F) Repeated parallel bands of ornamentation—detached details.
(G) Patterns animate and inanimate, enclosed

1500. Group VI (O).

1400. Group V (J).

1400. Group V (J).

1500. Group VI (P).

1500. Group VI (M).

1500. Group VI (M).

1500. Group VI (N).

1450. Group V (K).

GOTHIC FABRICS.

SPANISH GOTHIC.

ITALIAN GOTHIC.

TYROL GOTHIC.

GERMAN—NETHERLANDS.

Russian ornament has been at no time distinctive. Its arts were at first Tartaric, then Byzantine, then Celtic, Oriental and Italian.

1400. Group V (L).

1400. Group V (L).

1400. Group V (L).

in ogival framing and (H) combination circles or scale patterns as well as geometric straight line framing.

1200-1300 introduced as features of design (I) eagles, falcons, shields, hounds, swans, foliated crosses, crowns, rayed stars, lions, harts, boars, leopards, sun's rays and castle motifs, especially in the fabrics of Italy and Sicily.

1350-1500. Group V. A characteristic design of the Fifteenth Century was the use of (J) reversed curves so arranged that they made frames.

This form prototyped the Hogarth line of beauty. (K) Another form was the intersection of a Hogarth panel by two bold curving stems coming up through the bottom of the panel and capped by a cone, pineapple or fruit device.

Still another (L) showed a serpentine stem or winding trunk which ran through the Hogarth pattern in the midst of a variety of botanical forms.

1500. Group VI. Designs adopted a free treatment. (M) The plans of previous centuries were combined and elaborated.

(N) Ornament was arranged within ogival frames, springing out of the base of the frame to which it seems to be attached.

(O) Interlacings of two frames of which one is ogival.

(P) Ogival frames of leaves and flowers enclosing a large concentric pattern.

(Q) Elaborated ogival frames caught together by crowns.

(R) The use of vases, urns, crowns and animals became common.

1600-1700. Group VII. (S) During 1600-1700 we find an elaborate use of European garden flowers instead of the purely tropical Persian verdure, following, however, the general ogival form of arrangement.

FLOWER-VASE PATTERN LATE 16TH CENTURY VENETIAN.

DOUBLE MULLION PATTERN ITALIAN 16TH CENTURY MANCHESTER BOCK COLLECTION

SINGLE MULLION PATTERN FLEMISH 16TH CENTURY

1500. Group VI (M).

1500. Group VI (R).

1500. Group VI (P).

1500. Group VI (P).

1500. Group VI (N).

70

GOTHIC DINING-ROOM OF THE CHATEAU DE HAAR A HAARZUYLENS, NEAR UTRECHT.

PALAIS DE FONTAINEBLEAU.

1500. Group VI (P).

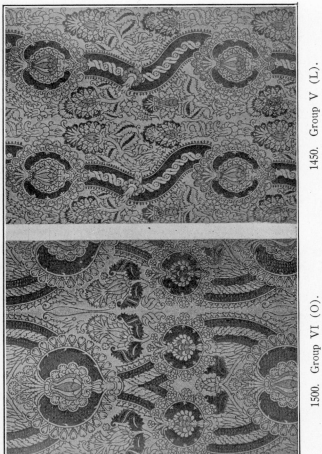

1450. Group V (L).

1500. Group VI (O).

1500. Group VI (Q).

SIXTEENTH CENTURY FABRIC DESIGNS.

1500. Group VI (P).

1700. Group VIII. (T) Pictorial tapestries and prints. (U) Pure Renaissance styles or developments of that style—Louis XIV or XV.

(V) Oriental characteristics of either the French or English styles, as shown in the scenic bits of Chinese or East Indian life.

(W) Louis XVI.

(X) Classic revival examples as expressed by the late Louis XVI, Directoire or Transition period in France and the Adam school in England. This period overlapped into 1800 and was generally adopted in the American colonies.

1800. Group IX (Y) Empire and Empire influence.

(Z) Art Nouveau.

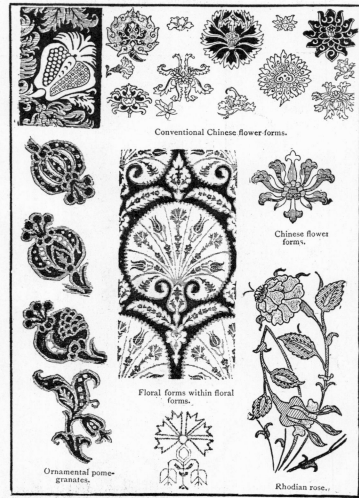

Conventional Chinese flower forms.

Chinese flower forms.

Floral forms within floral forms.

Ornamental pomegranates.

Rhodian rose.

PERSIAN CHARACTERISTICS.

DEVELOPMENT OF FLORAL TYPES

Iris, or fleur-de-lis. Seventeenth Century Venetian.

DURING the Sixteenth and Seventeenth Centuries there were three distinct types of fabric-design popular in Europe, (a) the Renaissance, (b) the Oriental-Renaissance, (c) the European floral.

(a) For centuries the textile weavers of Europe had been accustomed to follow Oriental design (chiefly Persian). Then came the pure Renaissance as developed in Italy (1400), in France (1500), in England and Spain (1500), and in Germany (1550), and the Persian pink and rose, the Rhodian lily, the pomegranate, cone and palm, gave way, as motifs, to the Roman, Greek and Egyptian details, the anthemion, lotus, iris and acanthus.

(b) During the Renaissance much confusion of types was precipitated by the commercialism of the Netherland States and the explorations of the Portuguese, who in 1140 had revolted from Spanish rule, under which they had been a province, and established the kingdom of Portugal; the Portuguese during the Fourteenth Century became famous sailors, and early in 1500 opened possessions in Persia and India.

Portuguese-Persian is the type of design (1500) showing the Persian influences merged in the Portuguese, which at that time was developing the Renaissance spirit.

For centuries prior to the opening of the East by Portugal, the twenty-one provinces of the Netherlands had been active in commerce and famous for the great cities of Ghent, Mechlin, Antwerp, Bruges, Amsterdam, Leyden, Delft, Brussels and Rotterdam. After the forty years' war with Spain, the Northern provinces, which had been known early in the Seventeenth Century as the Seven United Provinces of the Netherlands, formed the Dutch Republic and replaced the Portuguese in the settlement of trading posts in the East Indies (1610).

During the Sixteenth Century, involved as they were with the Netherlands and, subsequently, with France and England, who sympathized with the Netherlands, the Spanish, their sea power gone, had no means of continuing the commercial enterprises of Portugal, and the Dutch became paramount on the seas.

(c) The French developed still another form (the European floral) beginning about 1650 under Louis XIV, presenting the ferns and flora of Europe, especially the exquisite examples cultivated in the Royal Gardens.

Oriental influence in design has been stimulated at various periods by political and commercial developments. The Dutch brought East Indian types into England under the Elizabethan, Jacobean and Queen Anne periods, and English women perpetuated Oriental art in their embroideries. It seems like an anachronism in this Renaissance age. Chinese influence was strong during the period in France under Louis XV, and in England under George II and George III.

Then again as late as 1760 British rule in India began to stimulate a demand for Indian goods.

These phases must be considered in studying the periods.

Examples of Old Silk, 1750.

1200. Group IV (I). Saracenic Influence.

ITALIAN GOTHIC.

Fig. V.

Fig. IV.

Fig. III.

(See description on next page.)

FABRICS OF NORTHERN ITALY

FIFTEENTH—SEVENTEENTH CENTURIES.

SICILIAN 13TH CENTURY

THE Italian period of art brought great prosperity to Italy. Foreign courts adopted Italian customs and costumes. Vast quantities of rich hangings were used, and the most gorgeous form of d r e s s was affected. John the Calabrian was famous for a silk loom used in the Fifteenth Century and this loom was imported into France during the reign of Louis XI (1475) by the manufacturers of Tours. A loom associated with the name of Dangon appeared at the beginning of the Seventeenth Century and was hailed as remarkable in its ability to facilitate the weaving of fabrics in several colorings. As early as the Thirteenth Century Borghesano of Bologna had invented a spinning machine to which was due the superiority of Italian thrown silks. The processes of manufacture were, at this period, greatly improved. In 1500 armures became singularly rich. Cloths of gold were made, figured velvets, damasks with broché effects and fancy velvets.

When the Arabs under Mohammed had con-quered the countries of Persia and Syria they found the manufacture of silk a flourishing industry. From this period until the Fourteenth Century the silk industry was carefully fostered by the Mohammedans. Next in importance and value to the precious stones the chief treasures of the Caliphs of Bagdad, Cairo and Cordova were their silken goods. Silk fairs or markets were held periodically at Antioch, Rey, Orzeroum, Ispahan, Jerusalem and Mecca. The Jews then, as now, were the bankers in the Mohammedan districts and the purveyors of articles of luxury to the wealthy Romans of the South, the Gallic Romans of the West and the Goths of Northern Europe.

The Italians were first to travel over Asia Minor, and together with the Jews, brought Mohammedan products into Italy, Spain, France and England, eventually establishing silk manufactories in Europe. Notably in Sicily and Italy. Palermo, silk factory started 1100; Lucca, famous for silk weaving 1300.

Persia was the original seat of art, and thence Persian design spread and was adopted and adapted in North Africa, Sicily and Arabia.

In the Thirteenth Century Italian designers were inspired by Oriental art. In the Fourteenth Century they modified their treatment of animal motifs, aban-

75

Fig. 1.

Fig. II.

doning the fantastic type (See Fig. 1) and adopted a new school of flora, employing the vine and oak leaf. Venice gave special attention to compositions for altar decorations. (See Fig. 2.)

Specimens of the Fifteenth and Sixteenth Centuries display a lingering trace of Oriental art types which appeared and reappeared for possibly commercial reasons. (See Fig. 3.) Lobed leaves, rather Gothic in character, appeared in the Fifteenth Century and were abandoned in the Sixteenth Century. Thistles and flower artichokes often formed the center of the composition, and around the central motif the old geometrical lines were replaced by foliage forms, forming curvilinear or ogival borders.

The magnificent Venetian velvet shown in Fig. 4 illustrates a varied ornamental framework of the character described. Floral effects were in some cases the principal motif, in others the accessory ornament.

In Fig. 5 we show a fancy velvet of the Sixteenth Century; a pale yellow ground is in silk armure, the design produced by the cut velvet is in two delicate colors, mauve and light green. The design is known as the flowered Indian meadows, on account of the numerous shades employed.

Sixteenth Century designers were artists having remarkable facility of invention. The multiplicity of rich silken stuffs illustrates very forcibly the luxury in dress. Where gold or silver did not figure in the design it appeared in the form of embroideries on satin or velvet. It was a period of great prosperity in Italian manufacture, especially the factories of Lucca, Florence, Venice and Genoa. Italian workmen, moreover, were in demand and taught their arts contemporaneously at Avignon, Lyons, Tours, Barcelona, Bruges and London. Even at the end of the Seventeenth Century (1685) official Lyons records speak of Italian silk fabrics as forming the ideal models which the weavers of Lyons were to keep always in view as the standard of perfection.

During the Seventeenth Century, however, fashions were no longer dictated from Italy. Paris became the center and home of taste, and with the abandonment of long dresses the vogue for large designs had vanished. Smaller compositions were executed not only in dress but in upholsterings, and little by little Italy lost its prestige.

KEY TO FABRIC ILLUSTRATIONS.

Fig. I.—Italian cloth of gold of the Fourteenth Century. Fabric with two wefts following each other; the green silk weft forming the ground with the warp likeness in green silk; the gold weft forming the design.

Fig. II.—Italian cloth of gold of the Fourteenth Century; with figures. The ground is in satin weave, presenting a glazed effect; the warp is light yellow, the weft crimson. This crimson weft and the gold weft succeed each other. In the figures the face, the hand and the feet are executed with a supplementary weft of white silk. The turf is formed by another supplementary weft in green, producing a twilled appearance.

Fig. III.—Fancy cloth of gold, with velvet ground, of Italian manufacture of the Fifteenth Century. Pomegranate design. The cut velvet is of crimson shade; the design being formed by the gold weft. The center of the pomegranate, which is in small points, is in knotted gold weft; also called *bouclé* or *frisé*.

Fig. IV.—Fancy Venetian velvet, with gold ground. The cut velvet is in crimson; the design, produced by the gold weft, being raised.

Fig. V.—Italian fancy velvet, of the Sixteenth Century. Detached floral effects.

Italian, Sixteenth Century.

DEVELOPMENT OF THE RENAISSANCE

ITALIAN.

Alberti, 1404—1472.
Early Renaissance, 1400—1500.
High Renaissance, 1500—1540.
Late Renaissance, 1540—1643.
Florentine Renaissance, 1400—1600.
Brunelleschi, 1377—1446.
Borgognone, 1450—1524.
Fra Angelico, 1387—1455.
Luca della Robbia, 1388—1463.
Botticelli, 1447—1510.
Andrea del Sarto, 1486—1531.
Benvenuto Cellini, 1500—1571.
Venetian Renaissance, 1490—1600.
Palladio, 1518—1580.
Roman Renaissance, 1444—1643.
Donato, 1444—1515.
Giacomo Barozzio (Vignola), 1507—1573.
Michael Angelo Buonarroti, 1474—1564.
Raphael, 1483—1520.
Milanese Renaissance, 1400—1600.
Leonardo da Vinci, 1452—1519.

FRENCH.

French Renaissance, 1500—1643, a freely ornamented Gothic introduced by Fra Giaconda, 1502, under Louis XII, developed by Francis I, who reigned 1515—1547. Leonardo da Vinci, Seralio, Cellini, Italians, influencing the style.

ENGLISH.

English Renaissance, 1509—introduced by Henry VIII, through his architect, John of Padua.

FLEMISH.

Flemish Renaissance, 1507—
Antwerp was destroyed in 1584 and the famous manufactories were dispersed.
Dutch republic formed. 1581.

GERMAN.

German Renaissance, 1550—founded by Albrecht Durer.

SPANISH.

Spanish Renaissance, 1500—reflected the character of the Flemish Renaissance introduced by Flemish artists. Carlos I was born and educated in the Netherlands and upon attaining the crown his advisers were Flemish. The style was termed the Plateresque, and was a sumptuous mingling of Gothic and classic details.

Italian, Sixteenth Century.

ITALIAN RENAISSANCE.

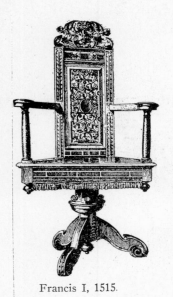

Francis I, 1515.

By Du Cerceau, France, 1550.

Francis I, 1515.

ITALIAN RENAISSANCE

See Chronology, pages 77 and 114.

DURING the Fourteenth Century religion, art and science expanded. Humanity broke the feudal fetters and a new social life prevailed, stimulated by the study of the ancient arts and sciences, and wider propagation of the Christian religion. This period was the revival period (Italian *Rinascimenta;* French, *Renaissance*).

ITALIAN—Brunelleschi was the first artist to study the monuments of classic art. To his genius we owe the Early Renaissance in Florence. The labors of Brunelleschi and his followers were soon felt in other Italian art centers, Rome, Milan, Bologna and Venice. Its spirit was brought to Rome by Donato, the teacher of Raphael. It supplemented the brickwork architecture of Lombardi. It developed in Venice under Palladio. The student who understands his Greek and Roman will very readily recognize the Renaissance spirit, although outside of Italy the classic motifs were often liberally interpreted in combination with cartouche, strap forms and shields; survival of Crusader motifs.

The centaur, showing the fore part of a man and the hind part of a horse, was frequently combined with a liberal system of scrolls. Masks, the female form, birds, animals and trophies were conspicuous.

The furniture was sometimes supplemented by painted decorations on gilt grounds prepared in a gesso material.

Italian *tarsia* (inlay) work was a characteristic type. Sometimes the inlays represented floral ornament, sometimes landscapes and buildings. The technique came from Persian sources, but the designs developed chiefly by the Venetians were usually classic. In the decoration of tables, chairs and cabinets ebony, ivory and metal were employed.

The marriage coffer, often in carved walnut, was a popular article of furniture. Chairs o f t e n carved a n d a l l gilt. Cab-

French, Henri II.

Italian.

French, Henri II.

78

ITALIAN RENAISSANCE, SIXTEENTH CENTURY.

Chair legs of early Sixteenth Century showed braces at bottom of legs.

Italian Tarsia or Intarsia Work.

inets were made with veined marble tops and panels. In the Seventeenth and Eighteenth Centuries painted plaques of porcelain took the place of these marbles.

In the Sixteenth Century Venice was renowned for glass manufacture. Looking glasses were invented 1507 by two Murano glass makers named Andrea and Dominico, who were given sole privilege to "make mirrors of crystal glass for a term of twenty years." Previous to this time mirrors were of polished metal. The frames of these Venetian mirrors were carved to represent doorways of windows, pilasters, friezes and cornices; sometimes gilt. Beds were often four-posters.

Discoveries of the stuccoes of ancient Rome aroused the Italian architects to a spirit of emulation and the mural work became extravagantly elaborate. Ground colors were laid on while the stucco was wet and the details heightened. Sometimes gilt frames en-

closed magnificent paintings. The work of Raphael and his followers was often applied to wall decorations. The superb friezes and panels constituted the best work the world has ever seen.

The age of oak extended from about 1500 to about 1660. The age of walnut was then generally taken up and extended to about 1700; mahogany 1730.

In 1530 furniture with a framework and panels as well as chairs began to adopt a really new order. Pieces of furniture became more complex, with columns, porticos, pediments, niches, friezes, cartouches, caryatids, etc., constituting veritable little monumental façades.

In France the Italian and Flemish tastes influenced development. In decorative art the form of Renaissance known as Henry II lasted for half a century.

Italian type of Cabinet work. Late Sixteenth Century.

ITALIAN RENAISSANCE.

ITALIAN RENAISSANCE.

RENAISSANCE—ITALIAN—FRENCH

See Chronology, page 114.

IT IS difficult to differentiate between Italian and the late French Renaissance. The French were saturated with the Gothic spirit and for a time it was difficult to displace the Gothic feeling. The new art was finally established in France through Cellini, Seralio, Primaticcio, Ilrosso and others who came from Italy and by French artists who finally went to Italy to acquire the newer style evolved from the classic remains of ancient Rome. The great French carvers of this period were Jean Goujon, Nich. Bachelier, of Toulouse, Du Cerceau, who published designs for all kinds of decorations and carvings, and Hugues Sambin, of Dijon. Towards the end of the Sixteenth Century and during the early half of the Seventeenth the superb furniture was covered over with fabrics to such an extent that little by little the frame construction ceased to be visible.

Wood carving was one of the great glories of the Flemish art throughout the Sixteenth Century. A Flemish chair of the second half of the Sixteenth Century is illustrated on page 85, and yet it might safely be regarded as Italian. During the Seventeenth Century the Flemings devoted themselves mostly to the carving of large pieces, chairs and small furniture being produced frequently by means of turning lathes not requiring the skill of the carver. The style was naturally Italian, although Spanish influence made itself felt during the Spanish occupation of the Netherlands in the latter part of the Sixteenth Century.

The term Renaissance in France, includes, according to many writers, the style of Louis XIII. An over-upholstered form eliminating the carved features may be said to characterize much of the furniture of Francis I, Henri II, Francis II, Charles IX, Henri III and Henri IV.

We are disposed to recognize Boule of the Louis XIV period as the promoter of marquetry work, but inlays went back to the tarsias of Italy, Fifteenth Century, and during the period of Francis I a great deal of Indian work, inlays of mother-of-pearl, was introduced by the Portuguese merchants.

Inlays in exotic woods, ivories, ebony and metal were also used in France, although French cabinetmakers, as a rule, confined themselves to carrying in relief and ignored the Italian colored marquetry in the style of *tarsia, intarsia pittoric* and *certosina*. The Gothic type lingered until 1525, and French Renaissance frequently showed Gothic traces. Unquestionably many Italians and Flemings were employed in France. As early as 1593 dressers, trestles, wooden bed-steads and wooden chairs were upholstered.

It is difficult to identify native French work because the cabinetmakers travelled frequently from one town to another wherever building operations might call them and good wages were paid. Thus the Italians were scattered over France and the work that they produced was handed down to native workmen who copied. French design may be characterized as an over elaboration of the more classic Italian forms, which latter copied the old Roman and Greek in strict conformity to tradition.

We fail to find any means of determining definitely the characteristics of the Norman school, the Lyons, Tours, or Burgundy. We do well if we determine approximately, a style like that of Francis I, by the end of whose reign Gothic characteristics, and especially those of the pointed arch had practically disappeared.

It must be recalled that the French had had broad experience in wood carving and naturally soon developed a boldness and freedom of execution which gave to their late Sixteenth Century work characteristics in no way to be confused with the more minute and restricted treatment of the Italians.

The castles of Francis I, Blois, Chambord and Fontainebleau were masterpieces of the French Renaissance.

French life under Henri II, Charles IX and Henri III, all semi-Italian princes, dominated by their Florentine mother, Catherine de Medici, was luxurious in the extreme.

Both Henri II and Henri IV styles showed a prevalence of interlaced strap-work, delicate reliefs and the use of the cartouche.

Late Sixteenth Century, Italian Renaissance.

FRENCH RENAISSANCE ORNAMENT.

Italy and France, 1530.   (See page 83.)

Flemish, 1560.

Francis I, 1525.

Henri IV, 1580.

Italian origin, 1550.

1580.

Louis XIII.

Italian origin, 1590.

FRENCH RENAISSANCE.

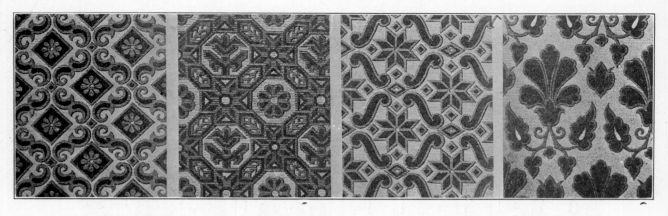

The illustrations above, as well as those appearing at the head of page 87, are reproductions of Venetian and Genoese velvets and gold brocades of the Sixteenth and Seventeenth Centuries. The reproductions are one-quarter the size of the originals which show colored motifs on gold ground.

FRANCIS I. 1515-1547.

FRANCIS I SALON, MUSEE DE CLUNY.

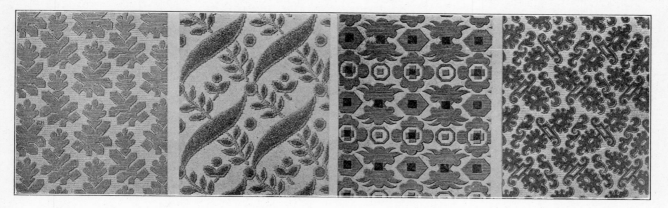

Venetian and Genoese velvet and gold brocades of the late Sixteenth and Seventeenth Centuries. Originals in the Museums of Berlin, Vienna, Munich, Dresden and Nuremberg.

FLEMISH RENAISSANCE

DEVELOPED FROM THE ITALIAN 1507.

See also page 114.

THE North country, now Holland, and the South country, which included Flanders, now Belgium, were, up to the period of Spanish domination, of homogeneous taste and character. With the Reformation came a gradual division of interests and sympathies. The North country, including about two-thirds of the Netherlands, established the Dutch Republic, while the South country, alienated from her Northern sister, soon lost supremacy in the arts. Upon the traders of Holland fell the mantle of the Portuguese voyagers, and, in India especially, they opened great avenues of trade.

For centuries the products of Flanders and later the products of Holland poured into Great Britain. England supplied most of the wool used in the manufacture of Flemish tapestries, and in Medieval days could always depend upon the support of the Flemings by her control of the wool situation.

From the date of the Dutch conquest over Spain, 1600, accomplished with English aid, the relations of the two countries became still more intimate, affecting materially the decorative arts of England from Elizabeth down to William and Mary.

In the Eleventh Century Cordova leathers, superbly gilded and painted, were introduced into Flanders; the term soon applied to similar leathers produced in Portugal, Flanders, France and Italy. Spanish leathers (Cordova proper) were usually in high relief and Saracenic design; leathers of Flanders and Italy, frequently of calf, were of low relief in exceedingly delicate design, mythological or ecclesiastical.

The earliest notable tapestries of Europe were

Flemish (1100). On account of the great importance of the arts, the Duke of Burgundy adopted the

Flemish type, early Seventeenth Century. The prototype of the later English type. Known frequently as Charles II. 1660.

RENAISSANCE ORNAMENT.

Late French showing influence of Flemish strap-work.

Golden Fleece as the title of the great order of Knighthood. In the Fifteenth and Sixteenth Centuries the tapestry makers of Italy, France, Germany and Spain borrowed the tapestry arts from Flanders.

The furniture of Medieval days was mostly of a fixed character. Cupboards, wardrobes and larders were built into the panelings. Up to 1300 the carver and carpenter were one and the same. Then came a division of labors. Carving was usually applied to fixed parts of the house.

Crude beds and benches were supplied with cushions carried in the chests. Walls were hung with printed linens and tapestries.

In the Fourteenth Century we find not only carved oak but inlays of ebony and ivory.

Hangings were the chief feature of the interior decoration. The Italians had a monopoly of the trade with the Orient, and Europe was supplied by them with Oriental rugs. Up to 1400 there was little movable furniture to be found even in the palace—simply benches, trestles chests and forms. The plain box or chest when raised on feet or legs was a dressoir, credence or sideboard. The armoire was developed by building chest upon chest with open fronts. In some old Medieval manuscripts we find chests so large that, covered with skins or matting, they were used for beds. The difference between a dressoir and buffet was simply that the dressoir was used for display; the buffet for use.

The number of shelves on a dressoir was regulated by etiquette. The common people could use a dressoir with two shelves, the nobility with three shelves, the royalty four or five shelves.

In 1420 we hear of Cordova leathers being used on the floor, around the bed, and of leathers for chamber hangings. Charles V of France (1380) used leathers on the floor in Summer time, and throughout the period we find leathers used for upholstering. During the Fifteenth Century Flemish workmen emigrated in great numbers to England, Spain, Italy and even Hungary.

The Flemish were almost as celebrated for their leathers as for their tapestries. Gold and painted leathers were common, and red morocco leathers from Spain were, from the beginning of the Sixteenth Century, generally used for wall hangings and table covers. In 1539 the tapestry factories of France sent to Flanders for her weavers. The Flemish cabinetmaker, architect and weaver was in great demand during the Renaissance, and in Spain, France and England he found congenial residence.

In the Seventeenth Century the Dutch commerce in the Far East not only brought into Europe vast stores of Indian art, but the masters of vessels were commissioned by nobles and potentates to bring home monkeys, parrots, peacocks, pheasants, cats and dogs.

In 1609, the East India Company issued letters for reserving "all strange fowls and beasts to be found there, for the Council." The cockatoo and the parrot in wicker cages were much in evidence in the paintings of that period. Naturally the artists were much im-

EARLY DUTCH

GERMAN RENAISSANCE (BEGINNING 1550).

FLEMISH RENAISSANCE (BEGINNING 1507).

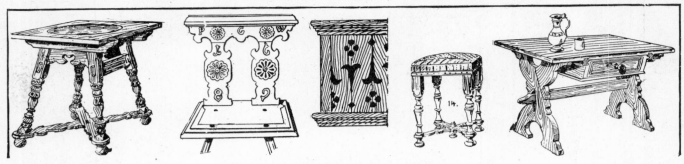

SWISS RENAISSANCE.

RUSSIAN RENAISSANCE.

SPANISH RENAISSANCE.

1

2

3

4

1. Detail of choir stalls, Convent of San Marcos, Leon.

2. Gothic chair, Fifteenth Century.

3. "Samson," carved choir stall of Leon Cathedral.

4. Armchair, Seventeenth Century. Museum of Salamanca.

5. Spanish cabinet and stand, carved chestnut, first half of Sixteenth Century, Victoria and Albert Museum.

6. Ivory box, Ninth Century, Madrid Museum.

7. Chair and table, Salamanca Cathedral.

5

6

7

SPANISH RENAISSANCE.

FINE OLD SPANISH LEATHERS.

The example at the upper left-hand dates from about 1720, the one at the right from about 1730. The specimen at the lower left-hand was made about 1660, and the remaining one dates from about 1730.

pressed, and the Dutch embroideries and prints of that age were full of Eastern character, floral and animal.

France owed much to Belgium and Holland during the first part of the Seventeenth Century, when Flemish and Dutch artists contributed so materially to up-building the French industries. But France repaid with interest, for in 1685 the revocation of the edict of Nantes sent 50,000 families of the best French blood, intellect, art, culture and craftsmanship into voluntary exile.

RUSSIAN RENAISSANCE — The Renaissance reached Russia through Italian artists, who worked always subordinate to Oriental and Scandinavian influences. Polish art, however, was more susceptible to Italian feeling, and the Renaissance ornament of Poland was purer.

NORWEGIAN RENAISSANCE — Norway and Denmark took the Renaissance feeling from Flanders. Norway peasants were natural woodworkers.

SPANISH RENAISSANCE—In 711 the Moors invaded Spain. In 755 they established the Caliphate of Cordova. In 1031 the Caliphate was dissolved. Subsequent to 1200 the Moors in Spain were confined to the Kingdom of Granada. By 1610 the Moors were expelled from Spain.

Early in the Middle Ages mansions of Spain were furnished in a style of rude grandeur. They were modeled after the Roman and Byzantine. In time the furniture of Christian Spain was affected by the Gothic and Renaissance arts, with always a trace of the Moorish. The furniture of the Middle Ages was much the same throughout all Europe.

The older Spanish furniture was frequently decorated with delicate ironwork and with columns of bone or ivory, painted or gilded, often exhibiting Moorish influence. Some specimens were richly inlaid with silver.

The bedstead was always a conspicuous feature of the house and was frequently of iron or bronze. Wood succeeded metal in the latter part of the Thirteenth Century and the beds grew even larger, rising so high above the floor that sets of steps were required to climb into them. Sometimes these steps were in themselves magnificent. Silver and rich carvings, elaborate mosaics, were common.

Italian turned rail furniture. Illustrations 1, 3 and 4, Italian. Adapted by Flemings, period Henri IV, France. Rail back chairs were common in Flanders, England, France, 1660. In the latter country called Chaise Cacquetoires. Chair in margin of page, probably Flemish.

A description of the furniture and furnishings would tax the imagination, velvets and gold and even precious stones being woven into fabrics.

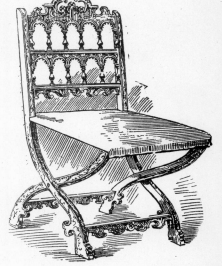

A PAGE OF SWISS COFFERS.

Spanish leather of about 1700.

The homes of royalty were of extraordinary magnificence, and while Gothic was the general tendency during the Gothic period the Oriental influences were conspicuous and the native Moorish a strong factor.

By the time of the Renaissance the love of luxury still further increased. We read of the one-hundred-and-twenty-pound silver balustrade of Dona Juana, sister of Philip II; it stood around her bed. We read of Turkish carpets, Spanish carpets, Toledo gold cloths, wonderful embroideries and tapestries.

According to the Marquis of Monistrol, Spanish furniture up to and including the beginning of the Renaissance, consisted of burial chests, storage chests, archive chests, treasure chests, brides' chests, chests for storing arms, and grain chests. The Spanish Moors employed but little furniture. The cushion was viewed with much favor by Spanish Christians. Among the Moors the cushion was used as a seat of honor because it raised the occupant above the level of those seated on the floor. The women of Christian Spain were always given cushions while the men made use of stools or chairs.

In the Seventeenth Century the dais or raised platform was introduced. In 1515 the municipal laws of Granada covered the "operations of the people who worked in the street of chair-makers and carpenters." These laws were found necessary owing to the false and faulty workmanship prevailing at this time. In Granada the laws provided, among other things, that the work must be bought at public auction, where all could discover its character. It must be thoroughly dry and free from flaws. The law also covered all the details of how a chair should be made and each chair had to be stamped with the city mark and a tax paid upon it.

During the Sixteenth and Seventeenth Centuries large arm-chairs of quadrangular form were used. The backs and seats were of leather and embroidered stuffs.

Cabinets were an important part of the furnishings. Cabinets and tables were inlaid with ivory, tortoise shell, ebony, bronze and silver. Frames inlaid in this way were hung on the walls. Women sat on low stools on the ground. Beds were hung with rich brocades embroidered in gold and trimmed with Point d' Espagne. On the splendid carpets were placed silver braziers which burned crushed olive stones. The walls were covered with tapestry and rich silks and from early times stamped leathers, painted and gilded "guadameciles" were used to a very great extent. This stamped leather was also met with largely in England. The word comes from the name of the village, Ghadames in Africa which was celebrated from the Twelfth Century for this industry. The art was imported by the Moors to Spain, Cordova becoming a great center of the industry, though this leather was made also at Seville, Granada, Toledo and Barcelona. In 1575 the fame of Cordova for such leathers was so great that the name "Cordova leather" was applied to those made in other parts of Spain as a general term. Leonard Williams, the corresponding member of the Royal Spanish Academy, has made a deep study of Spanish furniture and we are indebted to his book on "The Arts and Crafts of Older Spain" for the illustration here shown. Nothing more beautiful can be reproduced than the choir-stalls in the Cathedrals of Spain. The most notable example of Spanish Renaissance is doubtless the decoration of the choir of the Cathedral at Toledo.

Spanish Renaissance Chair, covered with Guadameciles.

Tyrolean ornament.

SWITZERLAND AND THE TYROL

IT IS not easy to describe the arts of Switzerland. Swiss museums are rich in the glory of the past. Museums which contain interesting specimens of the artistic productions of the different districts may be found in Berne, Basle, Zurich, Aargau, Zug and Geneva. In considering Swiss work we must consider the geographical position of Switzerland. To the west Switzerland was influenced by France, to the south by Italy, to the east by Bavaria. In the Fifteenth and Sixteenth Centuries the influences of Germany predominated. In the Seventeenth Century French art was an influential factor.

The Swiss have been always cabinetmakers and woodcarvers. Switzerland has been always famous for its coffers, sometimes used for preserving treasures or rare spices, garments or linens. In the houses of the wealthy they served the purpose of a treasure chest or safe. The lid was utilized as a seat and where large enough it served also as a bed. At Versailles, France, coffers were in general use as beds in about 1752. When traveling the coffer served as a trunk. In Switzerland these coffers were always elaborately carved.

Fig. 1 is a mixture of Gothic and Renaissance as a Swiss peasant understood it. It is dated 1594. The contours of the design are colored in order to throw the ornament into relief. At the Historic Museum, Basle.

Fig. 2, coffer from Canton Solothurm. The dolphins are peculiar to this Canton.

Fig. 3, dated 1626, probably a bridal chest with inlay. Now in the museum at Zurich.

Fig. 4, a monastery coffer, date 1614, now at the Zurich Museum.

Fig. 5, bedside coffer.

Fig. 6, Renaissance. The Renaissance began to make itself felt in Switzerland from 1520-1530. It is unusual at this period to find the field treated in divisions, preference being for long flat surfaces upon which to carve. In this example we have a different design upon each field.

Fig. 7, early Fifteenth Century, with the iron bands and clamps is decidedly Flemish.

Fig. 8, Fifteenth Century coffer. An excellent type of Fifteenth Century peasant carving.

The Tyrol district is an Eastern continuation of Switzerland, and is naturally influenced by Germany on the North and East and Italy on the South. The history of the Tyrol is partly German and partly Italian. In early times the Tyrol district was conquered by the Romans, 15 B.C. Subsequently it was overrun by German tribes.

For centuries the Goths occupied the district and the pagan creed prevailed here until the Sixth Century. Hence we have at all times the Gothic influence and in the furnishing of their homes, simple in the cottage life or elaborate in the palace structure, we have also the influences of Northern Italy. One must bear in mind that the Swiss are famous as woodcarvers and their skill in this direction follows natural forms, preserving usually the Gothic characteristics. In the use of fabrics the Tyrol people followed the work of Northern Italy, but in their panel carvings the work was typically native.

Tyrolean carved ornament.

ENGLISH RENAISSANCE
ELIZABETHAN—JACOBEAN—STUART—CROMWELLIAN.

A LIBERAL interpretation of what constitutes the English Renaissance must carry the student back to the reign of Henry VIII, and at the outset one must understand that the Renaissance covers all that period beginning with Henry VIII and extending through the Elizabethan (the reign of Elizabeth, 1558-1603), and the Jacobean (the reign of James I, Charles I and the Cromwell period, 1603-1659), the Italian classicism of Inigo Jones and the French classicism of Sir Christopher Wren, through the Stuart or Jacobean period well into the reign of George II. Indeed, what is generally regarded as the Georgian period, prolific with French Renaissance floriation, is really the termination of the English Renaissance.

Jacobean Chest.

The entire Renaissance development in England is full of confusion because subdivided by historical data in many cases confusing.

Under Henry VIII, Torrigiano, Ronezzano and John of Padua introduced the Italian style 1512-1536, but following upon Henry VIII's quarrel with the Pope, the consequent change in religion and the impoverishment of England, the Italians, now regarded with ill favor, returned home, leaving but little or no influence behind them, and their field of occupation was soon filled by Germans and Flemings.

Beginning with 1558, we have what is arbitrarily called the Elizabethan, but Elizabethan, although the reign ended with 1603, extended as a type clear through the Jacobean period, and the term Jacobean means simply, if it means anything, an Elizabethan development. The term Stuart relates to that period beginning with James I and extending down to Queen Anne—all subdivisions of the Renaissance.

As early as 1556 great quantities of Flemish cabinet fronts and other cabinet work were imported into England. Elizabethan houses were built by German and Flemish architects. Strap-work designs were common, male and female figures with strap-work on the front in lieu of clothes. To the Flemings we attribute the diamond-shapes superimposed, in moldings, on square panels; the numerous juttings, and angles; the extensive use of turned work plain and carved frequently

ELIZABETHAN—JACOBEAN.

JACOBEAN.

JACOBEAN OR JACOBIAN: From Latin *Jacobus,* James; pertaining to the style of decoration of James I.

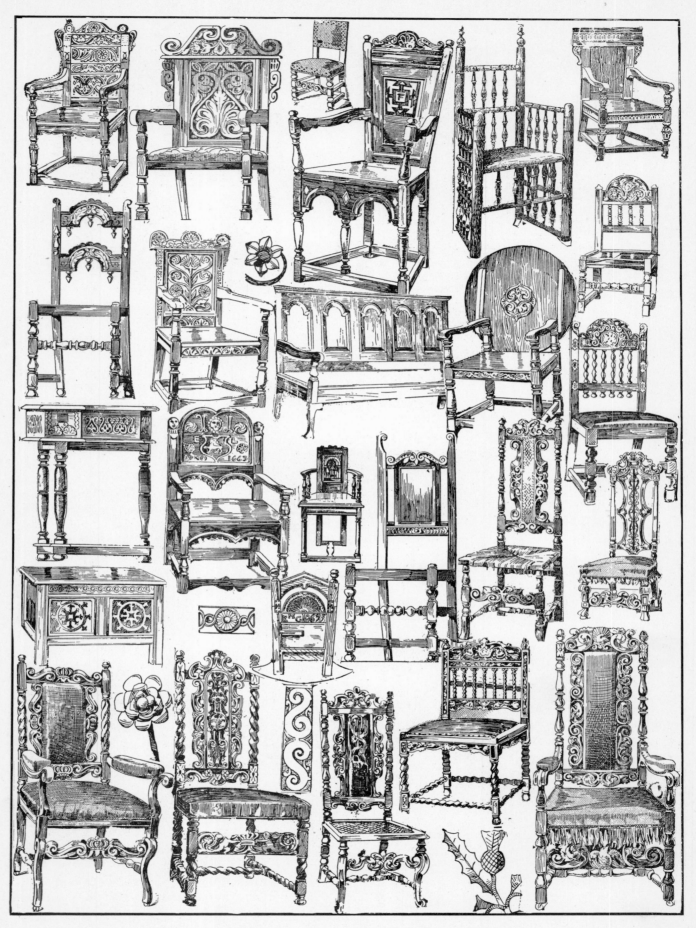

RENNAISSANCE—ELIZABETHAN—The chairs on the top row represent the types prior to 1610, Elizabethan or Jacobean. The second chair from the top is an English type beginning about 1650. The chairs of the bottom row are Charles II type, 1675 or thereabouts. The formation of the legs shows the French spirit, although the carving is of Flemish origin.

Elizabethan-Jacobean Embroideries.

glued upon panels on beds, round applied buttons, and pendants and ovals set in relief upon panels, as well as drop ornaments added below the table frames or the center of arches in panels.

It was all Renaissance, whether from Italy or through the more obscure channels of Germany and Flanders. The Renaissance movement, developed under Elizabeth, was contemporary with a similar movement in France, Flanders and Germany. ·Hence the presentation of styles closely related. We associate with the Elizabethan liberally-paneled rooms and stuccoed ceilings. We find the guilloche, common in Assyrian and Byzantine art, and other simple details, much used at this time owing to the fact that English workmen, who copied the foreigners, were restricted in their work to simple details, necessitated by the use of oak instead of the softer walnut, and this fact will aid one to determine the origin of work of this period.

Great importations came from Flanders, so great in fact that Elizabeth introduced prohibitive measures to stop the imports and encourage English workmen. Elaborate interiors were of terra-cotta. Stuccoed ceilings were of great beauty, but the work was confined mostly to palaces.

The same characteristics followed through the Jacobean period, 1603-1652. The cabinetmakers made

Flemish.

much of this patch-work furniture, and there was much use of the "S" curve in cabinetmaking. Carving was in low relief. The "S" curve, the semi-circle pattern and the interlaced semi-circle pattern and "C" curves became more common with this period.

From the architectural standpoint this period is conspicuous with the work of Inigo Jones (born 1572 died 1653), probably the first English architect who practiced the Renaissance style in its simplicity. Walpole says of him, "England adopted Holbein and Van Dyke; she borrowed Rubens, but she produced Inigo Jones." Inigo Jones studied closely the work of the Italian Palladio, and Charles I encouraged him liberally. Here we have, then, during this Jacobean period furniture and furnishings the work of the cabinetmakers which was of a decidedly hybrid type, and far removed from the exquisite, dignified and artistic work purely Italian that was accomplished by Jones and his contemporaries.

Inigo Jones died in 1653, and a few years later Sir Christopher Wren became famous in a further development of the Renaissance feeling. Sir Christopher studied in Paris and was saturated with the French Renaissance spirit, hence he was profuse where Jones showed restraint. His style was almost Baroque. Pendants of flowers, shells and fruits were used in a prodigal spirit. Carving was of an over-elaborate and highly-ornamented character. It gave the reputation to Grinling Gibbons, who was responsible for so much that was good in carved foliage, birds, fruits, shells, cupid faces, etc., that Charles II employed him on the palace work and subsequently, 1714-1721, he was "master carver in wood" to George I, with a salary of eighteen pence a day.

While we frequently refer to this prolific form of work made famous by the efforts of Wren and Gibbons as Georgian, we must understand that it developed in the late Renaissance and was a part of the Renaissance period, and the Jacobean, Cromwellian and Queen Anne belong in architecture to the Renaissance schools; thus we are confronted by confusing data, throughout this entire English history of decoration. The furnishings were of a commercial character and seldom, if ever, connected with the architectural spirit.

Frequently there was consistency in the wood trims of the house, mantels, panelings, wainscoting and stucco

work done by the architect, but the work was not carried into the furniture, which was usually of Flemish, Dutch or French origin.

Wood-paneled chairs were not generally displaced until the middle of the Jacobean period. Then the Flemish carved type appeared, which in England is sometimes called Jacobean, sometimes Charles I, and if cane-seated, Charles II. It is easy to trace the Flemish origin even if English details, crowned cupids surmount the back; and where the legs and the under-bracing convey something of the Louis XIV suggestion, we can account for the French influence. With the return of the cavaliers to England, just after Cromwell's downfall, 1660, the royalists brought back with their furnishings from France a good deal of its furniture, and thus we can trace the French spirit in what we now regard as the Charles II type.

This spirit was further accentuated at a little later period when, in 1685, the Edict of Nantes was revoked and the Protestant artisans of France, including many Flemish born, fled to England.

Late Elizabethan or Jacobean.

Illustration No. 1 represents a Flemish type common also with the Italian. In France, 1640, the time of Louis XIII, this type is called the *chaise perroquet* or *chaise cacquetoire*.

No. 2 is called by English authorities, a Derbyshire or Yorkshire chair, being made in great quantities, 1650-1660.

Illustration No. 3, a Lancashire chair, about 1675. No. 4, 1650. Derbyshire.

Illustration No. 5, English, showing Spanish influence, doubtless the work of Flemish designers when under Spanish domination, 1660. Yorkshire and Derbyshire.

JACOBEAN

JAMES I, 1603-1625, founder Stuart Period.   CHARLES I, 1625-1649, Commonwealth to 1659.

THE evolution of the spindle or rail-back chair comes from the Italian through the Flemish and French to the English, where it is arbitrarily called Jacobean and even localized as Derbyshire, Lancashire and Yorkshire.

Where the crown appeared, sometimes crown and cupid, it was a Royalist design, and followed Charles II's restoration. S and C shapes were frequently seen upon chairs that were unquestionably of French inspiration, a development following the social relations contemporary with Charles II.

Following the S-forms and the C-forms from 1585 to 1665, we find a chair with the top of its back finished off fan-shaped and later still shell-shaped, but this takes us well into the reign of Queen Anne.

Cane seats came in through the trading of the East India Companies, but the exact date cannot be fixed. It was in the neighborhood of 1650 in England, 1620 France; the poet Chaucer, in his "Canterbury Tales," 1400, mentions wicker chairs. Mahogany was not used until after 1700.

It must be recalled that all ceremonious and pretentious form was confined to castles, and not until late in the Seventeenth Century did the work of the

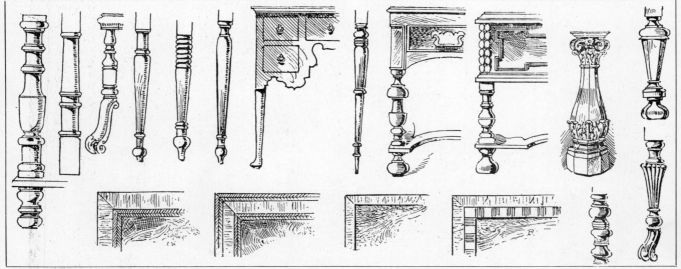

1680-1690. Note the French spirit in third table-leg, also those on extreme right. During the William and Mary period, about 1690, veneering became popular.

AN ELIZABETHAN DINING-ROOM

POSTLIP HALL, GLOUCESTERSHIRE
From Nash's "Mansions of England in the Olden Times."

ELIZABETHAN INTERIORS.

ELIZABETHAN

ELIZABETHAN

WROXTON ABBEY, OXFORDSHIRE, KNOWLE KENT—ELIZABETHAN.

HARDWICK HALL—ELIZABETHAN, 1599.

Elizabethan, showing Tudor-Gothic Mantel.

Jacobean ceiling of the famous Globe room, Reindeer Inn, Banbury, Eng.

ENGLISH RENAISSANCE.

decorator extend beyond the homes of the nobility. In the palaces the ceilings were superb, the interior woodwork was of a most elaborate character; one must realize this and in watching the development of furniture and furnishings one must not confuse the commercial work of the artisan with the more pretentious work of the architect.

In the homes of the wealthy the walls were frequently hung with tapestries, ceilings elaborately stuccoed often colored. Fabrics of elaborate character, velvet, brocades and damasks were used and the floors were covered with Oriental rugs, excepting in chambers for public use, on the floors of which they scattered rushes. It was an age of embroidering; Flemish leathers and embroideries of many varieties were used. Panels were full of heraldic devices and crests. In small rooms chintzes from India were used. India prints in the Oriental spirit were con-

Italian, wood-cut illustration from Dante's "Inferno," 1400.

spicuous in bed coverings, portières, table covers and balustrade hangings. There were no wall-papers used, but prints of cotton or linen or embroideries were in general favor.

The upholsterings were all that can be imagined.

Fabrics of every sort were manufactured.

Glass mirrors were made in Venice, 1507, when methods had been discovered of applying the metal leaf. Mirror makers had their own corporation.

During Elizabeth's time a mirror was a rare possession and worthy of a rich frame, but about 1685 the Duke of Burgundy installed a number of Venetians at Lambeth, where they made looking glasses.

Grandfather's clocks also appeared about 1680. Queen Elizabeth had chartered the East India Company in 1600, but it suffered serious competition with the Dutch, French and Portuguese companies.

The chair foot or the leg terminal indicates, in

1550	1550	1518	1640	1580	1578	1580	1550	1670	1670	1660	1690	1714

some measure, the period of the furniture. The scroll foot was Flemish with French influence, of the type that came in about 1670.

The fluted foot was Spanish in origin and goes back to 1600-1700.

The ball foot or bulb foot is Early Dutch or Flemish.

What is known as the spade foot came in with the Sheraton and Hepplewhite period, late in the Eighteenth Century.

The Renaissance feet were sometimes square blocks, discs or balls in flattened form. Frequently the legs rested upon parallel bars.

Various animal-feet were generally used by the Greeks and Romans and we therefore find them together with scroll feet in good Renaissance examples. They were not associated generally with Queen Anne until the Eighteenth Century. Sometimes we find the cabriole leg and claw foot in old Spanish pieces of the Seventeenth Century, but they can be distinguished

The Oriental motif from which Elizabethan and Jacobean embroidering took inspiration.

from the Queen Anne styles by the front, back and side stretchers that connect them near the base. The claw-and-ball foot was distinctly Queen Anne, but the form came through Louis XIV and late Jacobean.

FABRICS.

Tapestries applied above high wainscoting were in common use. Sometimes tapestry hung down over the panel. For a while during the Wars of the Roses tapestries were abandoned in England but under Henry VIII fresh impetus was given and later some superb examples were introduced in the Mortlake factory established by James I. Another very popular fabric was a "painted cloth," canvas painted in mottoes.

In "Much Ado About Nothing," Beatrice says that she "got all her wit from the painted cloth hangings." Embossed and gilded leather, cloths of gold and the richest kinds of silks and velvets were in use and what is referred to as a novelty is quoted by Pepys in his diary, 1663, "I bought my wife a chint, that is a painted Indian calico for to line her new study." The term study at this period must have referred to a sort of boudoir or library, although in some houses there were

On the right, typical of Elizabethan embroideries. Sixteenth and Seventeenth Centuries.

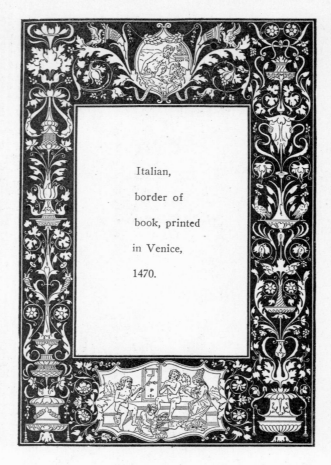

Italian, border of book, printed in Venice, 1470.

rooms set aside for study.

In a few houses ceilings were carved elaborately, which style was imitated in plaster. Windows were furnished with little diamonds or squares of glass and often in the center were armorial pieces. Even at this time floors of private chambers were of inlaid wood. Green, yellow and crimson were favorite colors for bed and window draperies and the materials were silk damask, worsted damask, satin, silk, or serge.

The names are not easy to define. We know that of the silken stuffs there is a constant reference in old documents to lustering, paduasoy, doubtless Padua *soie* (silk), tabby, taffeta, sarcenet, cheney (China). In woolen goods we have reference to serge, dorneck (linen print), perpetuana, mohair, camoca or camak, camlet, say, serge, rep, watchet, fustian, damask, and kitterminster or kidderminster, some of which were mixed with camel's hair or threads of silk. There were also dimity, flowered chintz, and callimanco (a glazed linen), as well as Turkey and "wrought-work" (which, of course, was needlework). East India goods, such as printed calico and seersucker were of this period.

White curtains for the bed were rarely employed, in-

| 1640 | 1650 | 1660 | 1690 | 1690 |

variably satin and dimity being employed, worked in colored crewels or worsted.

Valances were much used; leather, velvet, brass nails, needlework, embroiderings, were all popular.

As early as 1300 velvet is mentioned in English inventories and French documents. At that time it was a flock-like material. In Italy, beginning 1600, design was still influenced by the Orient, and France was a great producer of velvets and damasks.

While silken stuffs had been made in Europe at an early date (see page 35, chapter on Development of Textile Weaving), it was not until the commencement of the European trade with the East and the introduction of silk culture into Italy and France that the lower price of the raw material encouraged the manufacture. In the time of Queen Elizabeth a charter was granted to the Dutch settlers in Norwich for figured loom weaving, and damasks, flowered and striped, were made. The revocation of the Edict of Nantes, 1685, strengthened the English trade, and by 1700 Flemish and Huguenot weavers settled in London, Spitalfields, Cheshire, Lancaster, Derbyshire, Kent, Essex and Norfolk.

The illustrations on the right show the Jacobean panel work of 1600-1620. The rest of the pieces show the French development immediately following the restoration of Charles II, 1660, and the bulbous formations, distinctly William and Mary.

The eight-legged chair would be properly called Louis XIV, probably made by French exiles, who settled in England in 1685. These William and Mary styles were usually walnut, and need never be confused with mahogany of a later period.

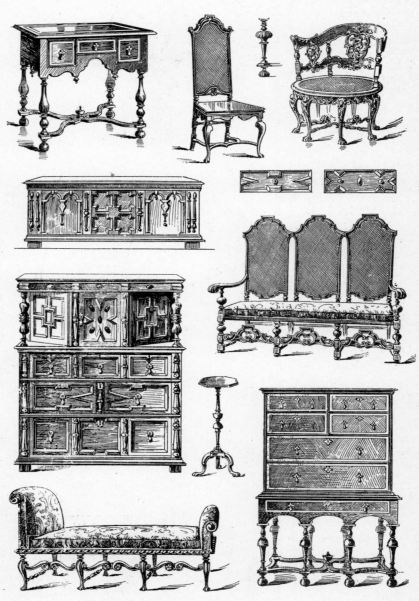

THE RENAISSANC

(See also page 77)

ITALIAN.

1400-1500. Early Renaissance.

1400-1600. Florentine Renaissance:
Brunelleschi, 1377-1446. Borgognone, 1450-1524. Fra Angelico,
1387-1455. Luca della Robbia,
1388-1463. Botticelli, 1447-1510.
Andrea del Sarto, 1486-1531.
Benvenuto Cellini, 1500-1571.

1400-1600. Milanese Renaissance:
Leonardo da Vinci, 1452-1519.

1444-1643. Roman Renaissance:
Donato Lazzari (Bramante), 1444-
1515.
Giacomo Barozzio, 1507-1573.
Michael Angelo Buonarroti, 1474-
1564.
Raphael, 1483-1520.

1490-1600. Venetian Renaissance:
Palladio, 1518-1580. (See England,
1603-1649 for Italian influence.)

1500. High Renaissance.

1540-1643. Late Renaissance.

FRENCH.

1515. Francis I.
Leonardo da Vinci and Cellini in-
fluenced the introduction of
Italian Renaissance.
Flemish workmen given generous
employment.

1549-1559. Henri II.
The furnishings up to Louis XIII
were similar to late Elizabethan.
(See English, 1603-1649.)

1559-1560. Francis II.

1560-1574. Charles IX.

1574-1589. Henri III.

1589-1610. Henri IV.
Edict of Nantes granting religious
freedom.

1604. Organization of East India
Trading Company.

1610. Louis XIII.

1643-1715. Louis XIV.

1642. Richelieu's East India Company.

1653. English cavaliers settled in
France after downfall of Charles I,
and on returning under Charles II,
brought back French influence in
art.

1685. Daniel Marot, one of the most
talented decorators who flourished
during the reign of Louis XIV, fled
with other Protestants at the time
of the revocation of the Edict of
Nantes, a measure originally granted
by Henri IV to allow toleration of
worship. When revoked in 1685 by
Louis XIV thousands of Protestants
fled to Holland and England. The
French style of Marot and his confrères became conspicuous in the
English period just prior to Queen
Anne.

FLEMISH.

1507 Development from Italian.

1576. All Netherland provinces united
and drove out the Spanish.

1581. Formation Dutch Republic.
Consisting of Holland, Zealand,
Utrecht, Gelderland, Groningen,
Friesland Overyssel.

1584. Antwerp destroyed. Famous
manufactures dispersed. Flanders,
Brabant, Limburg, Luxemburg, Ar-
tois, Hainault, Namur, Zutphen,
Mechlin became finally merged as
Belgium.
Dutch traders ruled the commerce
of the world.

1600. Spanish dominion overthrown.

1602. Dutch East India Co. incorporated. East Indian textiles and
pottery furnished Oriental motifs
for embroidery.

1613. New Amsterdam, America, settled by the Dutch.

1648. Republic of the United Province of the Netherlands recognized
by Spain.

1664. New Amsterdam was seized by
Duke of York, brother of Charles II,
and name changed to New York.

SPANISH.	GERMAN.	ENGLISH.

SPANISH.

1500. At first Moorish or Hispano-Moresque. Italian style was adopted gradually, developing what was termed the Plateresque, a sumptuous mingling of Gothic and classic details.

1550. Carlos I was born and educated in the Netherlands, and upon attaining the crown his advisers were Flemish, and the late Spanish Renaissance showed Flemish characteristics.

1500-1600. Portugal enjoyed monopoly of trade with India.

1600. Spanish withdrawal from the Netherlands.

GERMAN.

1550. Founded by Albrecht Dürer. Perpetuated by Holbein and Peter Vischer.

ENGLISH.

1509. Renaissance introduced by Henry VIII, who employed many Italian artists. This period is sometimes called Early English or Tudor, Henry VII having founded the Tudor line, 1485.

1534. Reformation. Departure of Catholic Italian workmen from England. Italian influence was soon forgotten in the employment of German and Flemish artisans.

1558-1649. Elizabethan style. Development along German and Flemish lines. Protestant element. Dutch commerce made such inroads that Elizabeth took measures to check it. The full development of Elizabethan style included what is popularly called Jacobean.

1600. English East India Trading Company incorporated. Charter renewed several times, and active up to 1813.

1603-1649. Jacobean (Jacobus, James), a continuance and full development of Elizabethan. Under James I came the classic development of Inigo Jones (1625-1652), who studied under Palladio, Italy.

1625-1649. Charles I. Charles beheaded 1649, and many royalists fled to France.

1653. Cromwellian.

1660. Charles II. To the Flemish spirit was added French characteristics through the sentiments absorbed by the exiled royalists who now returned to England.
New Amsterdam seized (see Flemish).

1685-1689. James II.

1689-1702. William and Mary.

WILLIAM AND MARY PERIOD, ABOUT 1690.

Early Jacobean.

FOLLOWING THE JACOBEAN

CHARLES II, 1660-1685.   James II, 1685-1689.   William and Mary, 1689-1702.

THROUGHOUT this entire period which follows the Jacobean epoch we have such a confusion of styles, adaptations of French, Flemish and Italian, that it seems absurd to attempt to distinguish definitely the beginning and ending of periods like the Cromwellian, which only lasted five years, or the James II, which only lasted four years, or the William and Mary, which lasted twelve years.

It is impossible to draw a strict line of demarcation between the end of the Jacobean and the beginning of the Queen Anne. Queen Anne reigned 1702-1714, but what is known in art as the Queen Anne Period had its inception in 1660. One may say of this immediate period that it is Charles II if French influences are particularly strong, or William and Mary if Dutch influences are prevalent, but Queen Anne in its entirety was strictly Dutch and, as will be seen later on, had a style distinctly its own. Before reaching, however, the narrowed confines of the period that began in 1702 we have to do with

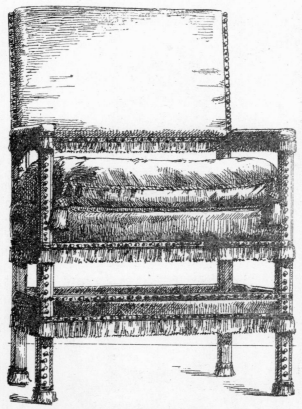

Chair with all covered frame, popular in France and England as early as 1600.

the French-Flemish and the Flemish-Dutch, which carries us through the late Jacobean and past the James II, 1685-1689, and William and Mary, 1689-1702.

Flemish characteristics began to depart and the French details of Louis XIV were adopted in the reign of Charles II. History tells of the lavish extravagances of his mistresses, especially Louise de Queroualle, who was presented to Charles through the instrumentality of Louis XIV, for whom she became practically a spy. The tastes of the court were distinctly French. Chairs with heavily upholstered seats and backs became popular. The cane chair took on the scroll leg. In 1675 marquetried furniture came in. Lacquered furniture became popular. Again in that year we notice the flat serpentine stretcher, drop handles and brass key escutcheons to doors. Bedroom chairs would often be made in sets and covered with velvet to match the hangings of the bed. Double-seated chairs or settees came into use. The French leg and foot came in 1680—the S-shaped leg, serpentine like.

In 1685 came James II and a marked development in furniture. With 1685 appeared the tall-backed French chair. It was a more severe style of furniture than that of Charles II. French dining-room chairs were tall, narrow-backed, without arms and with sometimes an upholstered seat. They had the French characteristics. Towards the end of James II and during the reign of William and Mary the crest at the top of the back was often placed as a finish to the back posts instead of between them.

The strong French characteristics were due largely to the work of Marot, a prominent decorator who fled from France at the time of the revocation of the Edict of Nantes, 1685. Many other French artisans worked in England at this time, just prior to the Queen Anne period, introducing what appeared to be anachronisms.

While cushioned seats were not uncommon at an earlier period, chairs made with fixed upholstering did not come into use until about 1550, the period of Elizabeth in England and Henri II in France. Henry VIII had gathered together a small army of French, Italian and German workmen and at this early date the Italian and Flemish X chairs were used, upholstered seats and backs. Prior to this date the furniture backs being carved did not encourage arm and back upholsterings and movable cushions were common. The chairs were without arms to accommodate the monstrous skirts of the women. At the period of James I the Farthingdale chair was popular. It had no arms and allowed the dress to spread in all directions. By 1620 we have the type illustrated where the frame is entirely covered.

CHARACTER OF THE WOOD-FINISH.

The use of varnishes goes back 3,000 years. The Egyptians were expert in the use of varnish, but the Europeans learned their art from the Far East Old English term, vernish; French, vernis; Italian, vernice.

Italian Renaissance furniture probably received an oil finish. Martin, a carriage painter, born 1726,

Above, types of inception Queen Anne; below, Cromwellian, 1653-1659.

rivalled the lacquers of China and Japan with a varnish which was hard and transparent, now known as Vernis-Martin. From 1744 to 1764 Martin was granted a monopoly to manufacture this lacquer.

Elizabethan and Jacobean oak furniture received only a light coat of dark oil varnish. The pieces were then rubbed with beeswax and given a rich tone.

It may be safely assumed that during the "Age of Oak," 1500-1660, and the "Age of Walnut," 1660-1700, little varnish was used.

Italian Renaissance furniture, 1400-1643, was of oak, lime, willow, sycamore, chestnut, ebony or walnut, and was wax polished, oiled or left natural.

The French, Flemish and Spanish Renaissance, 1500-1643, used a great deal of oak, chestnut and walnut polished, oiled or left natural. The Portuguese traders from about 1525-1576 and the Dutch traders subsequent to 1576, brought into Europe a great many foreign woods, but they were not to any extent employed in the manufacture of furniture until the middle of the Seventeenth Century. The finishing of woodwork was hand polished. Indeed, in England it was not until the Queen Anne style came in that we notice any efforts at even shellacking. The old-time cabinetmaker obtained his toned effects by exposing his woods to the light until the surfaces had darkened, then he rubbed in the oil and beeswax. Beginning about 1680 a spirit and shellac preparation was used. Then followed the Louis XIV period and soon afterward Vernis-Martin and a host of imitation varnishes.

As early as 1601 there are records of lacquer ware brought from China and Japan, hence the term japanned, as applied to lacquering. The Oriental method required a vast degree of patience and skill, sometimes requiring eighteen or twenty treatments and never less than three treatments. The Chinese and Japanese lacquer was derived from a juice of the varnish tree, which hardened into a black resin. Lacquer wares were brought into Holland, England and France in large quantities throughout the Seventeenth Century, particularly by the East Indian Com-

A Farthingdale Chair, 1620. See first column, page 118.

panies. Cane belongs essentially to the Jacobean period, England about 1650 and Louis XIII France. The earliest long clocks belong to the period of Charles II and were inlaid.

Excellent marquetry work following Dutch styles was popular in England during William and Mary's regime. Veneering was first used in the reign of William and Mary, until which time furniture had been made solid.

The beginning of walnut in England was about the period of Charles II. During the Queen Anne period the prevailing woods were walnut, beech, holly, birch and yew.

Cedar was used for room paneling in England as early as 1678; also for chests.

English elm has been always used, especially for chest drawers and tables. It has a plain straight grain and is not as attractive as oak. Some of the Queen Anne dressing tables were elm. Laburnum, a native wood of the Alps, was excellent as a veneering.

William and Mary.

Hardwick Hall, Derbyshire, from an old print. The Presence Chamber. No carpetings used, the floors strewn with rushes. Tapestry on wall.

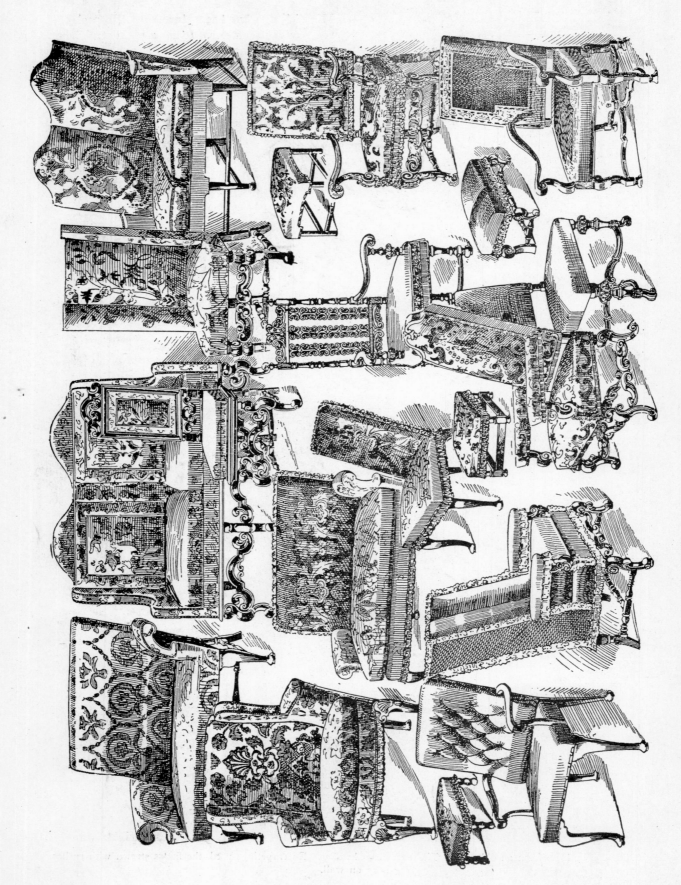

LATE SEVENTEENTH CENTURY ENGLISH FURNITURE, 1675-1590.

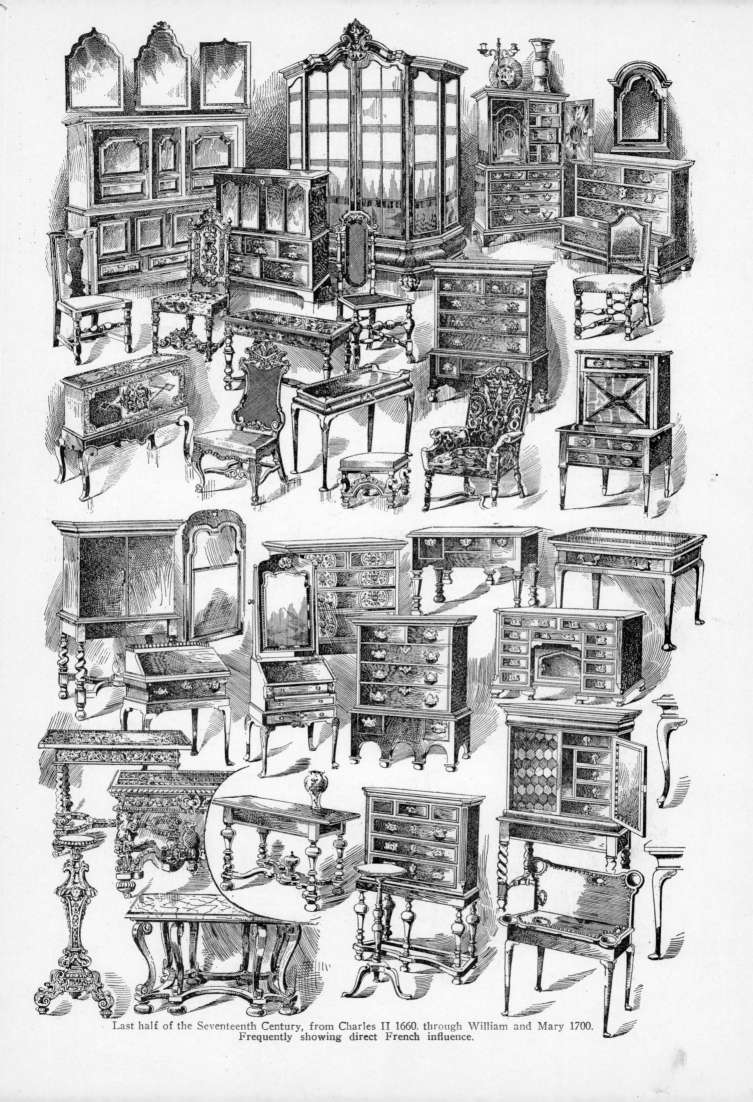

Last half of the Seventeenth Century, from Charles II 1660. through William and Mary 1700.
Frequently showing direct French influence.

LATE ENGLISH RENAISSANCE.

The ceiling is by Sir Christopher Wren and Grinling Gibbons (about 1680), the plaster is in high relief. The mantels are in Inigo Jones' best style, period James I. The cartouche shows the Baroque spirit of James Gibb. The table was made for King William, of pine inlaid with lignum vitae, amboyna and other woods. The bed is the State bed of Queen Mary. The firedogs are of steel, same period, William and Mary.

Reading from left to right, the portraits above are those of Rembrandt, 1607-1669; Van Dyke, 1599-1641; Franz Hals, 1581-1666; Rubens, 1577-1640.

THE FRENCH RENAISSANCE

Development of Baroque in Roman Renaissance, 1540—Classic influence of Inigo Jones (James I), Sir Christopher Wren (Charles II, George I), Louis XIII of France.

DURING the period known as the Late Renaissance, Michael Angelo, apostle of free thought in art, broke away from the fetters of classicism and produced some extraordinary results. These forms in the hands of a master were acceptable, but when others tried to follow the results were less pleasing and became known as Baroque.

Details were combined and superimposed in a fashion extravagant and frequently grotesque. It was the outcome of that universal spirit of unrest which revolts at rule or order, and the effort to do something different simply resulted in ornament that was impressive and astonishing at the sacrifice of taste and unity. The term Baroque became eventually an adjective expression for a corrupt style.

In France the Baroque was little in evidence.

In Germany it was passively accepted. We find little Baroque in England for the reason that apart from the work of John of Padua under Henry VIII there was no Italian influence until James I, and then the influence became Palladian or Classic, for throughout the period of Michael Angelo, Palladio was equally active in maintaining the integrity of the pure style — Venetian Renaissance — and Inigo Jones in England was a staunch Palladian. His work as well as that of John Webb, Edward Carter and Nicholas

Stone, expressed admirably the pure Italian spirit.

The work of Sir Christopher Wren, Nicholas Hawksmoor, Sir John Van Brugh, James Gibb, and other eminent architects, continued the classic spirit of the French style in architecture through the Cromwellian, Charles II, James II, William and Mary, Queen Anne and well into the period of George I. Sir Christopher died in 1723. Ceilings were all plastered, stuccoed, flat or in relief, divided into panels and circles, hexagons, and rhomboids, the borders being enriched with flowers and fruits of all sorts, well raised, following the extraordinary carvings of Grinling Gibbons; borders were often flat ornaments of Greek and Roman design or flowing Renaissance; the panels were often painted. Indeed, painted ceilings were common throughout the Seventeenth Century, the great artists, even Rubens, lending their talents to ceiling painting.

Sir Christopher Wren's work for William and Mary and Queen Anne was augmented by the ceiling and wall decorations of Verrio, the Neapolitan, who also did wonderful ceiling work for Charles II, prolific with goddesses, saints, satyrs, muses, cupids and inspirations of the New Testament and Roman History.

There was little or no Baroque in England; there was little in Holland, and even where it existed in

Reading from left to right, the portraits above are those of W. Jamnitzer, 1508-1585; P. Vischer, 1460-1529; Albrecht Dürer, 1471-1528; H. Holbein, 1497-1543.

Above, lambrequin ornamentation in the style of Louis·XIII—XIV. Below, Baroque furniture of the end of the Renaissance.

France it cannot be said to have become a style; it was rather a decadent taste indulged by the few and condemned by the many.

With Louis XIII, 1610-1643, the French Renaissance came to an end. It was a period of assimilation. French life under Henri II, Charles IX and Henri III, semi-Italian princes, was dominated by Catherine de Medici. Henri IV sent artisans to Holland to study carving, and at the time of Louis XIII, decorative art, as expressed by the work in his palace, was Italian, German, Flemish and Swiss. A definite French period did not develop until under Louis XIV.

In 1603 the Jesuits, who had been expelled from France in 1595, were recalled and in their religious zeal bent their efforts, especially in art, to the propagation of the classic styles. Not only marquetry, ebony furniture and painted furniture were made, but the Oriental spirit during the reign of Louis XIII became conspicuous in the woods that were used and the styles of the fabrics.

Cane was imported as seat coverings. Chairs were covered with leather or fabrics and upholstered heavily. The reception bed was introduced. Ladies received their guests *en déshabillé,* a fashion that pre-

124

vailed in the reign of Louis XIV. The fashion of covering furniture with drapery can be traced back to the Fourteenth Century in Italy. Bed draperies were then used and canopies were in vogue; but the Louis XIII period may be said to have introduced the use of table covers and scarfs.

The French silk industry developed rapidly and quantities of costly materials were to be had in France; they were hung upon the walls and displayed over tables and screens. See page 131.

The cultivation of the mulberry tree had been successful in the South. Lyons was manufacturing great quantities of taffetas. Weavers had come from Anatolia to do embroidering in the Oriental style (largely Arabian and Ottoman), and before long France was also making its first typical design, employing as motifs the exotic plants found in the royal garden. By the beginning of the Sixteenth Century fancy silk manufacture, including cloths of gold, velvet, satin, silk and silk mixtures, had been introduced in France; into Tours by Louis XI, Lyons by Francis I, Paris by Henri IV, Avignon by the Popes.

In the Seventeenth Century, Colbert provided regulations covering the manufacture at Tours, Lyons, Paris and Nimes. Contemporaneously were famous Venetian damasks, Luccan damascenes, Genoese velvets and mixtures called *filatrices,* poplins, *feradines,* Egyptian damasks, caffarts, Bruges satins, etamines, fustians and dimities.

Italian manufacturers lost a great deal of their German,

Above, pedestal of the Louis XIII—XIV period.

Swiss, Flemish, English and Spanish trade. Soon the American colonies were heavy buyers of French stuffs. Paris gained supremacy in matters of fashion. The French styles were accepted in all the capitals of Europe.

Jacquard has always received credit for inventing a machine which bears his name, but in 1605 Dangon made a machine which produced great complication of color effects. Gallatier and Blache in 1687 made a loom which enabled one to make easily small patterns. Bonchon originated the idea of needles pressed back by a cardboard on which was traced the design.

Falcon, his assistant, increased the number of needles and made the cards revolve on two quadrangular prism cylinders. The municipality of Lyons recognized the superiority of this new loom and allowed to Falcon a gratuity of 1,500 livres. Genin in 1749 received 1,750 livres for having invented a loom on which one could weave small fancy stuffs without the help of a draw-boy. Ponson in 1766 invented the loom for the weaving of several armures at one time. Vezier in 1798 made still further improvements. Philip de LaSalle invented a machine for reeding designs, which brought about a considerable development in the composition of fabrics. He invented an attachment by the aid of which the draw-boy was able to do all his work while remaining seated. Finally he created the flying shuttle.

Jacquard's machine was an improvement on former inventions, but what was accom-

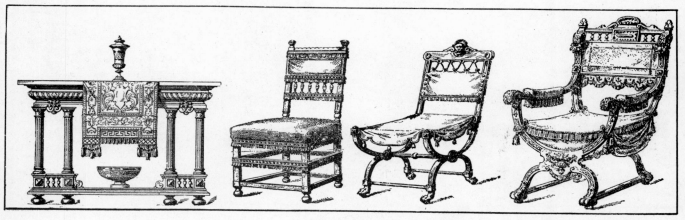

Louis XIII.

HENRI II, HENRI IV TO LOUIS XIII.

1500-1600 Group VI (R).

LOUIS XVI CEILING AND BORDER DESIGNS.

1710.   Group VIII (U).   Louis XIV.

1710.   Group VII (S).   Louis XIV.

1670.   Group VII (S).   Louis XIV.

1550-1650.   Group VII (P).   Late Renaissance, Henri II-
Louis XIII.

LOUIS XIII AND LOUIS XIV.

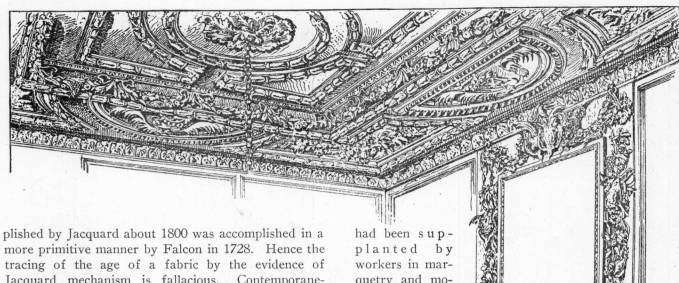

plished by Jacquard about 1800 was accomplished in a more primitive manner by Falcon in 1728. Hence the tracing of the age of a fabric by the evidence of Jacquard mechanism is fallacious. Contemporaneously we note the introduction through Italian channels of the crystal and glass chandeliers, sconces in the shape of arms fixed to the wall, the first holding the candle; also glass mirrors (invented in Italy, 1507), sometimes framed elaborately in gold and in ebony or appliqués of copper and silver.

This mirror was used in conjunction with the bureau, which followed the introduction of the cabinet. The term is carelessly used at present, but in the time of Louis XIII the bureau was a chest set upon a table and pushed back to afford a rest for the hand of the writer. About 1700 this table was provided with drawers and to-day this combination of drawers and chests we call a bureau.

Good wood carvers were becoming scarce. They had been supplanted by workers in marquetry and mosaic, after the Italian fashion, and spiral supports were generously used, the chisel being employed only on the tops of posts or important places. The upholstering of the furniture was heavy and comfortable and fixed

Above, illustration of a ceiling by Sir Christopher Wren, showing the exquisite carving of Grinling Gibbons.

Below, panel ornamentation frequently referred to as Gibbons' masterpiece.

1620.   Jacobean.   James I.   England.

1620.   Salon at Fontainebleau.   Louis XIII.

ENGLISH AND CONTEMPORARY FRENCH.

The pediment in the middle of the second row of illustrations shown above is the work of Inigo Jones. The two small pediments of the bottom row are attributed to Kent. The others are the work of James Gibb.

to the structure. The room was draped and as the woodwork was no longer beautifully carved, curtains and fabrics were hung in profusion.

At the beginning of the Seventeenth Century France greatly prospered. Damasks, damascenes, fancy velvets, cloths of gold, taffetas, silk, wool, cotton and other fiber mixtures, poplins, brocatelles, dimities, fustians, *filatrices* and *feradines,* as well as fabrics of low price were made, and Italy soon lost her ascendency. To cap the climax the discovery of the passage around the Cape of Good Hope (1579) turned from the Mediterranean the trade in silks from the Eastern part of Asia.

In the latter part of the Sixteenth Century and the beginning of the Seventeenth, the closing of the Renaissance, we find in fabric designs a great many of the pure Renaissance types, including griffins, birds, vases, bouquets, garlands, branches of leaves and fruits, masks, serpentine meanderings, birds and hounds, Oriental motifs, flowers, sprays, spots and curly-cues. Typical of the Louis XIII is the Arabian style, a survival of the Arabian popular under Francis I, sometimes called Moresque or Arabesque. As early as 1540 books of patterns were issued at Lyons and these Arabesque styles, which are conspicuous again in the Louis XIII period, were recommended as elegant and refined.

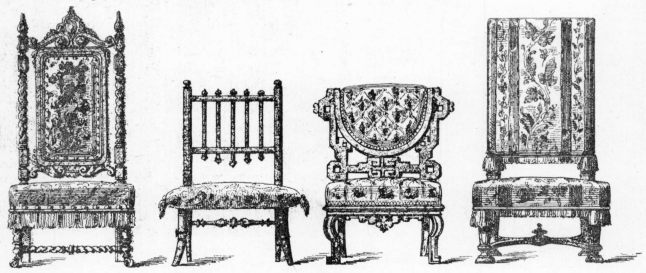

Louis XIII.

Louis XIII.

Under Louis XIII silk manufacture encouraged.
Note character of patterns.

Characteristic design.

INTERIOR AND FABRICS OF LOUIS XIII PERIOD.

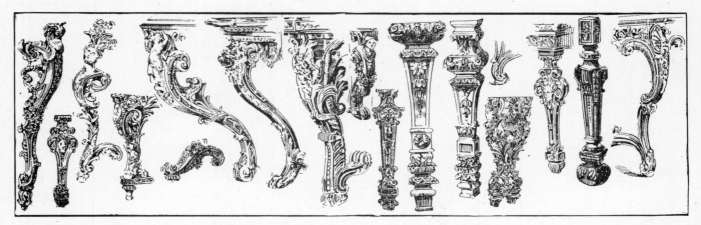

Characteristic furniture leg details of the Louis XIV Period.

LOUIS XIV

THE period of Louis XIV is supposed to have begun 1643, when the king was but five years old. The art period starts properly at 1667, when the *Manufacture Royale des Meubles de la Couronne* was established by Colbert, to promote the making of tapestries, jewelry, furniture and metal work, just as the Academy of Painting and Sculpture had encouraged the more *dilettante* arts. The Gobelin factory, and a little later the Beauvais works, were part of the enterprise, and French art may be said to have dated from this organization.

Le Brun, chief court painter to Louis XIV, became director of the Gobelin factory and gathered about him the most eminent artists of the day, Vandermeulen, Mansart, Hyvart, Monnoyer, the two Boullognes, the Coypel brothers, the ebenists Cucci, Poitou and the tapestry makers Jans and son. In

Boule Cabinet, Louis XIV.

1679 Jean Marot and his son Daniel, who left France for Holland and England, 1685, did much to emphasize and popularize the Louis XIV type. Jean le Pautre and his brother Antoine became authorities in wood work, and the designs of Jean Berain became also a type.

Mazarin, himself an Italian, drew many Italian workmen to France and naturally Italian art strongly influenced the Louis XIV style which closely followed the Renaissance. In tapestry work particularly we find pomp and much dignity, tableaux of classic grandeur: "Victory and Battle," the spirit of "Valor and Conquest," the "Purity of the Passions," the "Progress of the Arts and Sciences"— allegories of an exalted nature.

It was an ambitious period, stimulated by the enthusiasm of the Crown, and artists held high position and there was great incentive to royal favor. The art of the Italian Caffieri was gorgeous in gold and bronze. Andre Charles Boulle or Boule brought the arts of the inlayer to the highest possible degree. (Called also Buhl work.)

Mignard's ceiling paintings were superb. The richest velvets, silks and Oriental carpets were used. A great deal of gold stucco was employed together with bronze, and damasks following the classic models in an elaborate spirit.

Berain gave great freedom to the exercise of Renaissance form, and towards the end of the Seventeenth Century contemporary scenic and genre details were introduced, including Chinese. Ceiling work was massive or dainty, hand-painted, wood molded or stuccoed. Walls were covered with fabrics or decorated in paint, leather or wood.

It was a period of luxury in the use of superb beds and tapestries, hand-painted fabrics, damasks, brocades and velvets, rich upholsterings, curtains, bronzes, mirrors, clocks, screens, sideboards, porcelains and consoles. Huge pier glasses of great height were employed, the frames carved in imitation of palms. Bronze and marble were combined in mantelpieces. Marble-top tables held superb vases. It was the period of Louis the Great, *le grand monarque*,

and the decorations reflected that spirit. It was an age of conquest and naturally an age of absorption and adaptation.

In 1659 France received German and Flemish territory. In 1667 was the first war of conquest on account of the Spanish Netherlands. Then followed wars of conquest against Holland and the acquisition of territory. All this had its influence upon the character of the decorations. The style was classic and the Roman acanthus leaf was conspicuous until the Louis XV period when the rock and shell and even the stalactite forms were employed.

Wall decorations were usually of historical or biblical or legendary character.

Companies were established to trade with the East and West Indies in competition with the Dutch. The façade of the Hotel de Ville, commenced by Francis I, was now finished. All France was adorned with parks and public buildings and wall panels and fabrics frequently presented scenic and architectural designs. The French Academy was established. It was the age of Corneille, Racine, Molière and La Fontaine.

It has been said that Louise de la Valliere and

Ceiling and panels by Inigo Jones. English contemporary of Early Louis XIV.

LOUIS XIV.

IN THE DAYS OF LOUIS XV..

From an old etching.

LOUIS XIV.

Early Louis XIV.

Late Louis XIV.

Madame de Maintenon influenced the arts of Louis XIV. On the contrary, the arts were stimulated by the world force of conquests and state-craft, as distinguished from the arts of Louis XV, which were stimulated by social life, elaborate and European floriculture became for the first time an inspiration to the fabric designers. The shell introduced under Louis XIII became employed as a decorative motif; also plumes, feathers and bird wings.

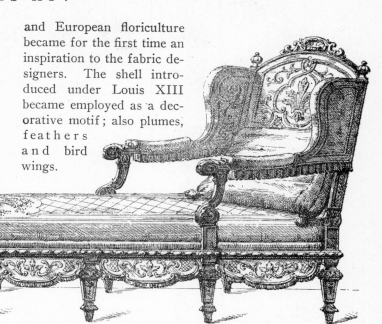

Chaise Lounge, Louis XIV.

ostentation and extravagance.

Under Colbert, lace, silk and porcelain factories were established, and as a result designers introduced as details of their patterns ribbons, festoons, vases, pottery, placques and statuary. Magnificent gardens were built

Daniel Marot, Louis XIV.

Berain, Louis XIV.

	ARTISTS AND ARCHITECTS.	CARVERS AND BRONZE WORKERS.	EBENISTES AND INLAYERS.
RENAISSANCE began about 1502. FRANCIS I–HENRY IV 1515–1610.	Aman. Du Cerceau, Jacques Androuet. Goujon, Jean. Hainofer, Philippe. Leonardo da Vinci, Seralio and Cellini (Italians) influenced this period. Martellange. Sambin, Hugues. Seibecq Francisque, called De Carpi. Stabre, Laurent.	Le Pot, Jean.	Bachelier, Nicholas. Baumgartner, Ulrich. Breughels. De Vos. De Vriendts, Floris. Francks, the.
LOUIS XIII, 1610–1643.	Bosse, Abraham. De Brosse, Salomon. La Sueur, Eustache. Le-Brun, Charles. Le Mercier, Jacques. Lorrain, Claude. Pouissin, Nicholas. Primaticcio. Villacerf. Vouet, Simon.	* Caffieri. * Cucci, Dominico.	Barbet, I. Bordoni, Francesco. Branchi. Giacetti, Luigi. Golle, Peter. Migliorini, Fernando and Horatio.
LOUIS XIV, 1643–1715. JEAN BAPTISTE COLBERT, MINISTER.	Bellin. Berain, Claude. Boullognes, The. Coypel, Antoine and Noel. D'Avilier, J. De Espouy. Francart Hedouin. Hongre, Louis le. Le Brun, Manager Gobelins, 1660. Le Pautre, Jean and Pierre. Loir, Nicholas. Mansart. Marot, Antoine. Marot, Jean and Son Daniel. Mignard, Paul (Manager Gobelins, 1690). Monnoyer. Rousselet. Van der Meulen. Yvart.	Auguier. Baronniere. * Caffieri, Jacques. Coysevox. * Cucci. Lespagnandel. Tuby.	Armand. Boule. Cucci. Denis, Louis. Oppenordt. Percheron. Poitou. Sommord.
LOUIS XV, 1715–1774. Regency, 1715–1723.	Albadier, Jacques. Audran. Blondel, J. F. Boucher. Briseux. Chamblin. Cotelle. Dagley (Le Sieur). Dantin. De Cotte, Jules Robert. De Cuvilles. De La Salle, Philip. Eissen, Ch. Fragonard. Germain. Gillot. Gravelotte. Huet. Jouy. Lancret, Nicholas. Lathuile, J. P. Leclerc, Sebastian. Le Moyne, François. Le Prince. Leroux, J. B. Martin, J. A. Meil, J. W. Meissonnier. Natoire, Joseph. Nilson, J. E. Oberkampf. Oudry, Jean Baptiste. Patte, Pierre. Pineau. Revel. Rubo. Slodtz. Tessier. Watteau.	Babel, P. E. Boffrand. Bouchardon, Edmé. Caffieri, Jacques. Cressent, Charles. Duplessis. Guibal. Hervieux. Lemoyne, M. Pigole. Pineau, Nic. Sally. Winant.	Arnoult. Bernard. Boudin, L. Dautriche, Jacques. De Lorme. Denizot, Pierre. Dubois. Garnile, Pierre. Germain. Gillot. Joubert. Leatz, I. P. L'Avasseur. Loriot. Mignon. Oeben, Jean François. Pillement. Riesener, Jean Henri. Sulpice.
LOUIS XVI, 1774–1793. FRENCH TRANSITION. DIRECTORATE, 1795–1799. CONSULATE, 1799–1804.	Berthault. Cochin, Chas. Nic. Coysevox. * David, Jacques Louis. De La Fosse, Chas. Desprez. De Wailley, Ch. Drud'hon. Dugourc, Jean Denis. * Fontaine, Pierre François. Fragonard. Goudouin, Jacques. * Gouthiere. Greune, J. B. Jouy. Lagrenée. * Lalonde. Le Doux. Leleu, Jean François. Leonard. Moreau, J. M. (Le Jeune). * Normond, Chas. Pierre Joseph. * Percier. * Riesener. * Rousseau, Jean Simon de. Salembier. Saunier, Claude Chas. Soufflot. Vanloo.	Bardin. Falconet. * Gouthiere. Hauré. Martin. Pajou. * Roentgen. * Thomire.	Beneman, Guillaume. Bergeman. Bertrand. Birkle. Blucheidner. Carlin, Martin. Degault. Feuerstein. Frost. Girard. * Jacob (Bros). Joubert. Leleu, J. François. Levasseur. Montigny. Pasquier. Richter, Chas. Roentgen. Saunier. Schmitz, Peter. Schneider, Gaspard. Schwerdfeger. Stokel, Joseph. Weisweiler.
EMPIRE 1804–1814.		Linereux.	Desmalter, Jacob.

* The asterisks indicate names of men who became famous in the Empire period.

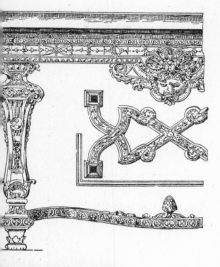

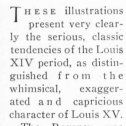

THESE illustrations present very clearly the serious, classic tendencies of the Louis XIV period, as distinguished from the whimsical, exaggerated and capricious character of Louis XV.

The Regency was the Transition Period between late Louis XIV and early Louis XV. At this time the classicism observed and the Renaissance principles followed by Louis XIV gave way to a predisposition to modernize, and the nymphs and satyrs assumed the dress of the day, a little low in the neck and a little short in the skirt, but nevertheless modernized.

The heroics of ancient Rome and Pompeii were succeeded by a comedy spirit, winged horses and fabled lions disappeared and monkeys, parrots, cats and dogs and farmyard creatures took their place.

Finally, the artists Watteau, Boucher, Lancret and Bouchardon abandoned altogether the legendary, historical and Biblical illustrations, scenes which found expression in tapestries, ceiling and wall decorations, and cultivated a modern spirit depicting the life of the people; idealized, to be sure, but of a contemporary character; social festivities, recreations, occupations, were the subjects treated, surrounded by a decorative treatment that developed finally into the Rococo.

Fig. 4. Group VIII. *Gros de Tours.* 1700. Sky-blue ground, flowers, fruits and leaves in blending shades broché. Design of Revel, the pupil of Lebrun. 1700.

Fig. 6. Louis XVI. Fancy fabric manufactured by Philip de la Salle. Medallion type. Ground of the medallion in yellow satin. The fancy design is in part broché.

Fig. 2. Group VII. Brocatelle. Period of Louis XIII. The design is executed in crimson on a yellow ground.

THE FABRICS OF THE XVI AND XVII CENTURIES

FRENCH manufacturers of the Eighteenth Century were equipped to produce exceedingly rich stuffs; foliage velvets in imitation of the Venetian broché cut velvets, crêpes, etamines, mixed cottons, Levantines, plushes, fancy velvets, fabrics with three and five colors in Turkish, Milanese, Genoese and Venetian fashions. At the end of the Eighteenth Century fewer metallic threads were used in weaving and the thick, heavy cloths of gold had fallen into disfavor.

Embroidery at the same time had done marvelously well. The refining and spinning of gold had been very successful in France, and in all the countries of Europe since the Fifteenth Century the art of embroidering official robes and ecclesiastical ornaments had developed considerably.

Oriental foliation and the vase which had for a long time served both before and during the Renaissance in the decoration of fabrics are now revived; one finds this combination in Figure 4, which shows a cut velvet on a gold ground. The warp threads of the

Fig. 1. Group VI (B). Dolphin design. Executed under Henry IV. 1610.

velvets which make the fancy effects are crimson. It followed the Chinese taste of the period. (See page 144.) At the end of the Sixteenth Century, designs were of small dimensions—detached floral pieces, palms and fleurs-de-lis. They corresponded with the less ample form of the garment. We reproduce (Figure 1) the sketch of a fancy fabric with gold ground, date 1610. The design is *Gros de Tours,* raised on a gold ground in a deep green shade. Many striped fabrics are noted at this period.

Under Louis XIII and Louis XIV, 1610-1700, the composition of fabrics took on a grandiose style. Brocatelle (Figure 2) is a beautiful specimen, Louis XIII; red in color composes the body of the fabric, and a yellow silk tram thread is intertwined in a serge weave in such a manner as to give a brilliant ground; the design is raised and is worked out in a satin weave with the crimson warp threads.

This fabric may be assigned to the latter years of the Sixteenth Century.

Fig. 5. Group VIII (U). Taffeta broché, about 1740, Louis XV. Rose-colored ground with lace effect in white. Flowers in gilt.

Fig. 8. Group VIII (U). About 1750, Louis XV. Pheasant design. Fancy fabric manufactured by Philip de la Salle. From the Lyons Industrial Museum of Design.

Fig. 7. Group VIII (U). Partridge design. About 1750, Louis XV. Fancy fabric manufactured by Philip de la Salle. From the Lyons Industrial Museum of Design.

The great vogue of gardens under Louis XIV brought about the adoption of architectural design—green arbors, trees in full leaf, bouquets, etc. Revel, the painter, a pupil of Lebrun, established himself in Lyons at the beginning of the Eighteenth Century, and gave a great impulse to this kind of ornamentation (Figure 4).

Under Louis XV rocks and shells entered into the ornamentation of fabrics in the Eighteenth Century. Fabrics reflected all the fantasies of fashion. One sees the feathers which women had placed in the coiffures, ribbons, knots, pastoral attributes, crooks, baskets, etc., finely garlanded, also Chinese and Japanese—whimsicalities.

Under Louis XVI the poetic spirit of the designers was inexhaustible and it is impossible here to indicate the innumerable paths in which it was successfully engaged under the impulse of the passing caprices of fashion. Decorative art was admirably comprehended and taste in composition was exquisite.

We have spoken of the numerous improvements in the art of weaving made by Philip de la Salle. In 1775 the Academy of Science commended his work in engrossed eulogies and presented him with a gold medal in 1783. An entire glass case in the Industrial Museum of Lyons is reserved for this remarkable manufacturer. It includes all types of composition, arabesques, foliage, flowers, figures, trophies, allegories, landscapes, country scenes and Chinese ornaments.

Fig. 3. Group VI (Q). Pomegranate vase design. Latter part of Sixteenth Century.

1750. Group VIII (V). A Jouy print.

1643-1715. LOUIS XIV.

LOUIS XV ROOM, METROPOLITAN MUSEUM, NEW YORK.

1643-1715. LOUIS XIV.

A fine old Buhl (Boulle) Secretaire, Louis XIV.

LOUIS XV

1715-1774.

SELDOM in the history of the world has there been greater exuberance of inflated wealth than that which prevailed during the early period of Louis XV. The first eight years constituted the Regency; medley of the mythological classic and modern; all parade and ostentation.

The austere, the serious and the heroic of Louis XIV became full of abandon, frivolity and extravagance. The monkey supplanted the Renaissance masque, and the Chinese utterly routed Pompeiian balance.

Then came another phase, the Rococo, an impressionistic form which, following in some degree the curved outlines of the late Louis XIV, displaced the acanthus floral motifs and substituted massings of rock and shell and stalactite shapes, and the independence of execution, already developed in the Baroque.

Carvers presented a flower the size of a man's head and beside it a pheasant no bigger than a canary. Occasionally the Louis XV period showed phases rational and charming, but the Regency and the Rococo dominated the reign.

Perhaps the greatest maker of furniture was Charles Cressent, who ranked with Boulle. Other artists were Caffieri, Duplessis, Riesener, Le Roux,

Oudry, Briseux, Pineau, de Cuvilles, Gravelot, Boucher, Blondel, Babel, Germain and Joubert.

Oeben was a pupil of Boulle and in great favor with Madame Pompadour. J. Henri Riesener was his foreman.

About 1720 Louis XV dispatched an embassy to the Emperor of China with goods of rare value, charged with a commission to encourage the opening of more extensive trade relations. The emperor was cordial in his reception of the king's messengers, and returned magnificent gifts lavishly decorated. This incident rendered the Chinese style fashionable in the upper circles of France, and for some time thereafter Chinese vases appeared in French textile designs juxtaposed to dragons, birds, human figures, pagodas and bits of scenery. A great amount of lacquer work was imported and the lacquers thus introduced were soon copied, the Vernis-Martin becoming especially famous. Pronounced stripes were affected as creations of Madame Pompadour.

The word apartment at this time meant a complete suite of living-rooms: vestibule, first and second ante-chambers (for the servants and attendants, sometimes used as a dining-room), principal chamber salon and company-room or reception-room, bedroom, several studies and wardrobe-room.

Each room had its own special decoration and coloring. The bedroom was usually hung with the same materials as the bed. Ceremonious visitors were received here. The ceiling was painted and pictures and mirrors wrought into it. White and gold was a favorite composition, but bronzes and colors and ma-

hoganies and all kinds of woods were also used. The room was usually longer than wide so that after the bed and side furniture were placed the balance of the room would be almost square. A niche or alcove was often provided to receive the bed. The walls were done often in hand-painted scenes, Chinese lacquered. Thick-pile French carpets or Oriental carpets covered the floors. Draperies were profusely used and

Beds of the Eighteenth Century, Louis XV spirit.

Designs by Antoine Watteau. Louis XV.

Watteau's designs became exceedingly popular. His ladies were depicted in fashionable attire and dainty landscape scenes were presented. Romance and fashion were merged. His subjects were "The Lady in the Sleigh," "The Lady in the Swing," "The Courtier

were introduced into his palace at Versailles by Louis l'Hongre. Thus we find that before Louis XV, the Chinese tendency was strong. Robert Martin, born 1706, as early as 1733 became known as *vernisseur du roi* Louis XV. A brother was engaged in making

By Marot: Chinese influence. Louis XIV.

and the Sheepherdess," "Frolic," "Folly," "The Dancing Girl." The nude was liberally presented in the great works of Boucher, Babel, Natoire, Fragonard and Bouchardon.

In 1692 there was record of three factories in Paris making "lacquer work and furniture in the Chinese style;" again under Louis XIV, Chinese lacquers

relief work in the Japanese and Chinese styles and two sons also followed the manufacture of lacquers. In 1744 the establishment of the Martin works, which in 1748 became a Royal Manufactory, is accredited to a Martin, born 1726, probably Simon Etienne Martin Jr., doubtless a nephew of Robert, and the work of the family was here concentrated. Vernis-

1715-1723. Regency—The transition between Louis XIV and XV.

Louis XV furniture and details,

Martin, or Martin varnish, soon became the finish for Louis XV furniture and hundreds of people were engaged in making lacquers in the Martin style: red, brown, gold, speckled bronze, even black, and the walls of the daintiest boudoirs were finished in this composition.

Ornamental bronzes also were much in evidence. Corners of furniture pieces were ornamented in bronze; panels were decorated in great profusion, and upon all sides we note exquisite mantel ornaments, clocks, vases, candelabra and sconces. Some furniture was almost completely covered with bronze work and wood carving was abandoned for this form of decoration. Charles Cressent, famous in this period, studied the Boulle methods, and we have in his work not only bronze or ormolu decorations, but tortoiseshell and marquetrie of the finest character. (See table of Intarsia.) Probably the Rococo spirit was carried to its best expression by Messonnier, who brought with him from Italy the decadent baroque and idealized it. He was designer to Louis XV and to the royal houses of Germany, Portugal and Poland. His interpretation of what was finally known as the

Rococo style became fashionable about the year 1730.

Walls and ceilings were decorated profusely with female faces and forms, costumed and in the nude, by Boucher, Watteau, Huet, le Prince, Gravelot and Bouchardon. Glass chandeliers were of the most gorgeous character. Huge mirrors were used not only for wall panels but for ceilings, cut up and surrounded by moldings and juxtaposed to painted scenes or decorations. Oudry's famous cartoons, illustrating the La Fontaine fables, were executed about this time in Beauvais tapestry, and some of the finest work of the Gobelins was undertaken, but the nudities of Boucher and the frivolities of Watteau were the fashion, and gave lasting imprint to the Louis XV period.

During the late years of Louis XV, and while the wildest extravagances were being encouraged by him, his favorite, Du Barry, and her satellites, his grandson was exploring the sciences.

The Dauphiness was a picture of refinement amid ribaldry, culture amid chicanery, but she held aloof from contamination, and the style known later as the Louis XVI was a style which reflected Marie Antoinette's personality.

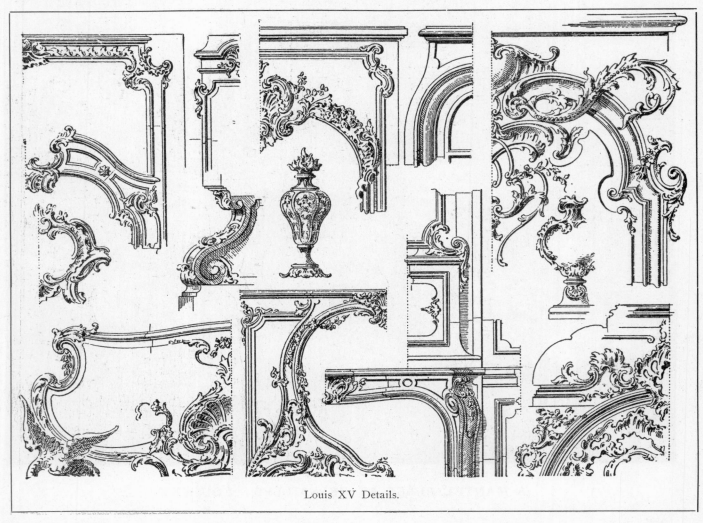

Louis XV Details.

A MANTEL PLACE AT VERSAILLES.   LOUIS XV.

Boudoir of Marie Antoinette; Louis XVI—Transition.

LOUIS XVI

1774-1793.

HERCULANEUM, for centuries buried beneath the ashes of Vesuvius, was discovered about 1709. By 1748 Pompeii also had been discovered and excavations were successfully undertaken in both cities.

The antiquities brought to light aroused great enthusiasm among French artists and in the latter half of the reign of Louis XV this purely classic feeling, this restoration of pure lines, Pompeiian lines, was strongly in evidence.

In the closing years of Louis XV's regime, the style had fully developed, and it continued under Louis XVI, to which period its development is popularly attributed.

The Louis XVI style was a reversion to the early classic. It came back to the straight legs of the early Louis XIV, but followed the models of the

Costume and Furniture of the Louis XVI period.

architectural columns, rounded, but smaller at the base or foot instead of smaller at the top. No longer did they use curved lines, the S shapes or the exaggerated curves in the acanthus forms. There was a well-defined effort to purify decoration, which had run the limits of extravagance. Moreover, the *petit salon* and *boudoir* had become fashionable, hence a demand for reduced proportions, daintier figures, smaller furniture. The tastes of Marie Antoinette were simple and her judgment and patronage stimulated the new styles, which following the lines of least resistance, adopted the classicism displayed in the Restoration work at Pompeii. So strong did this feeling become that notwithstanding the fanatical hatred and destructiveness which followed in the path of the Revolution, the style con-

LOUIS XVI FURNITURE DETAILS.

LOUIS XVI.

tinued through the Transition or Directoire and into the period of the Empire. We find the same spirit in the English styles of the Brothers Adam, Hepplewhite and Sheraton, modified but undisguised. Pagan deities, masks and caryatides were replaced by suggestions of pastoral simplicity: flowers, ribbons, festoons and the depiction of peasant life, a little unreal in the diminutive waist and high-heeled shoes and coiffures of the shepherdesses, but dainty and charming. Chinese lacquers were much in vogue and Chinese pictorial and scenic designs.

De la Londe published thirteen books of design during the Louis XVI period which he called "The Classic Taste." His work showed a fondness for the fluted leg laced with ribbon. He utilized the bow and quiver, the urn, lyre, garland, burning torch and the ribbon in many forms. Le Prince was particularly fond of pastoral accessories, groups of big pots, shepherd's crooks, spades, trowels, bird cages, thrown together in bunches with garlands and ribbons. Sometimes the oval frames of his chairs are supplemented by a quiver of arrows or a garland of roses wherein doves are nestled.

Salembier's books are devoted to the description of ornamental trailing foliage, the arabesque, the acanthus, and the thistle leaf. Although these are motifs which appeared for a hundred years previously they are treated now in a more delicate fashion. And this characteristic marks the style of the whole period—

delicacy, minuteness, grace. Vases were reproduced after the fashion of the vases discovered in the restoration, all Greek or Early Roman and all slender and graceful.

In textiles we find ribbons and stripes intermingled with flowers, winding ribbons and feathers, medallions, columns, lyres, and occasionally heads of Minerva or other classic subjects; and ever conspicuous was the stripe. Indeed Mercier in 1788 wrote, "Everybody in the King's cabinet looks like a zebra." To be sure Madame Pompadour had already set the fashion for stripes, but Marie Antoinette sprinkled her stripes with flowers and interwove them with ornaments. It is a singular fact that while the Germans did little for their own country they established through Riesener and Roentgen the fame of Louis XVI furniture. Riesener was particularly happy in his marquetry, introducing often painted porcelain, chiselled copper and Sevres plaques. Roentgen's marquetry also was full of the most minute shadings and he together with a number of other noted cabinetmakers followed the Boule (Boulle) style, and also utilized plaques and china.

At this period it is sometimes difficult to find the dividing line between the beds and sofas. Frequently the head and footboards were of equal height and exactly alike. The canopy was erected at the side instead of the head of the structure. They were sometimes upholstered, sometimes lacquered, frequently

Louis XV Terminals.

LOUIS XVI.

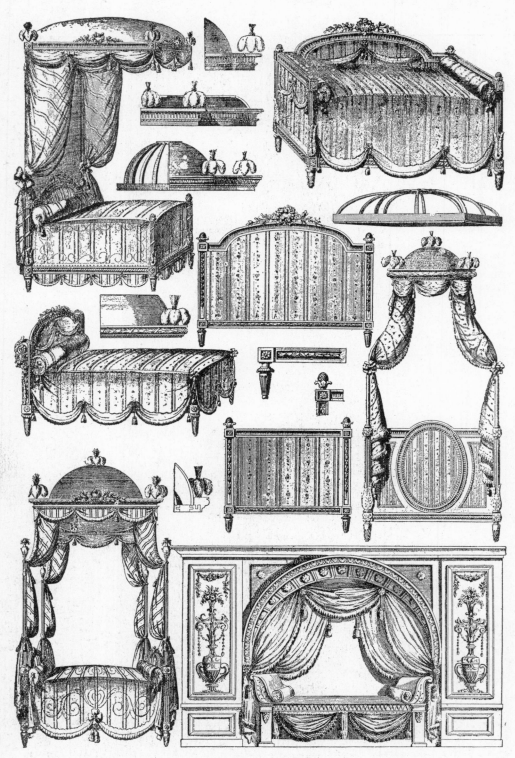

LOUIS XVI.

gilded or all white and paneled with cane or left in natural wood, ornamented with bronze, gilt or perhaps ormolu.

Muslins, prints and silks were profusely used for curtains, trimmed with cords and tassels. The beds were usually curtained. Cornices were used gilded and lacquered or white and gold. The commode became popular and was often made of mahogany or amaranth wood. The console or pier table held its place, but was composed of straight lines, with fluted legs, tapered. In the boudoir we find the Chinese lacquer as well as the Vernis-Martin. Flower tables were popular, writing tables, work tables, card tables, and in this period was introduced also the extension table. Dining-room chairs frequently had cane backs or were covered with material to match the walls.

Low ottomans were introduced, and while all kinds of carpets were utilized Moquettes were the most popular.

Louis XVI interior.

Louis XVI; the formal phase.

Louis XVI, heavy and formal.

APARTMENT OF MARIE ANTOINETTE, FONTAINEBLEAU.

THRONE ROOM, APARTMENTS OF NAPOLEON I, AT FONTAINEBLEAU.

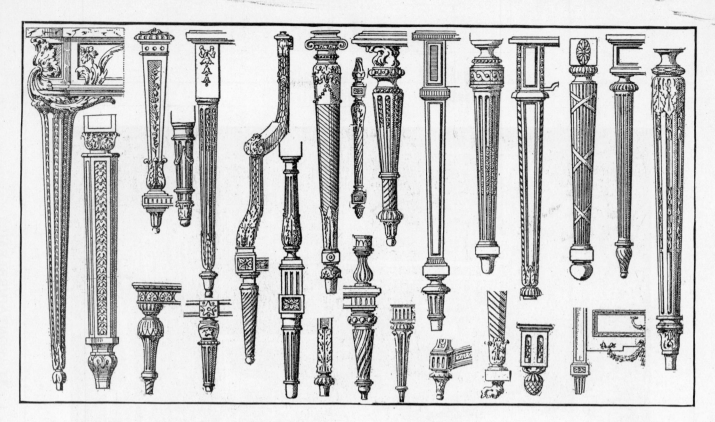

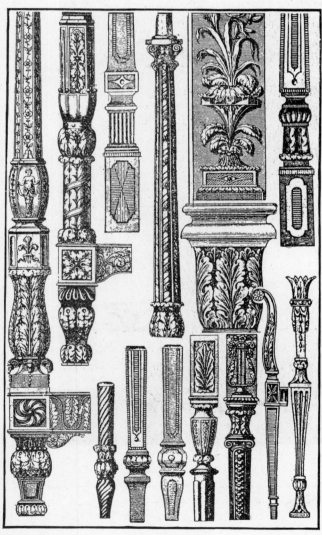

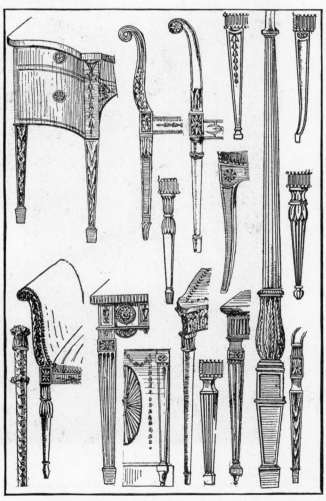

The Classic feeling, Early Eighteenth Century: Upper illustration, Louis XVI; on the left, Sheraton; above, Hepplewhite.

TRANSITION PERIOD.

Showing the detached as distinguished from the connected classic compositions of the Directoire and Adam work.

TRANSITION—DIRECTOIRE—EMPIRE

Following Louis XVI, the Revolutionary Period, 1793-1795.   Directorate, 1795-1799.
Consulate, 1799-1804.   Empire, 1804-1814.

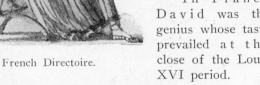

French Directoire.

THE period immediately before and after the Transition French was inspired by a common enthusiasm, the French and English developing the feeling contemporaneously. The English cabinetmakers, with the exception of Chippendale, who affected in many instances the Rococo spirit applied to Dutch structural lines, were especially active in this new classic school.

In France David was the genius whose taste prevailed at the close of the Louis XVI period.

Coming at this time, when the political atmosphere was unfavorable to the presentation of the styles of Louis XVI, David found ready acceptance for his rendition of the classic revival. He had studied in Rome, where also the brothers Adam of England had spent much of their early lives and naturally were interested in the restoration work in the burried cities. Thus the development which followed Louis XVI in France, as well as the contemporary period in England, was saturated with the Italian spirit.

The art was Pompeiian idealized.

Following the Louis XVI period came the Revo-

lutionary, from 1793 to 1795; then what is known as the Directoire, 1795 to 1804. This period, properly called the Transition, carried the delicate Pompeiian classicism of late Louis XVI into the more masculine type of the Empire.

It was a period that frowned upon all that was of royal suggestion, and designers and decorators endeavored to procure a style essentially new. The Transition period was largely Roman; but with Na-

Empire.

The Classic Inspiration in French Transition, Empire and Adam.

Empire.

poleon we had not only the inspirations of Italy but Egypt. In woodwork there was little or no carving. The decorative motifs were classic appliqués on massive frames; the wreath and laurel branch, the torch, Napoleonic bee and crown became conspicuous; winged figures were popular as emblematic of liberty; heads of helmeted warriors, trophies of lances surmounted by the Phrygian cap were significant details.

After the Italian and Egyptian wars the French adopted boldly all that was significant of conquest. Occasionally we find the sphinx carved into the arms of the chairs, a reminder of the French expedition in Egypt.

The furniture was of mahogany, rosewood and ebony, with brass mountings.

Sometimes the wood was inlaid. Vases found in tombs were introduced and the panther's muzzle and claw and other chimerical devices were introduced.

In some cases Egyptian and Roman examples were copied without alteration.

It was a style that was

Empire. Napoleon's room in the Grand Trianon.

massive, ponderous and ostentatious, and may be broadly designated as modern classic.

Examples of ceremonial work are apt to be pompous, but private work along the Empire lines was usually no more affected by what might be called national motifs than American home decoration is influenced to-day by the star-spangled banner or the spreading eagle. While it is true the flambeau and wreath are characteristic of the Empire epoch, their absence is not inconsistent with pure Empire.

Furniture ornament gilded or made of cast brass is not in itself a positive indication of the Empire period, but classic forms in metal ornamentation denote Empire.

The spirit of the Empire was influenced by a revival of the more dignified and pompous characteristics of Roman ornament, and its detection depends on the stately assembling of various decorative units in orderly and oft-repeated forms as distinguished from the more connected and elaborate ensemble effects of the Directoire style.

J.B. HUET — 1745-1811.

A Jouy Print.

EMPIRE.

Examples of exquisitely-colored floral motifs, Indian.

PRINTED FABRICS AND PAPER

WHEN one thinks of the steam-driven mechanically engraved cylinders of the modern print factories, it seems incredible that so much could have been achieved by the primitive methods of the Persian an' Indian printers, who in the late Seventeenth Century supplied all Europe with chintzes and calicoes.

There is no doubt that color printing was known to the early Egyptians, Persians, and Chinese. Ancient Mosul in the early Christian Era was famous for its muslins; and colored fabrics, printed, as well as painted, were used in Europe at an early age, impossible to fix definitely by any reliable data. Block printing on fabrics was undertaken in Italy during the Thirteenth

Toile de Jouy, engraved from museum example.

Century. In the Fourteenth Century printed linens were made in Flanders.

Painted cloths with stories or legends came into use during the time of Henry IV, England, early in the Fifteenth Century; some of them were intended doubtless as models for tapestries; at a little later period they were dyed and painted, possibly stenciled and printed.

The Portuguese, early in the Sixteenth Century, 1530, imported "painted" hangings from the East, but whether done by hand or by process and whether or not the term "painting" might now be regarded as printing, is a question. It is a noticeable fact that the French name for the early imitation of chintz was *Perses,* undoubtedly relating to the Persian

166

From an Indian cotton-printer's book of patterns.

origin of chintz, a fact reasonable to conclude when you consider that Persia was open to commerce at a period a little earlier than India or China.

While we are accustomed to examples of extraordinary richness of furniture and fabric during the reigns of Louis XIV and Louis XV—years of great decorative wealth—it is a fact little known that printed linens or painted linens, commonly called India prints, became so popular in France and threatened so seriously the prosperity of the silk trade that many French factories took up the manufacture, and Colbert, to protect his pet organization, prohibited in 1686, under pain of severe penalty, either the manufacture or importation of printed linen. Nevertheless they were manufactured clandestinely and persistently until finally the authorities instituted a plan of searching for and burning everything in the nature of a printed linen.

But the popularity of the fabric was too much for the law to cope with. Even Madame Pompadour herself had her chateau at Bellevue decorated with contraband prints.

The term "painted" linen is often confusing. In 1759, when the French ministry decided to authorize the manufacture of linens and cottons, the French industry may be said to have started, because heretofore all that was done was done surreptitiously. By 1789 a hundred factories were in operation and Christopher Philip Oberkampf, a German, had developed some new methods at Jouy, near Versailles. He introduced the "resist" method. The pattern was printed and then the whole fabric was dipped in a dye; a deep red, for instance. Again the fabric was submerged in an acid bath which withdrew the red color wherever it touched the lines of the chemically printed design, leaving the natural linen color. But at the beginning of the industry they knew only one mode of printing—that of the Orientals. The linen was laid on a table and the workmen pressed upon it by hand a block of wood

J. B. HUET — 1743-1811.

Intricate design worked out in colors; Jouy, 1745-1811.

engraved with the outline of the design. The piece then passed through the hands of the brushers, or painters, who filled them in with a brush of various colorings.

More slowly did they conceive the idea of printing uniformly certain colors with the aid of second plates which overlaid the lines or the outlines of the first plate. In 1780 printing by copper plates made its appearance. They were deeper plates and finer.

By 1797 such progress had been made that by cylinder printing, which at this date was introduced, they were able to print in one day, on one machine, the work ordinarily accomplished by forty-two block printers.

And now began not alone the art but the industry of linen printing. The vast amount of material now turned out was naturally of the French Transition or Empire character. France, during the period of Louis XV and Louis XVI, was rich in printed linens and they were used in enormous quantities.

Paper in quantity or size was not made until the Twelfth Century, and even then 13 x 26 inches was considered a large sheet. The first mention of rag paper we find is in Cluny, 1122.

Nobody knows when the first examples of wall-paper were made in Europe, but if the record of Herman Schinkel, the Dutch printer, is correct—that he actually made wall-paper in Holland in 1568, "printing roses and stripes on the back of common ballad paper and applying it as a covering for his attic walls," he was undoubtedly inspired by something he had seen or heard of, possibly by the cloth prints of early Flanders; possibly by the "Domino" papers of Italy or by the Portuguese imports, because it is fair to conclude that Indian or Persian papers had been introduced by the Portuguese traders following Albuquerque's settlements in Persia, 1505. The Dutch were not active in the East until the downfall of Spain and Portugal in 1600.

To be sure we have heard of Jehan Boudichon and his fifty rolls of wall-paper for the King's bedchamber in 1481, but they were not rolls as we understand the term; at that time paper was made in squares about 36 x 15 inches. Continuous lengths were not made until 1780-1800. The Boudichon papers were scrolls and not fastened to the walls. We have heard of colored papers for decorations at the time of the entrance of Louis XIII into Lyons in 1507. They were pictures on paper not applied to the wall, but loosely hung.

The term "domino" was Italian and used in Italy in the Fifteenth Century in relation to marble prints. At first the paper was used only for box linings and was usually stained irregularly, but French taste introduced arabesques and finally figures and the manufacture continued steadily and developed eventually to papers of larger size, and we have record, 1586, of marbled papers and papers of all colors, and printed with figures.

By 1700 there was hardly a house in Paris that did not utilize this domino work on walls or screens. They were printed from blocks of pear wood, finished off in distemper colors, or dusted with powder, or finished with a flock in imitation of flock cloths, sometimes referred to as velvets. In 1787 we find a decree of the King declaring that the art of painting and printing paper used in furnishings was a dependence of the governing board of the Merchants-Papetiers-Dominotiere-Feuilletinere, which shows that the term "domino" still clung.

We take exception to the theory that the Chinese were the first makers of wall-paper or that the Dutch were the first importers. The fact that a printer in Delft made paper in 1568 predisposes one to believe that something of the sort had been already introduced. Indeed we know that "domino" papers were already made in Italy. However, Chinese trade had not been opened at that early date, but the Portuguese early in the Sixteenth Century traded in Persia and India. There is no authentic record of Chinese paper until the reign of Louis XIV, 1643, when we began to hear of "pagoda" paper for walls.

Towards the middle of the Eighteenth Century wall-paper manufacture began to develop in France and England. It is probable that the first factory was set up in France in 1746. The industry thrived, but Chinese papers continued in popular use. Some of them, highly artistic, were utilized by the wealthy classes. Exquisite compositions of foliage and flowers, birds and butterflies, landscapes, water and sky scenes, the work of the Japanese as well as the Chinese. The paper was printed upon squares; continuous rolls were not undertaken until about 1790. The perfected process was patented in England about 1800, but our American records show that paper made in the roll was advertised in this country in 1790. There is no reason to assume that we were behind the times; there was wealth in America and the wealthy classes, even at this early date, enjoyed the latest luxuries from Europe.

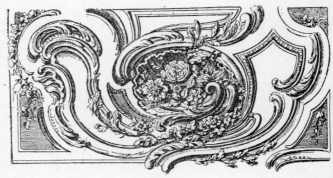

Rococo.

QUEEN ANNE, 1702—1714

Hogarth type of Queen Anne chair.

WHILE the term Queen Anne begins naturally with the reign of Queen Anne, 1702, it had its inception with the close of the Jacobean. We have illustrated already a number of examples of late Seventeenth Century English furniture, which brings us up to the period 1702. The influences of Louis XIV were disseminated both in Holland and England by Marot and other French artists, who had fled in 1685 at the time of the Revocation of the Edict of Nantes. Unlike the turned work, the bulbous forms of the periods from Charles II to William and Mary, we have the terminals, the cabriole leg, the stretchers and frequently the pediment forms of the French. The smooth splat is always a Queen Anne characteristic. The smooth stretcher instead of the carved and ornamented stretcher of the Charles II period was a natural development. There were probably no smooth splat-back chairs before 1700. There was probably no smooth cabriole leg until 1702.

While the cane chair was found in the beginning of Queen Anne's reign it had been identified with earlier work and was, subsequent to 1700, succeeded by upholstering of a substantial kind. Flat uprights were also used in the backs of the chairs which were now more comfortable than in previous epochs, being not only shaped to the back, but divested of carvings. The seat became broader and the top corners of the back were rounded. Shell details were conspicuous. The claw and ball finally came in about 1708. To the comfort-giving qualities of the smooth-backed, full-seated chair were added comfortable upholsterings, and the grandfather chair became popular, a form that was begun as far back as 1680, but was not developed to the full until well into the Queen Anne régime.

Double chairs or small sofas, called "love seats," were only wide enough for two. The sides were often in wings and when these wings extended very high they were called draught-chairs. The width of the chair seats at this time was due largely to the flaring, voluminous costumes worn both by the women and the men.

As far back as 1680 we find many examples of record where the cabinetmaker has not used stretchers between the legs of his chairs, but one may say approximately that the use of stretchers was practically abandoned by 1708.

The tendency to simplicity of form expressed in the furniture was extended to other woodwork of the room. Over-door fitments were frequently of simple pediment type. The woodwork was in most cases walnut. There are records of mahogany as early as 1708, but its use was unusual. Gilt ornament and marquetry and gilt furniture were common. A great deal of Chinese wall-paper and Chinese and Indian prints was used.

Commercialism prevailed to an extraordinary degree and both the Dutch and the English East Indian Trading Companies were active. At this period America naturally felt the effects of this commercialism and the colonies were saturated with the Queen Anne spirit. Indeed, to appreciate fully the Colonial furnishings at this time one must understand the Colonial relations with the mother country, for while many American cabinetmakers, upholsterers and decorators thrived in the larger cities of the new country they accepted the fashionable dictates of Europe and conformed to the contemporary styles.

While much Colonial furniture approximated the Queen Anne type, the same is true also of practically the entire Georgian period, so that any attempt to fix Colonial by its resemblance to Queen Anne alone is apt to be misleading.

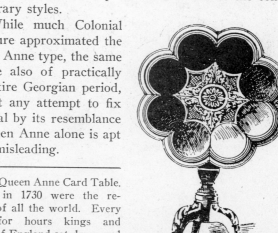

Queen Anne "Love Seat."

A Late Queen Anne Card Table. "Cards in 1730 were the resource of all the world. Every night for hours kings and queens of England sat down and handled their majesties of spades and diamonds."— *Thackeray.*

IN THE QUEEN ANNE PERIOD.

Bed in which Queen Anne slept on the occasion of her visit to Brympton.   The bed is entirely covered with rose damask.

IN THE QUEEN ANNE PERIOD.

Walnut bed, 1710, double frieze carved and gilded. Back is in four panels.

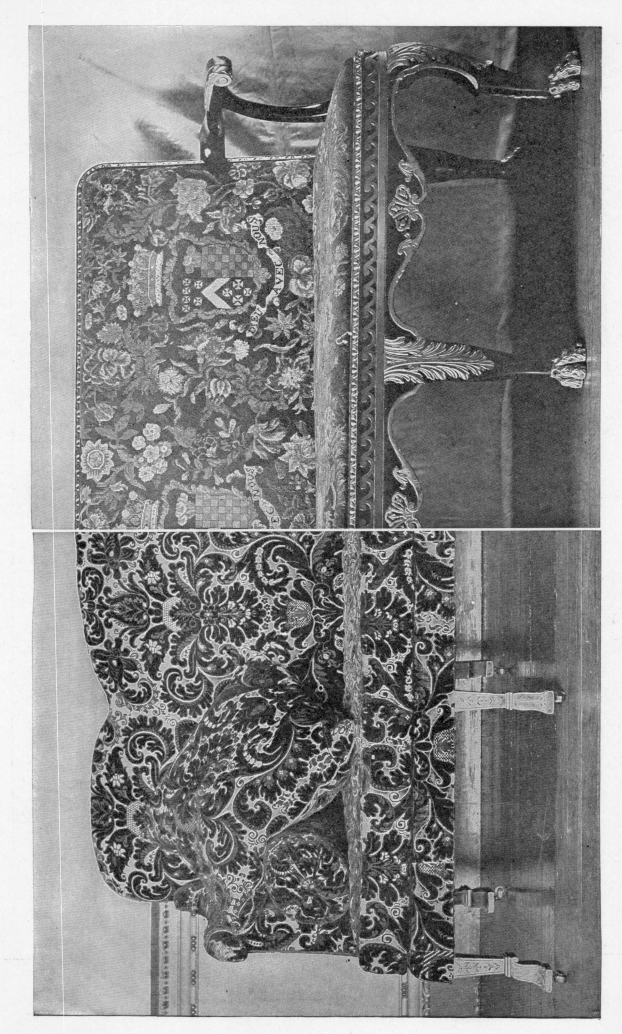

1723. About one-half the size. Walnut covered with needlework.

1730. From Walpole collection. About one-half of the sofa. Walnut and gilt.

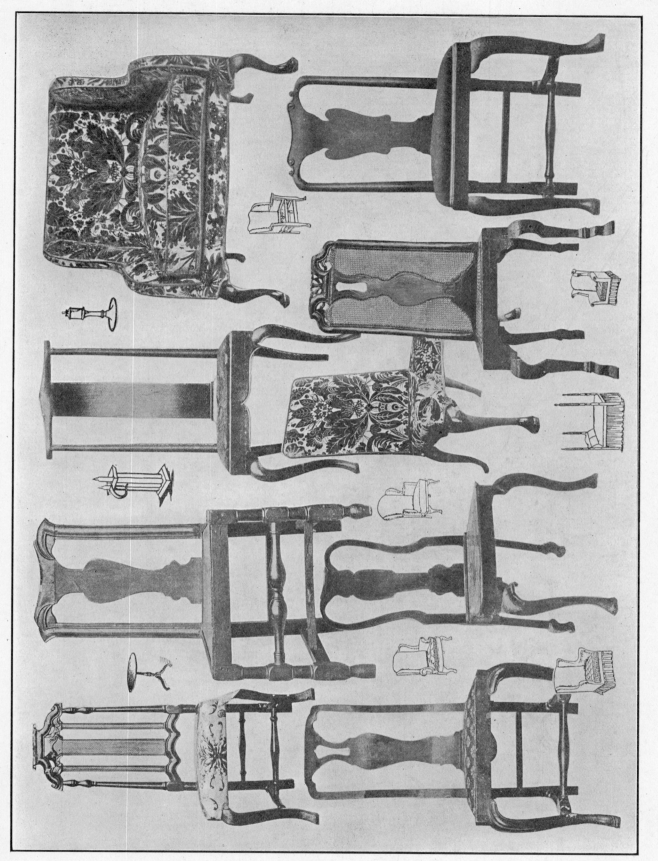

TYPICAL QUEEN ANNE CHAIRS.

QUEEN ANNE.

Queen Anne Chairs.

The term Colonial means anything from Jacobean to the end of the colonies and even beyond.

Indeed for a quarter of a century after the close of the colonies we have a definite style, called late Colonial or sometimes Jeffersonian, that is simply a reflection of the French Empire, the same type being adopted in England by Thomas Hope. The term Colonial covers a wide range of thought.

It was during the Jacobean period that the first settlers landed in New England.

During the commonwealth period of 1653-1659, Virginia and Maryland profited by the Royalist classes, out of power in England and many of whom were in exile.

During the Queen Anne period, which may be said to have had its inception with Charles II, 1660,

Queen Anne interior, showing characteristic furniture and draperies.

the English laws restricted American imports to England, and a great deal of East India goods came into this country through English channels.

In 1685 the Edict of Nantes caused French emigration, but it was not until later under George III that the French spirit had any material influence.

In considering the Colonial style we must always analyze it. We must determine always date and locale. The Cottage Colonial of New England, late in the Seventeenth Century, had nothing in common with the Ceremonial Colonial of the late Eighteenth Century. The styles covered a period of two hundred years. We copied from the English, the Dutch and the French. We benefited by the imports from Asia, particularly from the East Indies, and beginning about the middle of the Eighteenth Century, from China. There was wealth here in many of the cities and a fashionable element that profited by the best that Europe afforded.

History tells us of the progress of the American nation, and with the knowledge of the time and the classes we can

Queen Anne Period.

Georgian.

turn back to European chronology and fix pretty definitely the character of the Colonial style.

On the left, Queen Anne chair seats.

THE TRADES IN THE GEORGIAN PERIODS

EARLY in the century the gardens of the Emperor of China had been described by architects to assist the taste in landscape gardening. In 1750 William Halfpenny produced a book of new designs for Chinese temples, triumphal arches, garden seats, and he says that at that time Chinese manner of building was already introduced in England with success. Another book, by Edwards and Darley, which appeared four years later, was overcrowded with Chinese suggestions, particularly frets.

The work of Mathias Darley belongs more properly to the post-Chippendale period because it was more in sympathy with the Adam school.

Were it not for the literature of the times, the catalogues issued by the various cabinetmakers and even the architects, we would know little of the subject.

We know that besides the great masters there was an organization called the Society of Upholsterers and Cabinetmakers, doubtless composed of many capable men. A volume issued by this body is undated, but probably came out before Chippendale's book, "The Director."

Horace Walpole's interest stimulated the public taste for the Gothic style and no book was complete without designs for Gothic furniture; the "Society of Upholsterers," published probably about 1750, was full of Gothic suggestions.

Manwaring claimed that his book, published 1765, showed the first suggestion for rural furniture made from twisted limbs of the yew and apple trees. Manwaring seems to have imitated all that was weak in Chippendale.

Ince and Mayhew published a book that seems like a caricature of the Chippendale style, and adopted all that was flamboyant and exaggerated. They illustrated card tables with places for counters and stands for candles.

The English architects, decorators and cabinetmakers from the time of Inigo Jones developed rapidly. He with John Webb, Edward Carter, and Nicholas Stone, expressed the Italian spirit up to Cromwell, 1653. Sir Christopher Wren, Nicholas Hawksmoor, Sir John Van Brugh and James Gibb became famous up to and into the period of George I. From this point we can classify the great leaders as EARLY GEORGIAN, MIDDLE GEORGIAN and LATE GEORGIAN.

EARLY GEORGIAN.
Period of George I, 1714-1727.

Hogarth, artist and critic, 1697-1764.
Grinling Gibbons, 1648-1721.
Sir Christopher Wren, 1632-1724.
Nicholas Hawksmoor, 1666-1736.
Isaac Ware, published "Complete Body of Architecture," 1750.
James Gibbs, 1694.
Sir John Brugh (contemporary).
Colin Campbell, published many books, 1781, 1795, 1798.
Richard Harris, first connected the pendulum with a clock movement, 1641.
Thomas Archer (contemporary of Kent).
Abraham Swan, published "The British Architect," 1745.
William Kent, painter, architect and designer, 1684-1748.
W. Jones, published "Gentleman or Builder's Companion," 1739.
Sir Robert Taylor (contemporary).
James Paine, 1725-1789.

MIDDLE GEORGIAN.
Period of George II, 1727-1760.

Thomas Chippendale, 1708-1779; first known plates dated 1753. His "Cabinetmaker's Director" came out in 1754, 1759, 1762.
Robert Manwaring, published book, 1765.
Edwards and Darley, published book. 1754.
Ince and Mayhew, published their book, 1762.
Sir William Chambers, published book in 1760.
Copeland, issued work 1752.
Isaac Ware, best work about 1750-1756.
Mathias Lock, issued books, 1752, 1765.
Thomas Johnson, published volume of designs, 1758.
J. Crunden, published books 1765, 1770, 1776, 1796.
Milton (contemporary).
Josiah Wedgwood, famous for plaques and pottery, 1730-1795.
Overton (contemporary).
Francesco Bartolozzi, born 1710, removed to England, 1767.
Mathias Darley, published his book 1754-1769.
William Halfpenny, issued a book on Chinese architecture and furniture, 1750.

LATE GEORGIAN.
Period of George III, 1760-1820.

R. & J. Adam published their first volume on Italian art, 1764. First general volume of architectural details appeared in 1773, reflecting the classic taste following the discoveries of Herculaneum and Pompeii.
J. Carter, followed Adam style.
Antonio Zucchi, painter (worked for Adam).
Society of London Cabinetmakers, 1770-1800.
Angelica Kauffmann, ceiling and wood painter (worked for Adam).
Cipriani, Italian designer; worked in England, 1732-1785.
Pergolesi, painter, 1775 (worked for Adam).
William Clement, made first long clock case, 1780.
Columbani, 1775.
Sheraton, published great book, 1791.
Shearer, published book, 1787.
Hepplewhite, published book, 1789.
N. Wallis, published books of ornament, 1771.
George Richardson (contemporary).
Thomas Hope, published book in 1807.
George Smith, published book in 1808-1826.
Richard Gillow, 1800; improvements and methods of table slides.
W. Thomas and Joseph Rose, painters and decorators.

Chippendale chair backs.

GEORGIAN—CHIPPENDALE—CHAMBERS

IN THE reign of the early Georges, beginning 1714, there was a mania for everything French and for the Chinese motifs popularized in England by Sir William Chambers, to whom the cabinet-makers and architects were greatly indebted.

Chambers produced nothing strikingly new but adopted much that had gone before. He was decidedly un-English. He had made many voyages to East India and had spent much of his time in China studying the habits, customs and architecture of the people.

As early as 1757 Chambers described a Chinese room:

The side-walls are matted about three or four feet upward from the pavement, the rest being covered with white, crimson or gilt paper; instead of pictures they hang on them long pieces of satin or paper stretched on frames and painted in imitation of marble or bamboo, on which are written moral sentences or proverbs. Sometimes they hang a very large sheet of thick paper covered with antique Chinese paintings. The movables consist of chairs, stools and tables, made sometimes of rosewood, ebony or lacquered work, and sometimes of bamboo only. When the movables are of wood the seats of the stools are often of marble or porcelain. In the corners of the room are stands four or five feet high on which they set plates of citron or other fragrant fruits, branches of coral, vases of porcelain and glass globes containing gold

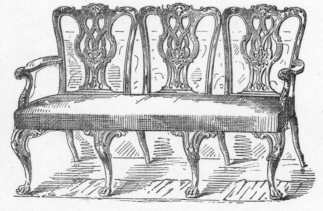

All Chippendale pieces. Square legs were made by Chippendale about 1750.

CHIPPENDALE.

These illustrations have been copied direct from Chippendale's first known book, "The Gentleman and Cabinetmaker's Director," dated 1754. They illustrate three characteristic types, the Classic, the French and the Chinese.

fish, together with a certain weed somewhat resembling fennel. On such tables as are intended for ornament they place landscapes composed of rocks, shrubs and a lily which grows among pebbles covered with water. But among the principal ornaments are the lanterns, of which there are generally four, suspended from the ceiling.

Chambers had no idea of the effect that his book would have, but the Chinese taste grew to extraordinary dimensions.

In the reign of Queen Anne the custom of paneling was partially kept up. The chimneypiece, however, only went half-way up the wall. White woodwork was affected. Low, marble mantelpieces were used, but with the beginning of the Georgian we had the greatest possible variety of taste—classic, Roman, Turkish, Pompeiian, French. Royalty having set the fashion, Chinese also became a special fad. Not only were Summer houses and other buildings erected in Chinese style, but it was mixed up with all the ornaments of the period. The walls of the rooms were simply covered with scenes of Chinese life, bridges and boats and impossible staircases and mattings and lacquers being abundantly in evidence. All the furniture was marked by the Chinese influence, and (Chippendale affected with rare abandon the use of the pagoda, the bell, dragons, and mandarins.) Other architects followed; even Lock, who was a student of the classic, followed blindly with Ince, Mayhew and Manwaring, and satisfied popular clamor. Rounded wood was used in the bamboo fashion, but of turned beech and painted in imitation of reeds or cane.

Gothic was also copied, and the flamboyant French was in evidence. Frequently in a room we find the Chinese spirit combined with Louis XV, just as in France this same combination

was very successfully effected.

Just before the death of George I, in 1727, the elder Chippendale came to England and began making furniture founded upon the Queen Anne fashions. He was accompanied by a son, a boy eighteen years of age, also called Thomas Chippendale, and the son absorbing the French taste of the Louis XV period, 1715 to 1774, soon showed his talent as a carver and a joiner. Chippendale was born 1708 and buried November 13, 1779. Probably he died November 10 or 11. His first plates are dated 1753, and his book "The Gentleman and Cabinetmaker's Director," came out in 1754. The second edition was brought out in 1759, and the third in 1762. This was the first furniture catalogue and it sold for sixteen dollars a copy. It was issued under the patronage of a long list of subscribers, members of the nobility as well as cabinetmakers, among them Ince and his partner Mayhew.

Although Chippendale was successful, he was no more so than others and his reputation was largely posthumous. It is seldom that we find records of his name. Even Walpole, who left many memoranda concerning designers and decorators, never alludes to Chippendale, and old American advertisements fail ever to mention his name. His contemporaries were Manwaring, Mayhew, Edwards, Darley, Mathias

All pieces on this page are Chippendale.

Lock, Copeland, Thomas Johnson, and Crunden.

The years of the first George, King of England, were the transition years of walnut and mahogany, 1714 to 1727. From 1715 to 1720 Queen-Anne styles became a little more squat and heavy.

From 1720 to 1730 there was a great deal of elaborate, gilt furniture and about this period we find what is known as the lion pattern, lions' heads on the knees of furniture legs. Sometimes the lion's head or mask is used as a center decoration. The lion's paw was used in place of the claw and ball for the foot of the leg.

As early as 1720 we find veneered mahogany, because from 1715 to 1720 the solid wood was not only very expensive but hard to manipulate. By 1721 Walpole was in power and set the fashion for mahogany in his use of it for the magnificent doors at Houghton, which he began to build in 1721. Kent was the architect. Much elaborate gilt furniture was used following the models of the Flemish fashions. The splat back was universal but this back was often elaborately carved. Middle-

Furniture on this page,
Chippendale.

class homes were furnished with furniture simplified by the use of straight legs.

By 1733, Walpole succumbed to the demands of the cabinetmakers and took the duty off mahogany, and from this date mahogany became generally used. By 1733 the lion's head was elaborated by the addition of a ring in the mouth.

By 1735, we find the splat back opening out into slits, sometimes vase shaped. The hooped or rounded top of the back departed and it curled up at the corners. This squaring up of the chair back caught the fancy of the trade generally. It seemed to lighten the appearance of a piece. The cresting also of the back became like a cupid's bow. This bow effect together with the claw-and-ball foot, dates between 1730 and 1750.

By 1740 the cabriole leg had shed its masks and lion's heads and was carved in low relief with the acanthus and similar effects. The splat-back was now being cut into strap devices which led up to the ribbon-back of 1750. The years 1737 to 1750 saw the rise of Chippendale and the full evolution of the square-backed chair as distinguished from the hooped back. Little by little the back had been punctured; little by little the corners of the back were lifted square. Then the puncturing of the back became more complicated until it developed finally the ribbon back typical of the late period.

We note also pierced rails and elaborate ornamentation, frequently uniting Chinese and Louis XV motifs.

We illustrate a page of Chippendale, showing the Chinese lattice and the mixture of Louis XV. We also illustrate three chairs above, which are in the Sheraton and Hepplewhite styles, and it will be noticed that the splat in the Chippendale chairs invariably comes down to the back rail of the seat, re-enforcing and strengthening the backs, while the backs of the Sheraton and Hepplewhite were above the chair seat always.

CHINESE INFLUENCE IN THE LOUIS XV AND CHIPPENDALE STYLES.

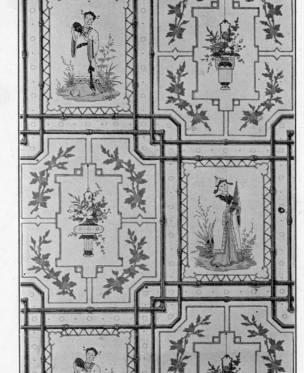

WHILE the popular adoption of Chinese decoration in England can be attributed to Chambers, the taste was felt as early as William and Mary, 1689; and even earlier in France, 1660, under Mazarin (Louis XIV). In 1720 Louis XV dispatched an embassy to China to encourage greater trade relations, and this step was followed by a rage for Chinese stuffs.

Japan, on the other hand, was a closed country for centuries, and Japanese art was not known to commercial Europe until after 1854, when Commodore Perry, who had entered the harbor a year previously, effected a treaty between Japan and the United States, followed eight months later by Japan's treaty with Great Britain, a year later with Russia, and three years later with France.

What we regard as the Chinese spirit is not necessarily pure Chinese. Frequently the Chinese spirit was merged with the Gothic or with Louis XV, or with some other French and English style.

Indeed the pure Chinese spirit, as shown, particularly in the rugs of China, was seldom seen. The form utilized was the adapted form wherein the Gothic, Louis XV or some conventional background was treated in Chinese motifs, plucked from the pottery and projected upon European composition. In the same way the architects reproduced bits of landscape and laid garden walks and grottoes, from the suggestions found in pottery.

ADAM—CEILING DETAIL FROM AN OLD ENGLISH HOME.

Hepplewhite and Sheraton desk, wardrobe and cabinet feet.

HEPPLEWHITE

Chippendale's great book, 1754.   Hepplewhite's book, 1789.   Sheraton's Cabinetmaker
and Upholsterer's Drawing Book, 1791.

Chippendale Cabinet.

PRIOR to Queen Anne chimneypieces were carried to the ceiling as part of the woodtrims, but by 1700 the chimneypiece never went above half the height of a room. White trims were also introduced at this period and have clung, more or less, especially to small rooms requiring greater light, to this day.

In 1755 Chambers, returning from Italy with Cipriani, brought back a number of Italian sculptors who made mantels. These mantels were put into a house independent of the architect and established a new height, sometimes four, five or even six feet, but independent of the woodtrims and usually marble or other stone. They became an article of general trade and were sold by the fireplace fixture dealers.

Another change came with Hepplewhite when wood mantels were introduced. Wreaths of flowers and classic details were painted on natural wood with plaques introduced. Fantastic elegance became the fashion, and plain wood was elaborately colored. Satinwood and mahogany were mainly used, painted, gilded and inlaid.

Contrary to the popular belief, glass knobs were not made at this period, but during the late Colonial period in America and introduced later into England, just as the use of mahogany was common in America for many years before utilized by the English cabinetmakers. Inventories and wills in this country dated 1708, refer to mahogany furniture, such pieces being solid and frequently in desks of the Queen Anne style, with claw-and-ball foot and serpentine front.

Hepplewhite had many contem-

Hepplewhite and Sheraton examples.

185

HEPPLEWHITE.

poraries, few of whom have survived in history. Among the cleverest was Shearer, a member of the Cabinet-makers' Society. He probably was as well known in his day as Hepplewhite. It is a curious fact that while Hepplewhite's book was full of chairs Shearer makes no reference to a chair, a fact possibly due to an understanding with Hepplewhite to avoid his specialty. Shearer's furniture, like Sheraton's, was full of concealed drawers, hidden receptacles. There were no safe deposit vaults in those days and one had to depend upon the cabinet-maker for devising hiding places. Shearer was not so well educated nor had he the artistic feeling of Hepplewhite; his furniture was heavy and he repeatedly utilized the Prince of Wales' feathers. His in-

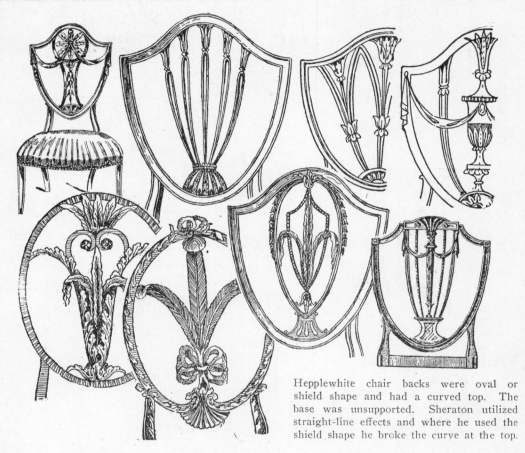

Hepplewhite chair backs were oval or shield shape and had a curved top. The base was unsupported. Sheraton utilized straight-line effects and where he used the shield shape he broke the curve at the top.

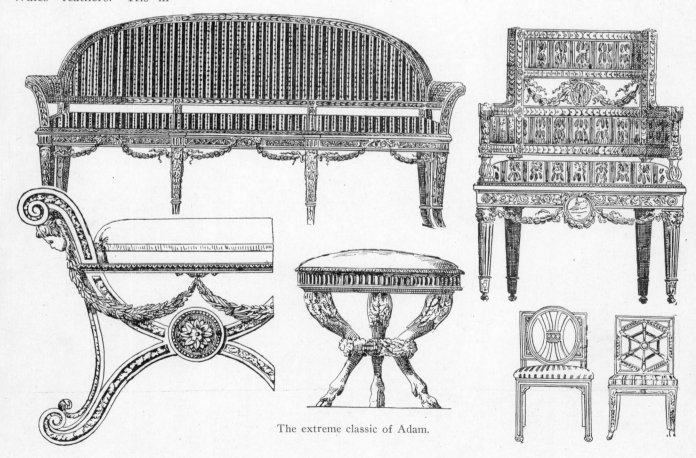

The extreme classic of Adam.

The illustration on the left-hand at the bottom of this page is an Adam piece; the second illustration is a Sheraton; the third and fourth Chippendale. The illustrations above are by Shearer.

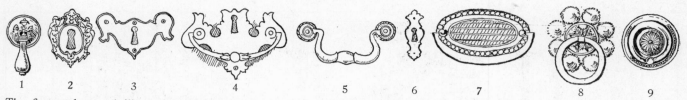

The first and second illustrations represent the hardware used from about 1660 to 1720. The second and third illustrations were used in the first half of the Eighteenth Century. The solid drop handles, as shown by illustration 5, were commonly used until about 1790, at which time the pressed brass became popular, shown in illustration 7. From this date through the Empire and late Colonial up to 1820 rosettes with inserted rings were used and in America glass knobs were common.

genuity in the invention of furniture was quite as great as Hepplewhite's.

It was about this time that the wardrobe came in. Hepplewhite produced wardrobes that supplanted in practical usefulness the highboy.

Hepplewhite's chairs were mainly for the room known then as the "parlour," a term that has clung.

We first heard of parlors in the Medieval times when it was part of the common hall but screened off for the privacy of the family. It gradually became a separate room often used as a bedroom. Later it was synonymous with the modern dining-room. According to Johnson, 1755, it was "A room for receiving company." Sheraton and Hepplewhite used the words parlor and dining-room as interchangeable terms. The chairs were frequently covered with horsehair in colored stripes and check designs, the edges finished with a close line of brass-headed nails; sometimes they were cane-seated.

The Duchess chair of Hepplewhite was an arrangement of two armchairs facing with a third chair or ottoman placed between them continuing the seats along one level and making one piece of furniture.

High clocks were very popular. The history of clocks would take us back to the Medieval ages—indeed, if specifically dealing with timepieces, to the prehistoric years. Our interest in the subject starts with the first making of household clocks. In the beginning of the Seventeenth Century clocks were made at a moderate price and were known as bird-cage, bedpost and lantern clocks. They were the kind that were wound by pulling down opposite ends of ropes on which weights were hung. None of them would run more than thirty hours. The pendulum was not introduced until 1670, and it is at this time that we fix the origin of the grandfather's clock. The bracket clock having a handle on top enabling one to carry it around, came in about 1675. Mantel clocks were another type, introduced at about the time of banjo clocks, so called on account of their shape, produced just after the American Revolution, about 1805, and very popular in America where they originated.

The Hepplewhite and Sheraton styles followed the Adam tendencies strongly and yet there was individuality in each man's work which gave character eagerly followed by their contemporaries.

In the mind of the modern decorator the differences are not clear. Broadly considered, while Hepplewhite and Sheraton were both influenced by their contemporary Adam, Sheraton leaned to Louis XVI.

To simplify the subject we have arranged the characteristics of the two schools in parallel columns.

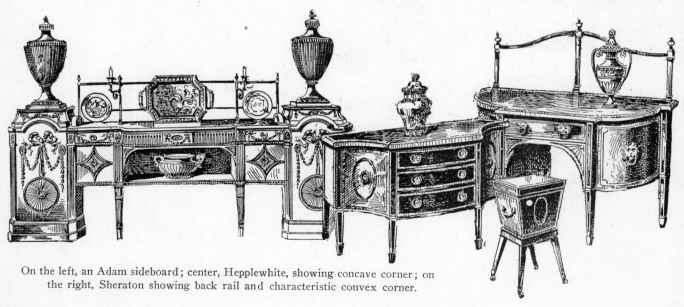

On the left, an Adam sideboard; center, Hepplewhite, showing concave corner; on the right, Sheraton showing back rail and characteristic convex corner.

189

Shearer furniture, with Hepplewhite mirror and chair of the period.

HEPPLEWHITE.

I. The HEPPLEWHITE chair backs are as a rule heart or shield shaped, and the bottom is unsupported by any rail. The top of the back of a Hepplewhite chair shows a sweeping curve.

II. The arms move out with a swing and join the leg as a part thereof. All Hepplewhite work is in sweeps and unbroken lines.

III. The chair legs are in most cases square. In the inexpensive chairs they are plain or with a simple reed or inlaid at the corners. In some chairs of the better type we find fluted legs.

A characteristic of most Hepplewhite chairs was

SHERATON.

I. THE SHERATON chairback is usually in straight lines and supported by a bottom rail. While occasionally Sheraton used a shield back, he broke the sweep at the top by some sharp straight line.

II. Sheraton arms moved out with a swing and joined the legs as independent parts, pedestal-like.

III. The chair legs run strongly to the Louis XVI style. Sheraton strengthened the back and ignored the under framing of his chairs. He used reeded and fluted legs, twisted pillars, festoons, husks, cornucopias. He carved swags of drapery and flow-

DRAWING-ROOM AT NOSTELL PRIORY.

The painted panels on either side of the mantelpiece emanated from the hand of the brothers Adam, who reconstructed and decorated the room.

the under-framing: Hepplewhite left the back weak and the legs strong. Mahogany and inlays were much used. The seats are upholstered frequently in horse hair, leather, cane, or in any kind of fabric.

IV. Sideboards were usually made with concave corners because of the decorative effect.

V. He became famous for his Pembroke tables. He indulged not only in inlays and carving, but in painting, japanning and brought into his services Angelica Kauffmann, Cipriani, and Pergolesi. The pole fire screen was just becoming popular. It was intended simply to screen the firelight from a lady's face and the screen itself was frequently no wider than eight or ten inches; a bit of embroidery, a mat, or bit of needle-work. The feet of the pole were loaded with lead to prevent its upsetting. Tea caddies were very popular. The Dutch did not introduce tea drinking until about 1660, and it was fully 1690 when the custom became prevalent.

VI. Hepplewhite's bookcases were furnished with glass doors, the glass being cut into patterns. They were called traceried doors, the lines or traceries being of mahogany or satinwood, brass or lacquered wood. These traceried forms in Hepplewhite doors were usually angular.

VII. His pediments over doors or windows were usually fragile and finnicky.

While Chippendale was one of the first to introduce the highboy, Hepplewhite improved it. He made also secretaries, secretary bookcases, bureau bookcases, toilet tables, washstands, chests, shaving stands, side tables, girandoles, wall mirrors, brackets, and innumerable other pieces, all treated from a decorative standpoint.

While bedsteads were draped in anything, Hepplewhite in his book commends particularly Manchester prints to be lined with white cotton. He also recommends specifically green silk as appropriate for mahogany.

ers; he used the vase and rendered all these motifs beautiful in carving. Occasionally he painted. He introduced the conversation chair, the sort of thing which one straddled facing the back upon which one leans.

IV. Sheraton sideboards had the added superstructure of a brass railing against which dishes rested. Sometimes the railing was balanced with candelabra, a plan seldom, if ever, adopted by Hepplewhite, who did not consider comfort and convenience so much as decoration. The interior of the sideboard was full of conveniences.

Sheraton's sideboards were made with convex corners, thus giving a little more room. In other respects many of the Hepplewhite and Sheraton sideboards are almost identical.

V. His Pembroke tables were furnished with scrap bags. As an instance of his ingenuity one of his tables was called a Harlequin table, so termed because in Harlequin exhibitions there is generally a great deal of machinery introduced. Some of his desks had disappearing drawers and pigeon-holes, leaving a space free for the breakfast table.

VI. In Sheraton traceried-doors curves were generally utilized, the oval and the vase being frequently used as centerpieces.

VII. Pediments were of a substantial character.

Sheraton introduced a form of horse screen, a larger lower set piece than the pole screen. Sometimes these screens were furnished with swinging toilet boxes on the side, or receptacles for odds and ends of the dressing table, also candle holders.

While he showed a preference for the round or turned leg for chairs he followed the square shape of the Louis XVI style very largely with his tables, sideboards and other cabinet work.

His grandfather's clocks were generally inlaid.

Sheraton's work will frequently be recognized because of its extraordinary ingenuity. He was an inventor and produced many pieces of convertible furniture, tables with concealed stepladders, bureaus with convertible desks. He made many little pieces of utility furniture. He considered not only grace of style but comfort. He anticipated the American roll-top desk by producing something almost identical.

A HEPPLEWHITE INTERIOR.

Sheraton's pediments, though showing somewhat the same characteristics as Hepplewhite's, were more substantially constructed.

SHERATON

A QUICK understanding of the character of Sheraton furnishings may be had in the knowledge that Sheraton cabinet work was a little more ornamental, a little more profuse, than Hepplewhite; the fabrics used were in harmony; little figure details of the Louis XVI order were particularly favored. Both Hepplewhite and Sheraton upholsterings and draperies were of a light and filmy type and rich in every possible variety of fine weaves. Sheraton leaned toward the French, although the decoration of houses into which the Sheraton furniture entered was frequently in the pure Adam. The styles of Sheraton and Hepplewhite were closely associated and the distinction is not always clear. Our previous chapter points to many of the differences.

Sheraton employed often the lyre form in his chair backs and used a form of needlework in burning or engraving panels of satinwood with rosewood inlaid; all of his work was at first of an original type, but little by little he copied slavishly anything French.

He originated intricate ornaments for legs and backs of chairs and turned work as well as inlay was much affected.

He picked out designs with gildings and employed cameo-like panels. He suggested in his book that ornament may be white and gold, japanned or painted, and

advised that the cove and ceiling be richly ornamented in paintings and gold. His use of satinwood or white mahogany was extended even to the production of mantelpieces. His drawing-room schemes provided for wall panels, mirrors and draperies a little more stiff than those of Hepplewhite, as a foil to the complexity of his furniture details.

When we consider that Sheraton designed many rooms and furniture for the Prince of Wales, afterwards George IV, and for most of the nobility, we can understand that he was not worried by any considerations of economy.

He confessed to an admiration for Shearer, and there are many examples of simple Sheraton inlay that strongly resemble Shearer.

Both men made the same little corner washstands and toilet accessories. Sheraton was an extraordinary inventor and not only introduced beautiful pieces, but pieces of great originality and far in advance of the times, full of quaint combinations, hidden drawers, parts that were convertible, turning from one use into another, cleverly hidden accommodations for boxes or writing materials or toilet articles—desks that became dressers and fancy tables that became washstands.

If he had never made a reputation as a cabinet-maker and designer, he would have become famous as a mechanician.

It was a period when bedrooms were frequently used as sitting-rooms and very many ingenious pieces

Chair and desk, Sheraton; balance probably Hepplewhite.

of bedroom furniture were concealed in bookcase forms or desks or writing stands.

Even washstands folded up and became cabinets. It is well to remember that in 1750 thousands of silk weaving looms were established in England at Spitalfields, Cheshire, Yorkshire, Essex, Derbyshire, Lancashire and Norfolk. Moreover, at this period up to the beginning of the Nineteenth Century an enormous lot of Indian silks and cottons were used; in 1759 the manufacture of printed linens was authorized and encouraged by the French. (See page 167.)

Sheraton died in what might almost be called poverty. He was not a good business man and his style was at its best in the beginning of his career. If he failed to gain material compensation for his art it was because he was unable to progress beyond the limitations which hedged him in and the work of innumerable competitors who had no hesitation in copying his style.

SHERATON.

THE ADAM SPIRIT WHICH INFLUENCED CONTEMPORARY FURNITURE MAKERS:
HEPPLEWHITE, SHERATON, SHEARER.

Adam furniture in which the classic spirit is emphasized.

R. AND J. ADAM—1765-1790

ROBERT ADAM, the elder of the two brothers, R. and J., was born in Scotland 1728. He was educated in the University of Edinburgh, studied in Italy under a French architect, became F. R. S. and F. S. A. and before he was forty he was architect to the King of England. He died in 1792 and was buried with high honors in Westminster Abbey. His brother was closely identified with him in all his work.

Herculaneum in a purer type than was expressed in the late Louis XVI adaptations, left its deepest impressions on ceilings, side-walls and mantelpieces produced under the architects' direction. They were tinted usually in jasper or palest gray colors. Circles and ovals were used as frames for pictures.

They utilized mythological ornament, the hexagon, circle, octagon and lozenge-shaped panel, wreath, fan, medallion, draped or with figures, the sphinx, griffin, sea horse, goat, faun, ram's head, the caryatid and innumerable other classic motifs found in Roman, Pompeiian and Etruscan work. They designed walls, ceilings, mantelpieces, even door knobs, escutcheons, locks—everything that went into a room, including table tops and furniture panels. While they were by

The Adam brothers were not furniture makers but architects, decorators and designers, employing Angelica Kauffmann and her husband, Antonio Zucchi, Cipriani, Pergolesi and a host of others. They built palaces for the nobility, houses for the middle classes, terraces, bridges, even streets and squares, and in almost every instance their work was classic. The Chinese craze cropped out now and then, but its popularity waned from the inception of this epoch. Their style, reflecting the spirit of Pompeii and

By Cipriani.

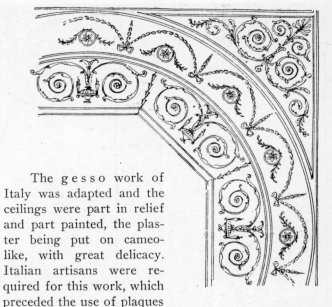

no means furniture makers, the brothers Adam always designed furniture to fit their rooms; many sideboards with urn-shaped knife-boxes and classic brackets, pedestals, clock cases and mirrors were designed by them. They even designed the carriages, the plate and the sedan chair for Queen Charlotte. Their style was a complete departure from the massive and ponderous compartment ceilings of the Jacobean. Instead they adopted light moldings, delicate stucco frames and painted ornaments. They advanced the theory that the dining-rooms being so often utilized for extended conversation should be finished with stucco and adorned with statues and painting and never hung with tapestry or damask, "which retains the smell of the victuals." As a result many of their rooms so largely depending on the work of the painter and sculptor lacked coziness.

They were often circular or semi-circular or with circular recesses.

The gesso work of Italy was adapted and the ceilings were part in relief and part painted, the plaster being put on cameo-like, with great delicacy. Italian artisans were required for this work, which preceded the use of plaques

By Adam.

and friezes furnished for late Adam work by Wedgwood, who caught the Adam craze and commercialized it. The brothers were so earnest in imparting their spirit to the entire room that they insisted upon even the carpets being in unison with the surroundings. The palest tints of color and neutral tints of carpets to match were utilized. Even the table cloths corresponded in

Paneled side-wall and furniture by Pergolesi.

DINING-ROOM IN SALTRAM, DEVON, HOME OF THE EARL OF MORLEY.

This room, with others of the ground floor, is remarkable for its harmonious decorations, which are the work of the brothers Adam. The carpet and ceiling are contemporary, and the paintings on the walls and ceiling are by Zucchi.

An Adam room.

1773. The period of their greatest success was contemporary with Chippendale, Hepplewhite and Sheraton. Being primarily architects, their mantels and sidewalls are conspicuous examples. Their moldings are usually of simple classic order; the vase and urn are favorite details, generally accompanied by swags or festoons of drapery, leaves or husks. While acanthus scrolls and chimerical creatures characterize their

pattern and the unity scheme was carried out in the silver plate, the table-tops, even the snuff-boxes.

Their first published volume on Italian art is dated 1764; next volume almost purely Pompeiian,

TYPICAL ADAM SIDE-WALLS.

work, they were not treated in the heavy Roman school, but with delicacy. Wedgwood ware was frequently utilized, in panels and plaques.

Michael Angelo Pergolesi is responsible for much of the fame which attaches to the name of the brothers Adam. In 1777 Pergolesi published a perfect storehouse of Italian designs covering plaster friezes, borders for painting on furniture, doors, sides of rooms, pier tables, settees and silver plate. Often he left a center of his panel work blank to be painted by Cipriani or Angelica Kauffmann in scenes of child life or nymphs. The same idea was often repeated in marquetry and painted furniture.

W. Thomas, a contemporary, followed the Adam style, together with N. Wallis, Columbani and George Richardson.

Richardson in 1792 published a work on wall treatment that was exceedingly interesting. He followed very closely the scenes from Greek mythology or Roman history, and bacchanalian figures and nymphs usually decorated the corners.

The same thing was frequently done by Zucchi, the Venetian painter, whose fame was gained in England. His walls were often tints of the lightest character, paneled.

To fix the relative influences of the conspicuous styles of this period we would explain that the first illustrated book bearing directly on furniture was that

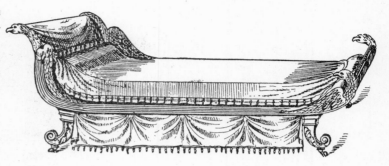

An Adam lounge or daybed.

of W. Jones, who published the "Gentleman or Builder's Companion" 1739.

Chippendale's first book was published 1754.

Adam's influence was approximately 1765-1790. George Richardson's book was published in 1776; Columbani's 1775; John Crunden's 1765, 1768, 1770; Wallis' 1771.

Hepplewhite's epoch-making book appeared 1789.

Sheraton published the book which made his name in 1791.

There were in all four Adam brothers. John inherited the father's business as architect. R. and J. were the second and third sons, while William Adam, who died in 1822, was the youngest brother.

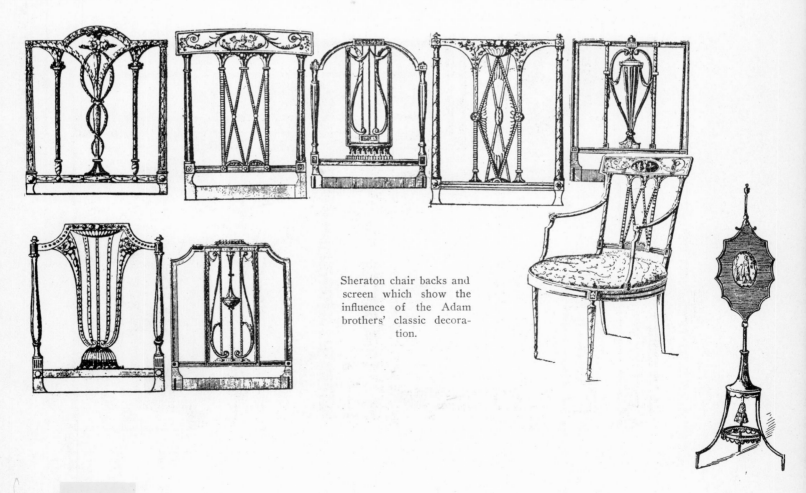

Sheraton chair backs and screen which show the influence of the Adam brothers' classic decoration.

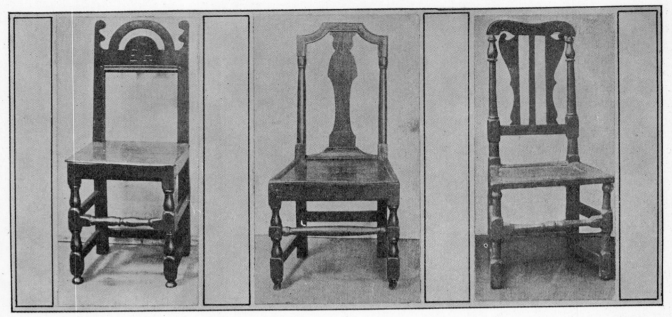

Oak chair with cresting rail of Charles II period retained and perforated, arched center peculiar to walnut designs.

Oak chair with elaboration and turned legs and uprights of William and Mary period retained and having Queen Anne splat of 1710.

Oak chair with sunk seat for cushion. Turned uprights and legs and curious back showing transition from lath back to splat back.

Windsor chairs.

Cricket table of about 1750.

Lancashire spindle-back chairs.

Cricket table of about 1700.

Windsor Chairs.

COLONIAL

COLONIAL furniture is simply the furniture used in the colonies. We can differentiate in the phases of Colonial furniture by localizing, and then we have New England Colonial, Dutch Colonial, Southern Colonial and the periods Seventeenth, Eighteenth or Nineteenth Century.

It is a mistake to assume that Colonial furnishings were necessarily primitive. Historians give ample record of wealth in the Southern States long before the beginning of the Eighteenth Century.

Pory, writing of Virginia as early as 1617, spoke of the growing wealth of the Southern colonies.

In 1607 Jamestown was settled by the English; in 1613 New York was settled by the Dutch; in 1620 the Puritans settled in New England. From 1650 to 1660, during the period of the Commonwealth in England, the Southern States profited by considerable immigration drawn from the Cavalier and Royalist classes then out of power. In 1674 the Dutch settlements of America went into English possession.

From this record we can form a fair idea of the character of Colonial furniture. The South was influenced by French styles, especially at the period of Charles II when the French styles prevailed in England.

New York and the Middle States were largely influenced by the Dutch.

New England took inspiration from all the periods, and from the beginning, skilled craftsmen, joiners, cabinetmakers and carvers settled in New England and during the Eighteenth Century a very small proportion of the furniture used in New England was imported. New England cabinetmakers were numerous and expert, and New England furniture from 1700 to 1776 found a ready sale all through the colonies. The principal woods used were oak, ash, elm, walnut, maple, pine and red cedar. Goods were brought to the colonies so quickly from abroad that the new fashions appeared in American homes quite as quickly as in the country houses of England.

Readers of history need not be told of the great wealth in the country even in the earlier half of the Eighteenth Century. Esther Singleton has gone into this subject very thoroughly and John Fiske, the eminent historian, says:

"The Puritan exodus to New England, which came to an end about 1640, was purely English. Like the best part of the emigration to Virginia, it consisted largely of country squires, thrifty and prosperous.... The best part of the New England immigration consisted of people prosperous in their old homes, from which their devotion to an idea (religious) made them voluntary exiles."

Again quoting from this authority: "Up to 1688 there were 26,000 New Englanders, and from this number, in the following one hundred and fifty years, there have descended at least one-quarter of the present population of the United States.

"The laws of the early colonies were discouraging to the poor people, who went to the Barbadoes, Honduras or elsewhere. Even as late as 1714 the immigration laws of the New England colonies were strictly enforced, forbidding one to enter who was unable to furnish proof of financial responsibility. During the fifty years preceding the American Revolution there was much wealth in the colonies, measured by the standard of wealth in those days. A fashionable social life centered about the representatives of the Crown, and the pride of the wealthy found expression in handsomely decorated homes. In Maryland and Virginia, where the High Church adherents and the Catholics settled, there was an aristocratic tendency, the happy combination of climate and agricultural facilities enabling the people to support a generous style of living as landed gentry."

There are no authentic records of mahogany furniture in American inventories prior to 1708, but the fact that mahogany was part of the inventories of that date indicates that the wood was used at an earlier period.

The Colonial styles followed closely the English. We used wall-paper at a time contemporaneously with that of England.

Mahogany trims for banisters, mantels, cornices and furniture were not generally introduced until 1750. At that period Isaac Ware wrote: "The decoration of an American room is of three kinds; first, where it is coated with a plastic material shaped into ornamental details; second, covered by wainscot; and third, where hung with silks, tapestries or paper." As early as 1745, Charles Hargraves was advertising wall-paper in Philadelphia, and a very few years later Peter Fleeson was making paper-hangings, although paper made in the roll did not appear till 1790, the same year it appeared in England.

At the Metropolitan Museum there are many examples of excellent American-made furniture covering the Jacobean types and at least forty pieces showing Elizabethan influence, the principal characteristics being wainscoting, flat carving, turning, straight legs and heavy underbracing, rails and stiles mortised, and the tenons pinned with wooden pegs. Other periods are also well represented, including twelve pieces grouped under the first decade of the Nineteenth Century and attributed to Duncan Phyfe, an American cabinetmaker of great skill.

It is very interesting in this connection to note the fact that small tables were not thought of in England until the abandonment of great halls and the construction of smaller rooms also the introduction of the new drinks, tea, coffee, and chocolate, from 1645 to 1658, and at that period they appeared also in this country.

Chests came over with the colonists, and when the use of chairs became common and the chest was no longer needed as a seat, it was raised upon a trestle and soon after drawers were introduced and we have then "a chest of drawers."

By way of Holland came the Chinese fashion of lacquering furniture.

As early as 1650 we find Connecticut quite famous for its chests. One in Hadley, Mass., was provided with a drawer and became a type. So many were made that they became known as the Hadley chest. See illustration.

Towards the close of Colonial history we have a type of furniture and furnishings called Late Colonial, which was a development of the Late Empire, in France developed by David and in England adopted by Thomas Hope.

In this country, especially during the Jefferson régime, Latrobe, the decorator and architect appointed

Bedstead,
late Eighteenth Century.

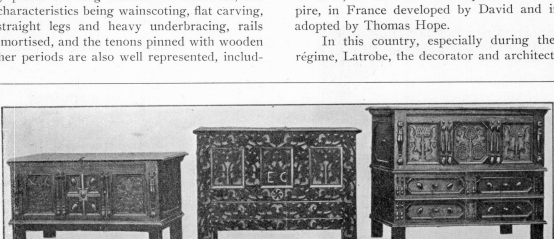

On the left, chest, Connecticut type, front in three panels, end ones having floral pattern in flat carving, center one divided into four sections with applied moldings and bosses.

In the center, "Hadley" chest with one drawer. Front covered with all-over design in flat carving; three sunken panels with conventionalized leaf and flower design.

On the right, chest with two drawers. Chest part divided into three panels with flat carving. Called the Connecticut pattern. American oak, with top, bottom and back of pine.

as surveyor of public buildings in Washington, exercised a great deal of influence. He eliminated the very extreme character of the Empire school, the personal elements interpolated by David, and the Egyptian and Roman symbolisms of victory and conquest, and retained the classic simplicity, notably the classic column, and in many cases the eagle's head appeared in the chair backs and as central pediments. If there is any one distinctive form of Colonial furniture it is this form.

Bureaus, sideboards, tables and sofas became famous and are still popular types of strictly Colonial character.

Colonial chronology begins with James I, but the American homes by no means adhered to the early Jacobean examples in architecture. The side-walls in the Elizabethan and Jacobean homes were largely wainscoted and often hung with tapestry. The ceilings were in stuccoes frequently colored, paneled and ornamented and in heavy relief. These features were not adopted in the colonies. The country was too young. Jacobean furnishings were in other respects in common use, and cotton, linen, chintzes and other fabrics were much utilized.

Field bed and tester.

Architectural features of the English home began to be copied with Queen Anne, and from that period down to the Georgian, we find many homes of distinction in America.

None more beautiful can be imagined than the Chase House, the Harwood House, the Hammond, the Lockorman, the Bryce-Jennings House, Byrd's, Carroll's or hundreds of other homes in Salem, Providence, Bristol, Annapolis and other thriving towns and cities.

As early as 1774 there was great wealth in the colonies, a condition obvious when we consider that it was from private sources that most of the money was obtained that sustained the eight years' war with England.

The variety of fabrics produced was unlimited. In silks Spitalfields was a vigorous rival to Lyons. From 1727 to 1750 innumerable silken fabrics were made, as: brocade lutestring, brocade tabby, brocade tissue, brocade damask, tobine, flowered tabby, figured tobine, four-comber damask, double tissue, gold stuff, double tabby, brocade satin, Venetian brocade, India figured brocade, tobine tabby, tobine lutestring, and so forth. The style of their patterns closely corresponds with that of contemporary Lyons silks.

In East Indian stuffs alone we have a list of forty terms.

Field bed and tester; on the right, an adaptation of the Windsor chair. Early Nineteenth Century.

1750

1740-50

1770-80

In 1759 "flowered damask for furniture" was imported. In 1760 "crimson, blue, green and yellow harrateens with tassels" were imported.

1762, Indian gimp and binding.

1768, fine striped lutestring (plain silk) Marseilles quilts.

1770, moreens, stout woolen curtain stuffs.

Harrateen cloth was made of combing wools.

Printed cotton, hand-printed, frequently of very large bird and animal designs.

The earliest example of a Windsor chair is found in an old Jacobean interior of Windsor Castle. It is estimated that the chair dates 1650. It was a common American article in cottage use in 1700. The illustration in the left-hand upper corner is the first example found. Immediately below it is the well-known Hogarth chair of about 1720, and to the right is a development of the Hogarth with turned rail back and Hogarth splat, about 1720. From this directly comes the type in the upper right-hand corner. The large chair is one used by Thomas Jefferson. Until 1830 various kinds of Windsor chairs were common in America.

Scarlet and crimson cassimere, calico and dimity. Durance, a stout worsted cloth.

Calamanco, a glazed linen stuff.

Turkey work, a coarse, plain ground with pattern tufted like a rug pile. Paduasoy, a strong silk.

Green cloth, crimson worsted, red cloth, red damask.

Shalloon, soy, watchet, linsey woolsey, fustian.

Silk muslin, chintz, Indian calico, tabby, sarcanet, taffeta, horsehair.

COLONIAL FURNITURE IN PENDLETON MANSION, AFTER CHIPPENDALE MODELS.

First three illustrations English Renaissance, 1550-1625.

Two mirrors on left, late Elizabethan. The others above them Jacobean, Charles II.

First three illustrations below and all above are either Queen Anne or early Chippendale.

Louis XV and Gothic styles, much affected by Chippendale.

Veneered mirror frames were popular under William and Mary. On the right pure Hepplewhite mirror

Mirrors upon stands. Hepplewhite or Sheraton

Camak, or Comacoa, was silk and camel's hair mixed.

Bancours, a kind of tapestry.

Shalloon was a coarse woolen cloth.

Darnix or darneck, coarse, taking its name from Dorneck, the Dutch for Tournay.

Perpetuana (1650), a very durable woolen.

Damask, first made in Damascus in such a way that "what is not satin on one side shows satin on the other side."

Green and red paly is the heraldic term for alternate stripes of these colors.

Camblet was a woolen, hair or silk twill, sometimes waved or watered.

Tabby, a kind of coarse watered taffeta.

Seersucker, a thin ridged and puckered material.

THE FOREIGN INFLUENCE OF COLONIAL STYLES

ELIZABETH. 1558-1603.

JACOBEAN. 1603-1625.

James I. 1603-1625. (Commencement Stuart Period.) Italian influence. Inigo Jones, dictator of style, 1573-1652.

1607. Jamestown settled by the English.

1613. New York settled by the Dutch, and for many years after India goods were brought over in large quantities.

1620. Puritan settlement in New England.

CHARLES I. 1625-1649.

LOUIS XIV. 1643-1715.

CROMWELLIAN. Commonwealth. 1653-1659.

During the period of the commonwealth, England, Virginia and Maryland profited by the immigrants drawn from the cavalier and royalist classes, then out of power.

CHARLES II. 1660-1685.

JAMES II. 1685-1689.

1674. Dutch settlements in America went into English possession.

1680. English laws restricted American imports to England and English possessions.

1685. Edict of Nantes caused French immigration to New York, Massachusetts and South Carolina, but influence on decorative arts was trivial.

WILLIAM AND MARY. 1689-1702.

Mahogany discovered (1597) by Raleigh. Came into use 1700.

ANNE. 1702-1714.

Dutch furniture largely imported.

1702-1714. Dutch furnishings prevailed owing to popularity in England and close political and commercial relations between England and Holland. First mention of mahogany in America 1708.

GEORGE I. 1714-1727.

Sir Christopher Wren and Grinling Gibbons, famous architects. Sir Christopher Wren and Grinling Gibbons took up the Renaissance movement where Inigo Jones left off.

GEORGE II. 1727-1760.

By 1714 the Colonies had reached that state of affluence that English styles appeared in American homes as promptly as in the suburbs of London.

LOUIS XV. 1715-1774.

LOUIS XVI. 1774-1793.

GEORGE III. 1760-1820.

Noted cabinetmakers and architects: Chippendale, Sheraton, Edwards & Darley, Thomas Johnson, Ince & Mayhew, Manwaring, R. & J. Adam, P. Columbiana, M. A. Pergolesi, George Richardson, G. B. Cipriani, Hepplewhite & Co.

George III, developed the work of Chippendale, covering the Dutch adaptation of the French and Chinese, the work of Thomas Sheraton. Hepplewhite, and the classic work of R. & J. Adam.

Empire, France 1795-1814.

1807. Works of Thomas Hope published, following the French Empire.

1800. Late Colonial. A form applied to the American acceptance of the "English and French Empire," which followed the French Empire and was successfully introduced in England by Thomas Hope and others.

Modern painted furniture in reproduction of Nineteenth Century chairs.

A Colonial interior of about 1630.

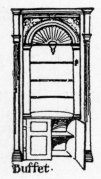

Buffet.

TO DEFINE the term Colonial we must fix the period not only chronologically, but geographically. We must discriminate between New England and the South, between early and late. We must understand the conditions, whether of town or country, because the types varied.

One is prone to regard in this country the characteristic Colonial form as that form which presented Oriental furnishings, brasses, Chinese porcelains, cotton prints, conspicuous in birds and flower details, rich lacquers, coppers and pewter. But this form lasted only from 1690 to 1740; in England it was broadly characterized as Queen Anne.

The early colonists enjoyed the same comforts as their English brothers, and sur-

prising as it may seem, the earliest settlements were furnished with window glass, at a period in England called Jacobean, when window glass was a luxury.

In 1629 one of the Salem settlers, Higgins, wrote to a friend in England, "Be sure and bring with you a supply of window glass."

The use of glass in dwelling houses began about the Fourteenth Century, although we have records of window glass used in Pompeii 79 A. D., and frequent references to window glass in the Fourth and Fifth Centuries; in the latter periods, however, the glass was an inch and a-half and two inches thick, sometimes discs or fragments joined. In the Fifteenth Century oiled linen was generally used. The Dukes of Burgundy used oiled paper, and as evidence of the general use of glass it will suffice to say that at the close of the Eighteenth Century, 1790, there existed in Paris itself a corporation for making window sashes filled with oiled paper. ("Glass Making," by Sauzay. Scribner.) Up to this date all glass used for mirrors or windows was limited in size to the lung power of the glass blower, which explains the little glasses in mirrors and cupboards.

It was not until

Kitchen at Van Cortlandt Manor.

Candle-mould

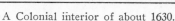

Knife Box

Glass

Pewter

209

the beginning of the Nineteenth Century that a method was produced for making larger sheets and for a long while the cost was very heavy. In 1702 a yard of looking glass cost $32.10. In 1802 a yard cost $39.90. In 1862 a yard cost $8.75.—Ed.

American patriotic societies have preserved not only many old landmarks and old buildings of Colonial reputation, but old furnishings. One must always bear in mind, however, the nature of a collection, whether a collection from the farmhouse, or the city house, the cottage or the mansion.

In the Northern States, where Winter comfort was considered, the rooms were smaller in size, the ceilings were lower, the windows were smaller than we find in the South, where weather conditions were diametrically opposite.

We hear a great deal of the rush-strewn floors of the Elizabethan homes; but they were only the floors that were open to the tenantry and the servants—rooms of a public character. We hear of the sanded floors through Pennsylvania, but they were the kitchen floors and inn floors. The same tastes prevailed here as prevailed abroad. All social grades were represented, and to those who are interested in the study of Colonial sociology we recommend the works of John Fiske, the eminent American historian, "The Beginnings of New England," "Child Life in the Colonial Days," "John Hancock, His Book," and "Examples of Colonial Architecture," a volume of interiors and exteriors of South Carolina and Georgian homes by E. A. Crane and E. E. Soderholz, published in Germany. The decorations of the ceilings, the sidewalls, the floors, even the wood finish followed the European styles, white woodwork coming in with William and Mary, about 1690. In 1749 Isaac Ware wrote: "The decoration of an American room is of

Eighteenth Century mahogany desk and bookcase combined.

three kinds—first, where it is coated with the plaster material wrought into ornamental details; second, where covered by wainscot, and third, where hung with silks, tapestries or paper," for in that year dealers in America were advertising "to hang rooms with paper or fabrics in the very newest fashion." Indeed, Charles Hargraves advertised wallpapers in Philadelphia in 1745, and only a few years later Peter Fleeson was making paper-hangings in squares, corner of Fourth and Chestnut Streets, Philadelphia. Nantucket, Portsmouth and St. Johnsbury, Vt., have yielded to the collectors some exquisite examples of wall decorations. Thomas Hancock, in 1757, wrote to an English friend to send him some paper-hangings showing a great variety of birds, animals, fruits and flowers and he adds to his letter: "I think these papers are handsome, better than painted walls." Colonial characteristics were simply the characteristics of modification or adaptation. Duncan Phyfe, in his time more famed in America than Chippendale in England, followed his English models with modifications. Latrobe followed the Empire styles, but with modifications. The larger cities and towns of this country were well equipped with cabinetmakers, who, at the time, were more famous than Chippendale, Sheraton or Hepplewhite, but they followed the English prototypes.

We have before us an extract from a New York paper of 1771, which dwells upon the exquisite work made by a New Jersey cabinetmaker who "served his time and was for eleven years foreman to the great cabinetmaker Hallet." If this advertisement is a mere catch-penny scheme it is evident the name of Hallet

was considered at that time a great bait in New York.

And so also American architecture was an architecture of modification modelled upon the work of Inigo Jones, who in turn modelled his style upon that of Palladio. But where the work of Jones was superb and elaborate, in America we followed his lines simply in much the same way that our late Colonial furniture followed the lines of the Empire, eliminating the specific ornamentation which in France made the style Napoleonic.

Not only in the South, but throughout the East also the Palladian spirit was well expressed. As early as 1738 the discoveries made in Pompeii and Herculaneum still further promoted interest and was received with great enthusiasm in America. Classic pillars were reared in front of every porch and by 1800 pillars appeared upon the ends and fronts of sideboards and bureaus.

The full development of this movement was felt in the latter part of the Eighteenth Century, and if there is any one form of architecture that may be said to be particularly Colonial and any one type of furniture that may be similarly characterized, it is the architecture and furniture of 1800 to 1820 when simplified classicism was universally

Above, mirror frame, about 1790; below, interior in Cowles house, Deerfield, Mass., 1752.

affected. Some of the old buffets and sideboards and bureaus of what we now call the Jeffersonian Period were purely American devoid of the Empire ornamentation which appeared in contemporary French and English work.

Up to 1810 the characteristics of our Colonial styles were built upon European prototypes, altered frequently, as Duncan Phyfe altered the Chippendale models, or as Latrobe altered the David models. Our cultured classes followed closely the prevailing fashions, and our American cabinetmakers and decorators learned in almost all instances their arts abroad.

Phyfe had a shop at 35 Partition Street, now Fulton Street, New York. His work from 1802 to 1810 was well known, following the Empire school.

The Dutch "kas" was a linen cupboard used largely in New York; seldom found elsewhere in this country; sometimes carved walnut, frequently of pine, cherry or maple, paneled or painted.

The heavily-carved mahogany beds with designs of acanthus leaves or pineapple, with high or low posts, came into use about 1790, following the Sheraton and Empire styles.

Candle Stand

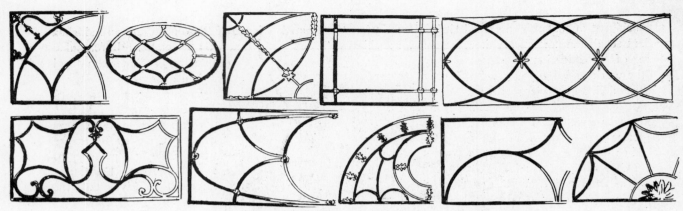

Window and door traceries.

The butterfly table, which appeared about 1700, was so called because the leaves were supported by wings which swung either way.

Turned woodwork came into America with the first settlers; from 1575 to 1620 we find a great number of examples of turned work in England, a development of the spiral work of the earlier Sixteenth Century.

The cradle that came over in the Mayflower, used for Peregrine White, was wicker, unquestionably made in Holland.

The first mention we have of tea-tables in America was 1660. We hear often of the French furniture of the South; the only part of the South where French furniture was used to any extent was Louisiana. That section had been settled by the French, who brought with them French fashions of the Louis XV and Louis XVI periods, and the French styles were adopted here in their purity. See page 203.

Chests, while utilized merely for travel, serving the purpose of trunk and bureau, for years also served as seats and tables. They developed in decoration and usefulness in

Cradle chair.

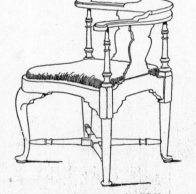

Roundabout chair, 1740.

America as they did in England, becoming finally chests with drawers and ultimately bureaus.

The use of the word form or bench applying to the primitive seats still used in some schools, has survived the style of seat that succeeded the chest. Frequently a room contained two or three forms and perhaps one chair.

At the dining table these forms were commonly used, excepting at the head of the table, where the master's chair was placed. Chairs of turned-wood and wainscoted chairs followed; then rush and cane chairs, then upholstered chairs, in the same order they appeared in Europe.

Rush seats continued popular until 1830.

The cradle chair shown in the center of this page is a curious piece of furniture, evidently having been planned with a removable rail at one end of the seat so that it could be used as a rocking settee. This removable rail would prevent a child from rolling off the seat while the free space at the end where the back is high provides a comfortable rocking chair for the attendant.

1820   Bed Curtains.   High Four-post   Field Bed   1727   1760   Chest.

Colonial Grouping—Everything except the bed and the right-hand chair of early Queen Anne or late William and Mary.

Late Colonial Room—Using William-and-Mary highboy.

OLD AMERICAN WINDSOR CHAIRS.

A TYPICAL COLONIAL INTERIOR OF ABOUT 1810.

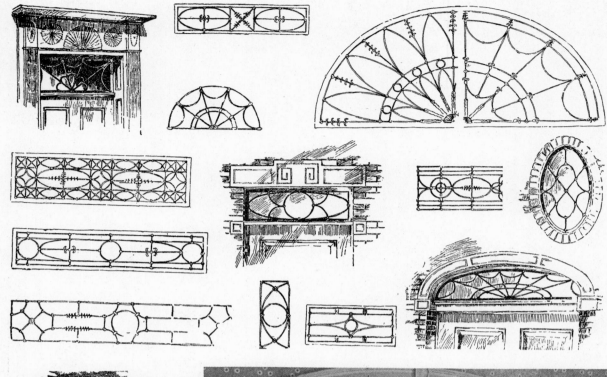

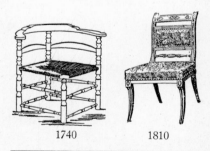

1740   1810

At the head of this page is shown a number of examples of Colonial transom window traceries.

Above in this column, Colonial doorway, about 1790, followed by two Colonial chairs.

On the right, a buffet showing the characteristic column construction of late Colonial times, made in New York, 1807.

Colonial, 1790, in the English spirit.

A Biedermeier interior from the Royal Palace at Ludwigsburg.
See definition of Biedermeier.

Modified L'Art Nouveau.

MORRIS, BIEDERMEIER, L'ART NOUVEAU

Extreme L'Art Nouveau.

THE development of the Empire Period in France inspired, coincidentally, a certain decorative feeling in England, America and Germany. In England the style had little vogue, but in America it developed structurally into what is popularly called "Late Colonial." From a recent issue of the Bulletin of the Metropolitan Museum of Art, over the signature of Luke Vincent Lockwood, we quote the following:

The evolution of style and decoration in furniture is one of the most fascinating and instructive of studies, and America is especially rich in specimens showing the various transition stages. In no other country has a style been so completely worked out as it has here. . . . Having once acquired the style the Colonial workman, adapting it to the needs of the people, developed it until it has reached a perfection not attained in Europe. The truth of the statement is particularly well illustrated in the development of the high chest of drawers. In England this article of furniture was abandoned, while yet in a rather crude state, for the French commode on the order of the modern bureau, but in America it was developed and the commode form remained comparatively scarce.

On the right, restrained L'Art Nouveau.

This statement was confirmed by the late Sir Purdon Clarke, who informed us that some of his best examples of furniture he found in America. The development of the Empire in this country resulted in great good, while in Europe all efforts at an absorption

of this style became a failure. In Germany the Empire school was so distorted by the effort to popularize it that it soon became known as the Biedermeier, a term of reproach.

Biedermeier was a fictitious character invented for the pages of *Fliegende Blätter,* a good-natured bourgeois with no aesthetic perception. Germany, after the Napoleonic wars, was either too poor or too prejudiced to follow the prevailing fashions in French furniture; hence the Biedermeier style which eliminated the ormolu mounts and expensive carvings naturally symbolic of Empire decoration, and substituted merely pretty forms, pretty details, unmeaning and weak. Not only was the studious work of Fontaine, Percier, David and

the brothers Adam pruned by the Biedermeier gardner, but a lot of petty florals were grafted in a sort of Dutch garden style. The acanthus, the vitruvian scroll, the lotus and the palmette were all displaced by a sort of barnyard flora. Symbolic animals were driven out and tame creatures adopted. The Biedermeier period began with 1800 and ended about 1830.

"With the glory of the Napoleonic era," writes Herr Lux, "vanished also the aristocratic Empire style. From cosmopolitanism and its political katzenjammer people fled back to the old land of romance. Uhland, Eichendorff and Schubert aroused enthusiastic love for nature. And the introduction of the moral element, as well as the influence of

Above, L'Art Nouveau chair; below, modern German-Empire or Biedermeier chairs.

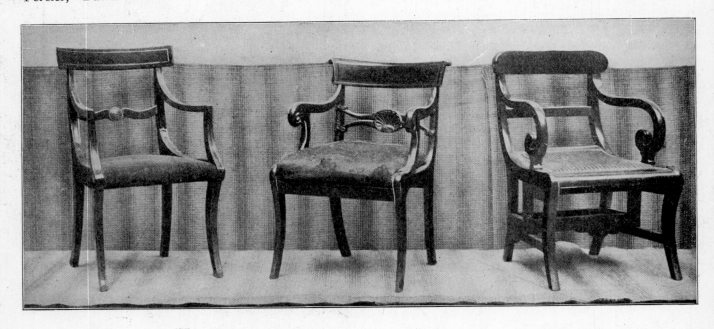

Two chairs which show modified L'Art Nouveau forms.

the top-heavy form of the Art Moderne prevailed, has there been any healthy or well-founded style.

In America a simple type known as the Mission school has been adopted quite generously, but it has represented not so much a school of ornament as a school for the elimination of ornament.

About 1870 a band of artists in Vienna, led by Wagner, produced a style of design arising out of the use of curved as opposed to straight lines. The underlying principle was based upon nature forms and Gothic and Japanese were drawn upon, and sinuous tree trunks and exaggerated vines produced occasionally such pleasing results that in the minor arts a great deal of encouragement was given to the movement. When applied to toilet articles and table, desk and dress accessories or even silverware there was little to offend, but when the same character of design was applied in broad and emphatic forms upon the walls and floors, it failed. Little by little Art Nouveau has been chastened, refined and simplified under various "movements," Secession, New Art and Art Moderne; some of the curves have been straightened out and the weird nature forms are no longer part of the structural character of furniture but are utilized only as decorations. In Germany this new development has made great strides; but not elsewhere.

It is surprising when we look back over the

England in matters of style, led to the solid, square and cylindrical forms of Biedermeier furniture, to which reminiscences of the Baroque and Empire styles remain attached as decorative details."

In England Thomas Hope made an ephemeral reputation with a rather clumsy adaptation of the Empire, but its vogue was brief.

In America, contemporaneously, the Empire grew and thrived; its influence was felt even in the farm districts, and classic pillared houses were erected with chaste doorways, columned and pilastered furniture was built and a taste was generally observed for lines that were simple, substantial and refined.

With the close of the Georgian period the great redivivus of art was ended, and while the Victorian period (Queen Victoria, 1837) has indulged in fitful spurts, nothing substantial has resulted and no phase developed that may be clearly defined.

We have had Eastlake and the Eastlake craze, William Morris and the Morris vogue, Sir Edward Burne-Jones, Walter Crane, Ruskin and the Arts-and-Crafts movements, but neither in England, France nor Austria, where Art Nouveau for a brief period became hysterically popular, and in Germany, where

serious utterances of Eastlake, whose book was written in 1870, that any success whatever attended his efforts. We are aware of the fact that much was produced by the manufacturers of Eastlake furniture which would have shocked the sensibilities of the author. The Eastlake school represented a simplification of Elizabethan and Jacobean. It was the application of factory labor and was full of jig-saw corners and cheap ornamentation, with metal and tile panels and squares inserted, and conspicuous hinges and handles obviously introduced for decorative effect. Sometimes the convex carvings were daubed with contrasting paint. Little by little this ornamentation became so vulgar and the operations of the jig-saw became so conspicuous that the Eastlake style died out.

While Eastlake was a man of education his work suggested nothing higher than the vaulting ambitions of a boss carpenter.

The work of William Morris and his confrères was important and far-reaching, establishing as it did the craftsman spirit in England. The Morris movement, so called because Morris was the managing head of affairs, employed the services of men who will live forever in the history of art.

William Morris was born in England, March 24, 1834. He died October 3, 1896. He went to Oxford in the fifties and beside him at the examinations sat Burne-Jones, who became his life-long friend.

He intended to study for the church. He knew nothing of art but became interested while traveling

An early Morris design, "Daisy and Columbine."

through Belgium and Northern France studying the churches of Amiens, Beauvais and Chartres. He had become acquainted with the work of the pre-Raphaelites, a brotherhood cultivating the Gothic arts and preaching the theory of individualism. Dante Gabriel Rossetti was the head, Ford Madox Brown, Holman Hunt and John Mullais were active members assisted by Ruskin's writings. Subsequently the coterie admitted William M. Rossetti, James Collinson, F. J. Stephens and Thomas Wolner.

As a child, Morris was possessed of a vivid imagination and a romantic, poetic temperament. At an early age he became a poet. Buildings had interested Morris from his childhood. The Gothic period appealed to his nature, the beauties of the Gothic art stimulated it and before he was through Oxford he had decided to study architecture and Burne-Jones was to become an artist. Morris studied under George Edmond Street, an architect whose enthusiasm for the Thirteenth Century made the foundation for all of Morris's work. Street was engaged at the time Morris went to him in restoring ancient churches and designing Gothic buildings. While never an artist in the broad sense—in the ability to depict the human form—and while never an architect, Morris developed along lines of adornment or ornamentation. In 1855 Burne-Jones and Morris took lessons in painting under Rossetti, and in 1856 Rossetti wrote enthusiastically of Burne-Jones predicting his fame as an artist, and of Morris he said that "in all illumination work of that kind he considered him quite unrivalled." When he was twenty-five Morris married Jane Burden, and the house into which they moved, known afterwards as "The Red House," possessed many furnishings contributed by their artistic friends.

A Voysey design showing the pre-Raphaelite influence of Morris and his colleagues.

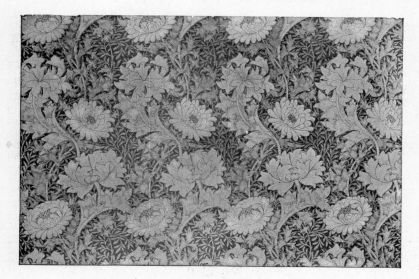

Chrysanthemum design, by William Morris.

The firm of Morris, Marshall, Faulkner & Co., as it was first called, appears to have followed their success of this early effort at decoration. Rossetti explains that the suggestion to organize a firm was a whim. "One evening a lot of us were together, and we got to talking about the way in which artists did all kinds of things in olden times—designed every kind of decoration and most kinds of furniture, and someone suggested that each put down five pounds and form a company. This was done. Morris was elected manager simply because he was the only man among us who had time and money to spare."

The associates were Morris, Rossetti, Burne-Jones, Madox Brown, an artist of reputation, Webb, the architect of the Red House, also a designer of furniture, Peter Paul Marshall and Charles Faulkner.

Naturally their work was of the highest character, covering mural decoration, carving as applied to architecture, stained glass, metal work, furniture, fabrics, s t a m p e d leathers and decorations generally, including draperies and wall-paper.

They affected f u l l, luscious colorings, tabooed fadey effects and dingy colors were abhorred by them.

In 1858 some of the

furniture made by Ford Madox Brown was described by him:

"Adapted to need of solidity and of a kind of homely beauty; above all, free of false display in carving, veneering and the like."

He tried to exhibit his furniture at the Hogarth Club, but the work was rejected as not fine art. But he persevered, and to-day his masterpieces, the frescoes in the Manchester Town Hall, are recognized as unequalled.

Rossetti describes a room which he was furnishing for his bride:

"Our drawing-room is papered from a design printed on common brown packing paper. The trees stand the whole height of the room; the stems and fruits are of Venetian red; the leaves are black; the fruit will have a fine line of yellow to indicate roundness."

The Morris factory took up finally printing on wall-papers or fabrics, which, together with the furniture, was based upon Gothic lines influenced in the modern spirit. Occasionally his floral treatment was classic, utilizing the acanthus or flora of England. His wood tones predominated as a background for vivid colors. His designs were never in straight lines and were always Medieval, and even where his motifs were modern flora the colorings and technique were Medieval.

In 1875 the original firm of Morris, Marshall, Faulkner & Co. was dissolved and Morris carried on the business alone, though Burne-Jones and

A typical Morris treatment; designed by William Morris for St. James's Palace.

Webb continued to help him with designs for stained glass and furniture. His enthusiasm was aroused in 1877 (in spite of his great interest at this time in public affairs), by the establishing of calico and chintz printing, the manufacture of brocades in silk and silk and wool, a Frenchman being got over to teach brocade work. He also began to think of tapestry, though this could not be attended to till later in the year, and it was when he took Kelmscott house, on the upper mall, Hammersmith, that he had a tapestry loom put up in his bedroom, rising early to practice the art of tapestry weaving. Carpet looms were built in the stables and here the first Hammersmith carpets were made.

The most important development perhaps was the production of printed cotton goods, i. e., "Morris' chintzes," which are more used than any of his other fabrics.

Between seventy and eighty wall-paper designs and nearly forty chintzes were invented and carried out by Morris, though if the various colorings were counted separately his designs would amount to 400. The sum total of his designs for paper-hangings, chintzes, woven stuffs, silk damasks, stamped velvets, carpets, and tapestries (excluding the hand-made carpets and the arras tapestries, which were each specially designed and as a rule not duplicated) which were

Chair designed by Charles L. Eastlake.

actually carried out, amounts to little short of 600, besides countless designs for embroidery.

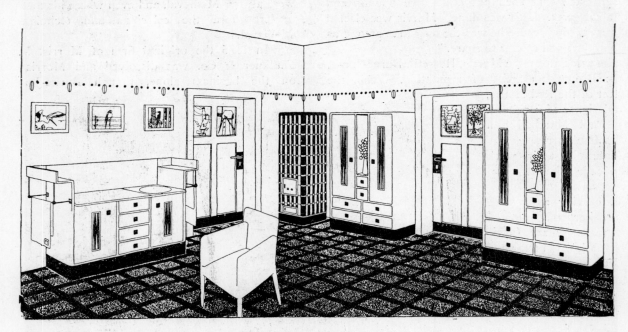

Modern Arts-and-Crafts.

APARTMENTS OF MARIE ANTOINETTE, PALACE OF FONTAINEBLEAU.

MISSION

On the left, chair in relic-room, Santa Barbara; on the right, chair in relic-room, Santa Clara.

THE Mission style is a commercial style. Originally it made pretense to reflect the character of the furniture found in the missions of old Mexico and the countries now New Mexico, Arizona, Texas and California; but there was never any serious effort to conscientiously follow the style which, after all, was simply primitive Gothic—the simplest style of carpenter work made for or by the missionaries under conditions which neither invited nor permitted the exercise of an artistic touch. It was simple, crude furniture bearing naturally the influences of the Spanish architecture which constituted the environment. The woods used were those most easily manipulated and obtained.

Ponce de Leon discovered Florida in 1512; in 1513 Balboa discovered the Pacific; in 1519 Cortez set forth to conquer the countries of Mexico.

In the early part of the Sixteenth Century Mexico proper and all the newly-established Central American provinces were being flooded with missionaries from Spain; churches by the hundred were built and missions established on every hand, in what are now the Mexican provinces.

The colonization of Mexico by Spain naturally meant the introduction of Catholic missions. In the early times the furnishings of these mission chapels

Modern Mission.

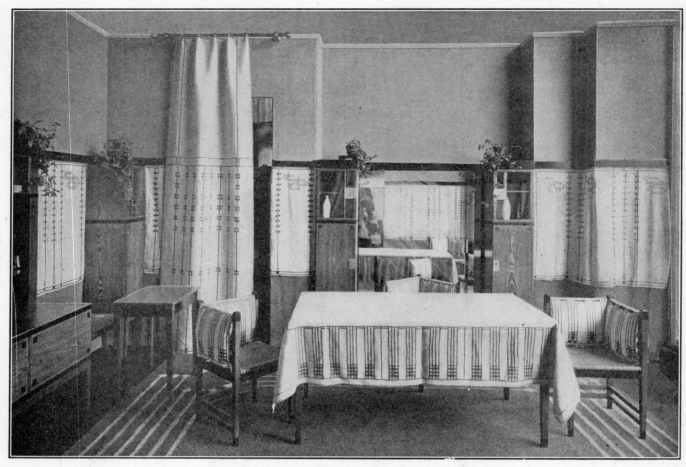

An Arts and Crafts Interior, from the German School.

were crude in the extreme, but in the Eighteenth Century the missions gathered strength and prosperity.

It has been often claimed that the Mission style was a purely American style. Unfortunately, the Mission style could have been historically accurate were it not that it was at an early age subjugated to the exigencies of commercialism.

Lumholtz, in his extraordinary work on Mexico, gives a vast store of illustration and data regarding the work of the Aztecs, that dominating people who possessed a civilization in Mexico before the Spanish invasion under Cortez, 1519.

One finds a very good example of this work at the American Museum of Natural History. While the furniture is probably not authentic in style, it approximates the character of furniture which even at this early date was found by the missionaries, and with slight alteration, was adapted to their ideas of Gothic structure.

Mission ornament was necessarily ecclesiastical and to present the old Mexican or Aztec decoration as a background to the Mission furnishings is wrong, for whatever the charm of Aztec decoration, we doubt if the representative of the Christian Church adopted it in any particular.

The United States Department of Agriculture is authority for the statement that the woods of California covered a wide variety, and it is illogical to assume that Mission furniture was made of any one particular wood.

In SOUTHERN CALIFORNIA what is known as the Pacific Coast forest yields Douglas fir, spruce, larch, western red cedar (arbor vitae), hemlock, redwood and big-tree, yellow and white pine, incense, port Oxford and yellow cedar, fir (balsam), juniper, yew, cottonwood, maple, alder, birch, madorna and laurel.

In ARIZONA, COLORADO, NEW MEXICO and NORTHERN MEXICO, what is known as the Rocky Mountain forest yields yellow pine, Douglas fir, fir (balsam), spruce, juniper, pinon pine, aspen, cottonwood and oak.

In other parts of LOWER MEXICO we find all of the sub-tropical and tropical woods, mahogany, pine, prima-vera, santa maria, logwood, Mexican rosewood, zebrawood, mesquite, aliso (alder), ash, elm, mulberry, cottonwood, silk cotton tree or ceiba, linden, china, pimienta, John Crow wood, buttonwood, black maba and salm-wood.

In CENTRAL AMERICA and WEST INDIES, mahogany, lignum vitae, logwood, sabicu, rosewood, fustic, quiebra hacha, zebrawood, calabash, cocobola, cork-wood, panama, jaqua, amarillo, laurel, sarsaparilla and cocoa-wood.

It is doubtful if any Spanish furniture was brought over by the early missionaries for the furnishing of their pioneer structures. Their work was attended with great hardships, long marches and struggles for a living and a foothold in the interior of a new country. And it is unreasonable to suppose that they added to the hardships of their progress any unnecessary burdens. The famous missions of to-day are the missions of California, and in their construction the builders utilized black oak, laurel, juniper, live oak, red wood, scrub oak, sycamore and walnut.

The Arts and Crafts style has gradually become a general term for any furnishings of an unperiodic and unconventional character. Originally, it stood simply for individuality. It represented a movement that advocated the association of art and labor and had its first practical inception some forty years ago, when Morris built his famous Red House, ignoring the prevailing styles and factory products and producing through individuals an independence that was effective. But the work of Morris and his confrères was saturated with the spirit of Medievalism, hence the move-

ment at the very beginning presented a consistency of decorative thought.

Morris developed along the ideas instilled by Carlyle and Ruskin, who preached what was practically the socialism of art, expressing contempt for the purely artificial, the carving that is plaster, the luster that is varnish, the bronze that is sheet brass, the painted woods—all the dictates of commercialism or tradition, and in no way representing an individual ambition. In the beginning the movement was undertaken by men who had something worth saying.

But to-day the movement simply expresses a contempt for all rules of order.

While Carlyle and Ruskin advocated the application of individual thought, the movement would never have developed were it not that the individual thought was born of culture, and followed with respect the pre-Raphaelite traditions.

The doctrine that no man can accomplish anything worth accomplishing if he is not free to express all that is in him, is good theory if the man is an artist, but it is dangerous to extend this encouragement to the inexperienced and uneducated.

As a result the Arts and Crafts movement has become simply a cloak behind which one hides his inability to produce a period style.

Chair-back stencil pattern of eighty years, a photographic reproduction of the original stencil plate.

PAINTED FURNITURE

IN OUR "Chronology of Inlays and Marquetry" we covered the subject from 1100, when marble and vitreous paste were much used in Southern Italy, to 1779, when David Roentgen, appointed by Marie Antoinette as "marqueteur to the Queen," produced extraordinary work. The Dutch marqueteurs were famous in the middle of the Seventeenth Century and in England as well as France they practiced the art of intarsia—the inlaying of woods.

We have already gone into the distinction between intarsia, marquetry and parquetry.

In the Queen Anne epoch the designs were rich in colors, obtained through the use of tropical woods, and lustrous with the use of ivory and mother-of-pearl. But from the latter part of the Eighteenth Century down to date, little has been done until the School of Nancy (France), stimulated by the vogue of Art Nouveau, introduced intarsia of quaint and unusual form.

Contemporaneously the Austrians, Germans, French and English went in for this style during the latter part of the Nineteenth Century.

After the Revolution many types of painted furniture were brought to America, not only from England, but from the South of France. They were frequently called japanned work, but the term is a misnomer, for the decoration is usually an ordinary paint and not lacquer work or japanned work, so called because at an early period it came from Japan and China.

The Dutch about 1750 took up

On the right, typical painted chairs of the Nineteenth Century.

the fashion for painting furniture, much after the style of Vernis-Martin, painted under lacquer, not unlike the work of carriage panels.

All sorts of subjects were followed, from flowers to ship scenes, a type familiar even to those of the present generation is the work of the New York stage coaches, sleighs of the old seventies, and snow chairs, which of late have been much sought. The work was frequently of a highly-artistic character.

In Holland of late years dealers have bought up old sleighs by the thousands, utilizing the painted work for cabinetwork. Similar work was done in Norway and Sweden.

Lacquered furniture was brought into England and France in large quantities throughout the Seventeenth Century, particularly by the East India Company. It gave inspiration to much of the work of Adam, Hepplewhite and Sheraton, who, however, made no pretense to do lacquer work; they simply applied good painted motifs to certain parts of their furniture.

Angelica Kauffmann and Pergolesi were particularly successful, and in some cases their work was highly lacquered or japanned; but the hosts of unknown artists who followed this style and painted humbler types of furniture, bedsteads, washstands, chairs and toilet articles, used common paint, and some exceedingly simple effects, which finally deteriorated into stencil work, became popular and continued in vogue well into 1830. Indeed, the work became so common that the broad splats were introduced in chairs especially to give space for decoration.

AMERICA'S MOST DISTINCTIVE NATIVE FURNITURE TYPE.

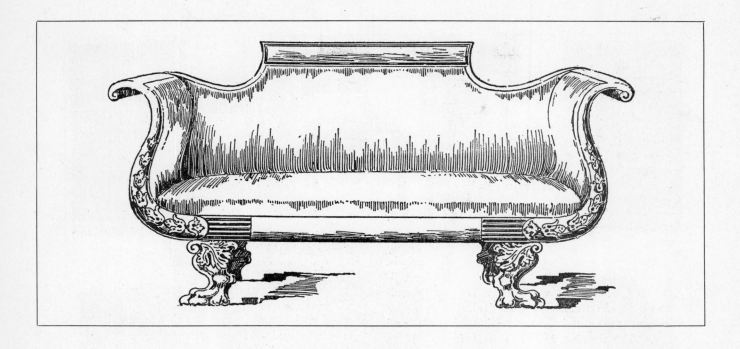

AMERICA'S MOST DISTINCTIVE FURNITURE TYPE

FEW authorities have covered the subject of furniture and furnishings in America 1790 to 1830. English authors stopped with the early Georgian. They felt that with the end of Sheraton and beginning with the abortive efforts of Thomas Hope, who in some degree followed the Empire, there was an end to the periods, and the Victorian age was approached apologetically.

Nevertheless there was a distinctly American type produced early in the Nineteenth Century, the outgrowth of the Empire form, simplified and beautified.

The Chippendale, Sheraton and Hepplewhite schools were dainty and delightful examples of carving, painting and inlaying. Empire shapes were more massive and employed brass appliqué. From the beginning the Americans eliminated the brass or

A type of 1770.

ormolu ornamentation, and while there was considerable carving on the backs of lounges and on the table legs, little by little this disappeared and only the simple shapes remained with broad flat surfaces made beautiful by veneers highly finished and polished. Prior to the Nineteenth Century veneering was an expensive art; the wood was cut by hand and it was impossible to cover large surfaces excepting at heavy expense.

In the pieces of William and Mary and Queen Anne veneering was used frequently as an economy. It was applied very often as a surface to cheap woods, but the veneerings of the late Colonial period were not applied because cheap, but because of the possibilities of a high, lustrous finish, and the veneers were often attached to a solid mahogany base.

It is a mistake to assume, as so many do,

Above, American chairs of the period 1790-1830; below, tables of the same epoch.

that veneer is shoddy and undertaken as a pretence and deception. Veneering is one of the oldest arts and in some form or other, as marquetry or as inlaying, has been practiced throughout all periods. Moreover, it gives strength to the frame, as best illustrated in Queen Anne work when frequently walnut was veneered on oak or yellow deal.

Veneers are cut in two grades—saw-cut and knife-cut. The first vary in thickness from 1-32 to 1-16 of an inch and are cut from a log with a large circular saw producing twelve or fourteen sheets to the inch. Knife-cut veneers are thinner. Before the introduction of machinery veneers were almost invariably an eighth of an inch thick and the decorative beauty of some of the veneers used is due to cutting through the burrs or excrescences of the tree. The "curls" and "feathers" are produced by the separation of the heart at the junction of a branch with the main trunk.

Mottles and figures, which are noted particularly in maple and mahogany, come from certain conditions of the wood when cut across the grain. Machine-made veneers opened up a wide field of usefulness and constituted a type coincident with the beginning of the Nineteenth Century.

CHRONOLOGY OF WALL AND CEILING TREATMENTS

WOODS USED AND RUGS.

[4500 B. C.—1603 A. D.]

Egyptian, 4500 B.C.—324 B.C.

WALL treatments confined to frieze decoration on plain walls; full of gold and brilliant colors; ornaments frequently hieroglyphics and Egyptian symbols; beautifully hand-painted stucco and fresco work much in vogue; illustrations representing industries.

Chinese, 3500 B.C.—238 B.C.

Modern art described by Chambers 1757. Sidewalls, matting four feet high, the rest colored or gilt paper, overhung with pictures and proverbs.

Assyrian, 2286 B.C.—608 B.C.

Stone work overwrought in bronze and gold; human faces showing profile; Assyrian symbols used, following largely the Egyptian. Walls of King Solomon's temple were covered with carved cedar and olive wood.

Greek, 1900 B.C.—168 B.C.

Fresco on plaster in strong colors, usually in deep friezes and dadoes; also stucco, fresco and tempera or distemper painting practiced; borders frescoed and painted in religious and legendary subjects, full of color; painting of still life, city and country shown; ceilings elaborate, divided into geometric sections; mosaics brought to perfection.

Roman, 753 B.C.—455 B.C.

Similar to Greek.

Pompeiian, 100 B.C.—455 A.D.

Following the Greek and Roman style, but walls were also completely covered with paintings, sometimes divided into panels with small pictures and fine mosaics; sometimes wall space divided into dado, middle and upper section and ornamented with delicate garlands, fruit, masks. In England the Adam style almost reproduced the Pompeiian.

Byzantine, 328—1451.

Closely related to Roman. Magnificent in tiles, largely Oriental.

Romanesque—Affected materially by the Byzantine and Saracenic. Tiles and tile treatment; stained glass windows recorded 525 A.D. Tapestries made by Flemish weavers, 1170 A.D. In the Eleventh Century Cordova leathers, superbly gilded and painted were made in Flanders. The term was also applied to similar leathers produced in Portugal, France and Italy.

Gothic, 1100—1550.

Beginning with 1200 walls of houses were wainscoted and painted, often decorated with romantic, biblical or legendary subjects. In the Thirteenth Century walls were treated with tiling forms called Cosmatic mosaic, and frequently hung with tapestries. Wall-paper used prior to 1500 was simply pictures on paper and was hung like banners and not stuck to the wall.

About 1500 large hall of house was generally sitting-room, reception-room and dining-room combined. Raftered ceilings were common.

Italian Renaissance, 1400—1643.

Discoveries of the stuccoes of ancient Rome aroused Italian architects to the spirit of emulation and Roman and Greek mural work was generally adopted. Ground colors were laid on while the stucco was wet. Raphael and his followers applied themselves to wall decoration. Superb friezes and panels, the best the world has ever seen, was the result. Both wainscoting and rich tapestries, leathers, gold and silk fabrics were liberally used in all the phases of the Renaissance. Marbleized paper called "domino" was made in Italy during the Fifteenth Century in small squares and used on walls.

French Renaissance, 1500—1643.

Covering practically the same characteristics as the Italian Renaissance, years of great magnificence embracing the reigns of:

Francis I, 1515-1549.
Henry II, 1549-1559.
Francis II, 1559-1560.
Charles IX, 1560-1574.
Henry III, 1574-1589.
Henry IV, 1589-1610.
Louis XIII, 1610-1643.

The domino papers of Italy were improved and instead of being marble or plain papers were printed in figures, and by 1700 there was hardly a house in Paris that did not utilize "domino papers."

Continuation of the use of fabric side-walls, rich paneling, stuccoed ceilings, carvings, rich paintings. Louis XIV, 1643-1715, side-walls frequently paneled in fabric. Ceilings painted or in rich plaster.

Elizabethan, 1558—1603.

Reflected the Italian spirit. Moldings were much used and strap-work carvings, wood side-walls clear to the ceiling, stucco ceilings. Oak prevailed. Period lasted from 1500 to 1660. Painted linens and hangings, tapestries, embroideries.

CHRONOLOGY OF WALL AND CEILING TREATMENTS

[1603—1800.]

Jacobean, 1603—1649.

Continued the Elizabethan style. Still the age of oak. Side-walls of oak but in some of the finest residences the ceilings were beamed. Side-walls hung with tapestries. Magnificent stuccoes. Ceilings frequently of the most elaborate type, often colored. Heavy relief work, massive reproductions of panels full of heraldic devices and in small rooms chintzes from India were used. Cotton and linen embroideries were hung on the wall. Embossed and gilded linens, cloths of gold, painted cloths.

Louis XIV, 1643—1715.

Gobelin Tapestry Works became royal property. Beauvais Tapestry Works established. Richest silks used on the walls, damask, brocade and embroidery. Magnificent ceilings, paneled, painted and stuccoed. Magnificent Chinese papers popular for walls.

Louis XV, 1715—1774.

Chinese characteristics introduced. Wealth of his predecessor continued. Paneling rich in gold and bronze. 1746—first factory established in France for the manufacturing of wall-paper squares. French Ministry, 1759, authorized the manufacture of printed linens, and by 1789 one hundred factories were in operation, some of them working from copper plates. Wood side-walls disappeared. Everything rich in fabrics.

Louis XVI, 1774—1792.

Continuation of fabric effects following the daintier classic feeling; ceilings beautifully hand painted, cleverest artists of the day contributing to the work. Walls paneled in fabrics, surrounding the same with elaborate compositions of plaster and molding work. White and gold conspicuous. Continuous rolls of wall-paper were undertaken in 1790.

In 1787 we find a decree of the king declaring that the art of painting and printing paper used in furnishings were a dependence of the governing board of the Merchants-Papetiers-Dominotiere-Feuilletinere, which shows that the term "domino" still clung.

Empire, 1804—1814.

Walls stronger in gold effects. Continuation of fabric treatment with the added use of bronze and gold in profusion. Walls hand painted on plaster or canvas.

Charles II, 1660—1685.
James II, 1685—1689.
William and Mary, 1689—1702.

Wainscoted side-walls began to come lower in height and by Charles II's time began to disappear; the French method of treating walls in fabric came in. The ceilings, however, continued to be of magnificent proportions, elaborate in stucco and relief work divided into panels, circles, hexagons and rhomboids, borders enriched with flowers and fruits similar to the extraordinary carvings of Grinling Gibbons. Borders were often flat ornaments of Greek or Roman design. Ceilings were magnificent reproductions following the Renaissance, also prolific with goddesses, saints, muses and Cupids.

Queen Anne, 1702—1714.

Frequently side-walls followed the French style. The custom of paneling the side-walls was partially kept up. Chimneypieces, however, only went halfway up the wall. White woodwork was affected. Walls were often without any paneling or wainscoting and covered with squares of Chinese wall-paper or painted directly on or hung with fabrics, particularly prints.

Colonial, 1700—1800.

The American colonies adopted the European styles. White woodwork was popular, little wainscoting was attempted about 1690. In 1749 Isaac Ware wrote: "The decoration of an American room is of three kinds—first, where it is coated with the plaster material wrought into ornamental details; second, where covered by wainscot, and third, where hung with silks, tapestries or paper," for in that year dealers in America were advertising "to hang rooms with paper or fabrics in the very newest fashions." Indeed, Charles Hargraves advertised wall-papers in Philadelphia in 1745, and only a few years later Peter Fleeson was making paper-hangings in squares, corner of Fourth and Chestnut Streets, Philadelphia. Nantucket, Portsmouth and St. Johnsbury, Vt., have yielded to the collectors some exquisite examples of wall decorations. Thomas Hancock in 1757 wrote to an English friend to send him some paper-hangings showing a great variety of birds, animals, fruits and flowers and he adds to his letter: "I think these papers are handsome; better than painted walls." Fabrics were used on the walls contemporaneously with the European use of them.

CHRONOLOGY *of* RUGS ACCORDING *to* PERIODS

THE chronological or the period uses of rugs is in no way confusing if one knows the history of rugs. For centuries the only rugs in use were Oriental rugs, and when the making of Oriental rugs was introduced into Europe by the Saracens, Ninth and Tenth Centuries, the patterns continued to be Oriental. The history of Oriental rugs goes back to Assyria, Egypt, Old Persia, ancient Greece and Rome.

In 711 when the Saracens began swarming into Spain and later when they settled along the southern countries of Europe, particularly Sicily, they took their looms with them. We find as early as 900 A.D. traces of Oriental art as far north as Scandinavia and in later days, the Thirteenth and Fourteenth Centuries, we have a distinct type of Oriental rug known as Hispano-Moresque, and a little later Portuguese-Persian was evolved.

We have record also of looms set up by the Saracens in Palermo, Twelfth Century; Poland, Twelfth Century; Venice, Fourteenth Century.

During the reign of Henry IV of France, 1600, rug weaving was undertaken. The first European influence developed in design character, and right here it is well to emphasize the fact that we must differentiate between a tapestry and a specific floor covering.

The term carpet was one which in the early days applied to hangings, and the references to ancient carpets which we frequently find in literature have doubtless reference to tapestry. The French term *tapissier* means to carpet, to hang or cover with tapestry; *tapis,* a carpet; *tapete,* carpet or tapestry. Hence when we read of the Flemish, French, English or Italian "carpets" of an early period, we must remember that the term was synonymous with tapestry. An Englishman today who carries a traveling shawl speaks of it as his "rug."

THE PERIOD USES OF RUGS

The making of rugs in Asia goes back to the Prehistoric Ages.

English Romanesque 1066
French Romanesque 700-1100

Gothic Early Period 1100-1500
Late Gothic and Italian Renaissance 1400
French Renaissance 1500
    Francis I, Henry II, Louis XIII.
English Renaissance 1500
    Henry XIII.
Flemish Renaissance 1507
Spanish Renaissance 1500
Portuguese Renaissance 1500
German Renaissance 1550

Elizabethan 1558
Jacobean, English 1603-1650
James I 1603-1625
Charles I 1625-1649
Cromwellian 1653-1659
Charles II 1660-1689
William and Mary 1689-1702
Queen Anne 1702-1714
Georgian Period 1714-1820
    Chippendale-Sheraton-Hepplewhite and Adam.
American Colonial Period 1727-1820
Henry IV, French 1589-1610
Louis XIV 1643
Louis XV 1715
Louis XVI 1774
Directoire 1795
Empire 1804

Oriental rugs from Asia or of Spanish origin the results of colonization.

From 1100 to 1400 the Mediterranean merchants established rug industries in Spain, Sicily and Venice and supplied Europe with Oriental carpets of European manufacture, besides the vast quantities of native examples imported from Anatolia, India and Persia; all of Oriental design.

Early in the Seventeenth Century Shah Abbas introduced Renaissance characteristics in the Persian rugs of his court, in order to demonstrate his antagonism to the influences of Mongol character. Contemporaneously the manufacture of Turkish carpets, but of *European design* was introduced at Arras, Fontainebleau, Tours and La Savonnerie. Results of practical productions began 1620, and by 1660 this manufacture was well developed. Frequently heavy wall tapestries were utilized for the floor. Prior to 1745 English-made carpets were crude products similar to ingrain. In 1745 a cut pile carpet called Wilton was first produced. In 1749 the Brussels loom was erected in England. During Louis XV and the period of Chippendale Chinese rugs were much used.

Inlay or Marquetry woods are in *italics.*

ENGLISH.

Applewood.
Ash.
Beech.
Birch.
Bog or Black Oak.
Brown Oak.
Cedar.
Cherry.
Chestnut.
Elm.
Holly.
Lime or Linden.
Maple.
Oak (English).
Oak (Pollard).
Pearwood.
Planewood (Buttonwood or Lace-
    wood).
Sycamore.
Walnut.
Willow.
Yew.

EUROPEAN.

Austrian Oak.
Baltic Oak.
Birch.
Black Sea or Circassian Walnut.
Boxwood.
Cedar.
Cherry.
Chestnut.
Cypress.
Elm.
French Walnut.
French Oak.
German Oak.
Holly.
Italian Oak.
Lime or Linden.
Maple.
Olive.

Pearwood.
Pine.
Polish Oak.
Planewood.
Riga Oak (Russian).
Spanish Oak.
Sycamore (Colored varieties called
    Hairwood, Mousewood, Grey-
    wood).
Walnut (Italian).
Willow.

ASIATIC.

Andaman Redwood.
Cedar.
Calamander (Blackstripe, India).
Cherry.
Coromandel (Yellow Ebony, In-
    dia).
Ebony (India).
Green Ebony (India).
Indian Mahogany.
Ironwood (India).
Pearwood.
Porcupine, Pheasant or Partridge.
Rosewood.
Satinwood.
Teak (Pheasant or Graniteware).
Zeen Oak (India).

WEST INDIAN AND SOUTH AMERICAN.

Angelique (Mahogany).
Cedar.
Cocobola.
Greenheart.
Green Ebony.
Kingwood or Violet.
Lancewood.
Lignum-Vitae.
Mahogany.
Mora (Mahogany).
Purplewood.
Rosewood.

Sabicu (Mahogany).
Santa Maria (Mahogany).
Santine (Mahogany).
Satin Walnut.
Satinwood.
Snakewood or Leopard.
Tulip.
Yellow Oak.
Zebra.

AMERICAN.

Ash.
Basswood (Lime).
Beech.
Birch.
Bird's Eye Maple (Sugar Maple).
Black Walnut.
Butternut.
Cedar.
Cherry.
Chestnut.
Cypress.
Elm.
Hickory.
Holly.
Live Oak.
Maple.
Pine.
Poplar.
Planewood (Buttonwood or Lace-
    wood).
Red Oak.
Redwood.
Sycamore.
Walnut (many varieties).
White Oak.
Whitewood (Known as Tulip, Yel-
    low Poplar and Canarywood).

MISCELLANEOUS.

African Oak.
African Teak.
African or Golden Walnut.
Citron (Africa).
Mahogany (Africa).

INTARSIA OR MARQUETRY.

INTARSIA—Tarsia, from the Latin, *interserrere,* to insert, applied to the inlaying of woods. When in metal, as practiced at Damascus, called *damascening.* MARQUETRY—Synonymous term adopted by the French from *marqueter,* to spot, to mark. PARQUETRY applies to coarse work for floorings or wainscotings. The process of inlaying goes back to the early Assyrian and Egyptian methods on metal, ivory, marble and wood.

1100—Intarsia of marble and vitreous pastes produced in Southern Italy.
1259—Beautiful examples of inlaying produced in Siena.
1300—Germans worked in inlays, and beautiful examples were brought from India, Arabia, Egypt, Venice and Spain.
1331—Famous stalls inlaid with ebony, boxwood, walnut and white poplar were produced by the Siennese and reached a high degree of artistic merit.
1416—The Duc du Berri's furniture was illuminated with pictures in intarsia, doubtless of Italian workmanship.
1490—Exquisite work done in France.
1500—Germans understood intarsia work in colored woods.
1550—Italians revived the ancient styles of marquetry and the furniture of this Latin Renaissance or Baroque Period was often of marquetry arranged in the form of actual pictures. Sometimes furniture was also painted, gilded or decorated with oil paintings.
1550—Ebony and ivory work successfully undertaken in Germany. Fine examples in Mosque of Cordova, Spain.
1550-1650—Dutch marquetry, highly artistic, employing Asiatic woods in great number. Rich chairs were commonly decorated with marquetry, usually huge tulips and birds.
1600—Marquetry made itself felt in the Netherlands and Flemish artists copied the work in precious woods.
1603—Some excellent work was done by Englishmen during the Jacobean Period. Jean Macé of Blois is thought to be the

first to practice intarsia in France under the name of *marquetrie.* He learned the art in the Netherlands. French designs usually ran to landscapes, ruins and classic scenes.
1650—Under Louis XIV Dutch *marqueteurs* were employed to teach the art to Frenchmen. The name Boulle has become indissolubly connected with the application of copper and tortoise shell mosaics upon wood. The Portuguese carried on the work in the Seventeenth Century, employing metal plates cut and pierced in elaborate and fanciful patterns fastened upon black wood, the beginning of Boulle work, which was characterized by the sinking of the metal into the wood.
1672—Andre Charles Boulle, born in 1642, was granted apartments in the Louvre as "joiner, marqueter, gilder and chiseler." Boulle's work covered Louis XIV and XV Periods. J. F. Oeben was famous during the Louis XV Period, also J. Henry Riesener and Chas. Cressent.
1700—Marquetry fashionable in England in the Queen Anne Period. The designs were rich in foliage with bands of ivory and mother-of-pearl.
1760—Satinwood used for inlaid lines of Sheraton furniture; also holly, tulipwood, decidedly reddish, and later lancewood.
1770—All of the tropical woods utilized by the inlayers. Wonderful effects obtained by David Roentgen, German, who secured shadings by subjecting woods to various degrees of hot sand baths.
1779—David Roentgen appointed by Marie Antoinette as *marqueteur* to the Queen.

FINISH.

1200—Gothic and early Renaissance furniture was left untouched. As the forms of furniture became more ornamental a deep colored varnish was applied or the wood was much oiled and waxed.
1500—Amber was known from time immemorial. It was a recognized commercial article in the Sixteenth Century, and it is probable that it was used for the manufacture of varnish for violins.
1600—The gums used in the manufacture of varnishes coming from Asia, South America and the West Indies, there was probably no commercial supply for the general manufacture of varnishes until late in the Seventeenth Century. Unquestionably varnishes have been made at almost all periods, but they were rare. In small quantities they were used for jewel boxes, violins, musical instruments. Japan and China have long been skilled in the art.
1700—Towards the close of 1600 the craze for Oriental ware induced Louis XIV to enact laws to protect native industries.
1710—In 1710 the French japanners claiming that the lacquers and japans were equal to the Asiatic ware, asked for protection, and throughout this period there is constant reference to lacquered tables, screens, chairs, lacquered trunks, panels fans and furniture.
1733—Imitations of lacquer found fame in the Netherlands through Huygens, and contemporaneously in France through Martin (Vernis-Martin) Royal factory, 1748.

INDEX

NOTE:—The innumerable racial names, divisions and nationalities, not indexed hereunder, will be found comprehensively grouped under the charts, "Developments of Nations," pages 3 to 6.

INDEX

INDEX

INDEX